Dr Martyn Lloyd-Jones and Evangelicals in Wales

Bala Ministers' Conference
1955–2014

D Eryl Davies

© Author 2014

First published 2014

ISBN: 978-1-78397-056-8

All rights reserved. No part of this publication may be reproduced, stored in a retrieval system, or transmitted, in any form or by any means, electronic, mechanical, photocopying, recording or otherwise, without the prior permission of the Bryntirion Press.

Unless otherwise indicated, Scripture quotations are from the New King James Version (NKJV)®. Copyright © 1982 by Thomas Nelson, Inc. Used by permission. All rights reserved.

Evangelical Movement of Wales
The EMW works in both Welsh and English and seeks to help Christians and churches by:
- running children's camps and family conferences
- providing theological training and events for ministers
- running Christian bookshops and a conference centre
- publishing magazines and books

Bryntirion Press is a ministry of EMW

Past issues of EMW magazines and sermons preached at our conferences are available on our web site: www.emw.org.uk

Published by Bryntirion Press, Bryntirion, Bridgend CF31 4DX, Wales, in association with EP BOOKS, Faverdale North, Darlington, DL3 0PH, UK.

EP BOOKS are distributed in the USA by:
JPL Fulfillment, 3741 Linden Avenue Southeast, Grand Rapids, MI 49548.
E-mail: sales@jplfulfillment.com
Tel: 877.683.6935

Printed and bound in the UK by 4edge Limited

"Although small, the town of Bala has played a key role in the religious life of Wales. Indeed, one has only to mention Bala's strategic part in the establishment of the Bible Society to realize that its contribution to the history of evangelical Christianity has extended far beyond the Welsh border. For over twenty years, between the 1950s and 1970s, one of the annual highlights in the life and ministry of Dr D. Martyn Lloyd-Jones was the Ministers' Conference which was held for much of that period in Bala. It is difficult to overemphasize the importance of that Ministers' Conference in the recent history of evangelicalism in Wales, and its influence has also been felt much further afield. We are indebted to Dr Eryl Davies for this pioneer overview and analysis of the Conference's context, development and significance, which draws not only on his extensive research, but also on his first-hand experience of this crucial—if controversial—Conference."

Professor E. Wyn James, School of Welsh, Cardiff University

Dr Eryl Davies has made a major contribution to the history of Evangelical Christianity in Britain with his clearly written, interesting, and scholarly book on Dr Lloyd-Jones and the yearly ministerial conference in Bala (from 1955 to 2014). I was there in the mid nineties, and took away with me a sense of profound Christian earnestness of the ministers, of unction of the Holy Spirit upon the meetings, of loving fellowship, along with academic honesty and biblical fidelity. It gave me hope for the Church in the future, and it still does. Dr Davies honestly and bravely addresses the major issues still faced by evangelicals in our secularized West; that is why this book will have relevance and influence far beyond Wales, and even into China and Africa. I delight in his emphasis upon the need for revival in our churches, but appreciate his realism and balance, and his call for sound theology, biblical preaching and fervent prayer. I shall recommend it to my classes.

Douglas F. Kelly, Professor of Systematic Theology, Reformed Theological Seminary, Charlotte, North Carolina

In this absorbing study, Dr Eryl Davies has provided us with a vivid insight into the role played by the great preacher Martyn Lloyd-Jones in developing evangelical thought and practice in post-War Wales. Although its focus is specialized, the impact of the Bala ministers' conference was wide and for many has been profound. This volume affords a fascinating glimpse into the stresses as well as the achievements of twentieth and twenty first century Welsh evangelicalism. It is an admirable contribution to our understanding of recent Christian history in our land.

**D. Densil Morgan, Professor of Theology,
University of Wales Trinity Saint David**

Dr Eryl Davies has written an excellent summary of the influence of the ministers' conference run by the Evangelical Movement of Wales, tracing how it has encouraged and developed evangelical leaders in Wales and beyond. He gives a fascinating insight into the leading personalities of the period and what they have contributed to the church. The chapters are very readable, making it ideal for dipping into when reading time is limited. The book gives an inspiring overview of the work of God during the period it covers and will encourage all who read it.

**Dr Tom Holland, New Testament Research Supervisor,
Wales Evangelical School of Theology (WEST)**

Ministers who are no longer able to attend the Bala Conference shake their heads, smile and sigh, "Ah, the Bala Conference" full of regret and the happiest memories of the three days spent there. The fellowship after the meetings, on the lawn, around the meal tables, the prayer times, the ministry of the Word of God. It is an egalitarian conference with no big personalities strutting their stuff. Unassuming, with usually less than a hundred attending, spiritual, with a subterranean longing for God to awaken the dying testimony in Wales, a place of encouragement and refreshment and laughter and books of course. "What are you preaching on now?" we ask. "How are things in the church?" We begin, "Did you have a good Sunday yesterday?" Dr Eryl Davies' brilliant book captures in detail the blessed ethos of Bala.

Geoff Thomas, Pastor, Alfred Place Baptist Church, Aberystwyth, Wales.

As we wind our way into the 21st century interest in the preaching ministry of the late

Commendations

Dr Martyn Lloyd-Jones is unabated. Now comes one with unquestioned scholarly and personal credentials whose relationship to Dr Lloyd-Jones and the Welsh Church will be welcomed by all. Dr Eryl Davies' new book provides a faithful guide to the ministry of the Doctor in his native land and gives not only an eyewitness account of the glory years of Lloyd-Jones' preaching in Wales, but now bequeaths to the Church a pastoral theological gold mine of insights, illustrations, applications, and Biblical diagnosis and treatment from the Doctor. As I read through Dr Davies' work I was carried away to times of revival, but rather than creating nostalgia to go back, the book cultivated prayer for God to come down.

I commend my former professor's work to the Church with an appeal to set other books aside. This is the first book to read as soon as you can get it. For we need revival desperately. Dr Davies' book is a wonderful blessing and a gift to the Church that I pray will be used of the Lord to stir us up to God's glory in our own generation.

Rev. Professor Michael A. Milton, Ph.D. (University of Wales), Chancellor, retired, Reformed Theological Seminary, USA
President, Faith for Living, Inc.

Dr Davies's book is an excellent resource on Evangelicals in Wales, especially on the life and influence of Dr Martyn Lloyd-Jones. Dr Davies based this book on research conducted over 20 years, having lived in Wales his entire life and being personally acquainted with Dr Lloyd-Jones. In today's constantly evolving era of biblical preaching, this book will become an outstanding guide and encouragement for preachers, missionaries, and serious disciples of Christ who are seeking to know God and the power of the Gospel.

Won Sang Lee, Ph.D.
Senior Pastor Emeritus of the Korean Central Presbyterian Church, Centreville, Virginia, U.S.A.
President of SEED International

Contents

Preface	9
PART ONE: THE BACKGROUND STORY	**15**
1. An Exciting Story: Evangelism in Wales	17
2. Exciting Background	22
3. Further progress	28
4. An important diversion	35
5. A New Development The Evangelical Presbyterian Ministers' Fellowship	44
PART TWO: THE EARLY YEARS—1955–1961	**55**
6. The 1955 Conference in Context	57
7. The 1956 Cilgwyn Conference	65
8. Cilgwyn Conferences 1957 and 1958	75
9. Unforgettable but with tensions Cilgwyn 1959–1961	83
Summary of Parts One and Two	93
PART THREE: TURBULENCE, QUESTIONS AND PROGRESS —1962–1978	**95**
10. Relocation to Bala	97

11. Digging for Bible Answers to Big Questions	105
12. Another Big Question	114
13. A Significant Milestone: 1968–1969	121
14. 1970–1973 Conferences	133
15. 'Crammed to Capacity': 1974–1977	137
16. The Last Conference for Lloyd-Jones	146
Summary of Part Three	152

PART FOUR: GROWTH, EVANGELISM AND REVIVAL —1979–2009 — 153

17. Evangelism and Revival	155
18. Covenanting to pray	163
19. The Wind of Change	173
20. 'Complacent and Satisfied?'	182
Summary of Part Four	190

PART FIVE: CONCLUDING THE STORY—2009–2014 — 191

21. Change and Encouragement: 2009–2013	193
22. The 2013–2014 Conferences	202
Summary of Part Five	210

PART SIX: CONCLUSION AND ASSESSMENT — 211

23. Looking Back and Forward (1)	213
24. Looking Back and Forward (2)	225
25. Lloyd-Jones's Pastoral Role	238
26. Lloyd-Jones's Piety	245
27. Lloyd-Jones and Gospel Preaching	252
28. Lloyd-Jones and Revival	259
29. Word and Spirit (1)	270
30. Word and Spirit (2)	283

APPENDICES 1–15   303
Appendix 1: 'Why are we where we are?'   305
Appendix 2: 'why could we not cast him out?'   308
Appendix 3: Strain and stress in the Christian ministry   316
Appendix 4: 'Why are we failing?'   321
Appendix 5: Looking back on 1966   326
Appendix 6: The next steps   332
Appendix 7: An affirmation concerning the Nature of the Church   337
Appendix 8: Some fundamental questions   341
Appendix 9: Religious life in Wales since the turn of the Twentieth Century   345
Appendix 10: The Living God   352
Appendix 11: Faith healing   357
Appendix 12: Importance of sharing our experiences   360
Appendix 13: Life and teaching   364
Appendix 14: The place of extraordinary phenomena in Revival   370
Appendix 15: 2 Timothy 1:7   377

Bibliography   384
Endnotes   391

PREFACE

Two books on this subject! That was the plan until recently. One was intended as a brief, popular outline of the Conference's history and influence. The second book was to be more academic in nature. However, for several reasons, I decided to write only one book, namely, this semi-popular history and evaluation of the Conference and Lloyd-Jones's ministry in it.

Readable
I have endeavoured to ensure that readers will not feel discouraged by the book's length or contents. I am influenced by my doctoral supervisor in Cardiff University (1968–1971), Professor Humphrey Palmer, who insisted that academic research should be written for 'ordinary' people to read and appreciate.

Thanks
My thanks are due to pastors with whom I have enjoyed fellowship in the Conference, including contributors to this book. The Rev. Iain H. Murray, Edinburgh, provided valuable

information on the 1956 and 1969 Conferences for which I am grateful.

I appreciated John Emyr's kindness in loaning me notes of early Conference addresses written by his late father, Emyr Roberts. Conference members esteemed him highly for his knowledge of Welsh church history, theology and culture; they also enjoyed his delightful sense of humour. His notes on some of Lloyd-Jones's addresses appear as appendices. I am also indebted to Philip and Jennifer Eveson for their editing work.

I am deeply grateful to those who have prayed for me, especially over recent months, while I was completing this book.

New information

A considerable amount of new information and primary sources are published here for the first time. I hope this book, therefore, contributes significantly to Welsh church history and will also be an encouragement for people to pray for the ministry of the Word. The final two chapters are more theological and demanding as the Conference theme of Word-Spirit is discussed in the light of contemporary writings and criticism.

I assume full responsibility for the views expressed here, including the critical evaluation of the Conference. I am not in any way expressing a formal Evangelical Movement of Wales (EMW) response nor am I representing the views of any group or other organisation.

Longing

I long that Conference and churches will enjoy the favour of our Triune God so that prayers for the widespread success of the gospel and for revival will be answered soon in Wales and in other countries as well.

Eryl Davies
Cardiff
April 2014

Questions and answers about this book

Why this book
To tell the story of what pastors/churches learned and experienced through the Conference between 1955 and 2014.

- To encourage more prayer for the preaching of the Word.

- To fill a gap in Welsh church history for this period.

- To make available previously unpublished details and primary sources relating to the Conference and Dr Lloyd-Jones's ministry there between 1955 and 1978.

What is its message?
- God's Word is true and should be believed and preached; His love in Christ is amazing and lies at the heart of the Bible; God keeps His promises and answers prayer.

- The Holy Spirit makes the preaching of the Word effective.

- The Lord breaks into people's lives and into difficult church situations. He is active TODAY.

- Relevant and important application of pastoral theology.

Who is this book for?
- For ALL Christians, irrespective of background, location, position or church.

- For pastors and church officers as a contemporary case study.

Will I be able to read it?

- The book is intended as an interesting and easy read.

- It is user-friendly. Many chapters are brief and challenging.

- It is ideal for use with a friend/family or group. The choice is yours.

- Each chapter includes study questions to assist readers.

- Chapters 29 and 30 are more theological and demanding but very important.

PART ONE

THE BACKGROUND STORY

Chapters 1–3   Evangelism in Wales

Chapter 4   Dr Lloyd-Jones's Early Relationship with Evangelicals in Wales

Chapter 5   Evangelical Presbyterian Ministers' Fellowship in Wales

1

An Exciting Story: Evangelism in Wales

This book is a story, a true story,[1] covering an important yet turbulent period of church life and Christian witness in Wales from 1955–2014.

Lloyd-Jones

Dr Martyn Lloyd-Jones's ministry and influence in the annual pastors' Conference in Wales figure prominently. Originally from West Wales, he was a medical consultant in London who reached the top of his profession by the age of twenty six.[2] Feeling an irresistible call to preach, he became a church pastor and an outstanding preacher. Some influential leaders regarded him as the greatest preacher in Christendom in the twentieth century.

Between the years 1955 and 1978, Dr Lloyd-Jones normally attended the annual Evangelical Ministers' Conference in Wales. He was usually one of the speakers and many details concerning his contributions to the Conference are published here for the first time. The book majors on this formative period[3] but before assessing his influence, it is important that the story is brought up to date.

Exciting

This is an exciting story relating how some pastors became Christians and how God worked in their lives and churches, especially through this pastors' Conference over a period of nearly sixty years. It is impossible to recapture in print the excitement felt in the earlier years while God was working, creating a deep sense of interdenominational unity in the gospel. It was unexpected but thrilling.

Warning

One warning, however! We should not idolise anyone named in this book. They were all, including Lloyd-Jones, fallible people and sinful like ourselves. There were occasions when division and sin were apparent. Some examples are included in the story; and this is a challenge to us because fractured relationships within and between churches still occur.

Our story begins in the 1930s when one teenager was converted and later became a powerful preacher—another thrilling part of the story!

A newspaper reporter turned preacher

Glyn Owen was born (1919) in Woodstock, rural Pembrokeshire,

South West Wales. After leaving school he worked in nearby Carmarthenshire as a local newspaper reporter. His editor, a Christian, prayed that Glyn would be converted and his prayers were answered. When Idris Davies, an Ammanford teacher, was preaching at evangelistic meetings in Carmarthenshire, the editor sent Glyn to report on what was happening. During one meeting, he stopped taking notes as he came under conviction of sin. Hearing of the Lord Jesus dying to bear the punishment of our sin, he trusted in the Lord.

Soon afterwards in 1940, Glyn enrolled at Cardiff University where he met other Christian students.

Sitting on a plate of jam tarts!

Another new student, Gwyn Walters,[4] from Llanelli in South West Wales, had been impressed at his grammar school by Tom Jones, a former school prefect and a keen Christian. When Tom heard that Gwyn was going to Cardiff University, he urged him to attend the IVF Christian Union. As a result Gwyn went to the opening meeting. It was held in a small crowded room with no empty chairs or spaces, so Gwyn sat on top of a piano. Later he realised he had been sitting on a plate of jam tarts!

The speaker was a local Presbyterian minister, Rheinallt Williams[5] who spoke on John 3:7: 'You must be born again.' Students listened intently as they heard that being born again 'formed the only foundation of the Christian life. Without ... regeneration, Christian living was impossible.'[6] There was an encouraging response with some identifying themselves with the gospel witness in the University. Slowly, as he joined in Christian

Union prayer meetings and Bible studies, Gwyn became assured that he was a Christian.

Prominent

Both Glyn Owen and Gwyn Walters were to become prominent early members of the Ministers' Conference. As students they became part of a group who longed to tell others about Christ in the University as well as in the towns and villages. Consequently, Cardiff students, with students from other colleges in Wales, held evangelistic meetings—referred to as 'campaigns' or 'missions'—during the Easter or summer vacations. Glyn and Gwyn usually preached at these meetings.

Glyn Owen became a powerful preacher, pastoring churches in Cardiff, Wrexham, Belfast, London and Toronto. After completing doctoral research in Edinburgh, Gwyn Walters was ordained, like Glyn Owen, as a Presbyterian minister and served in Cardiff before going to the United States in 1956 to teach theology. By 1962 he was Professor of Homiletics at Gordon-Conwell Theological Seminary in Massachusetts.

It was an exciting period. Meetings were held by students in various parts of South and North Wales; their aim was to share the gospel with unbelievers.

Important background

This is important background to the main story, so in the next two chapters I refer to more missions to illustrate what was happening in the 1940s and 1950s in Wales, before the Conference was established in 1955.

But even in 1937 in the Llanpumpsaint, Cynwyl, Llangeler and Carmarthen districts of West Wales, as well as in other areas, God was powerfully at work. Many people came to faith in Christ. But that is another story.

Questions for reflection and discussion

How can we avoid 'idolising' preachers and others?

What do you find challenging in the conversions of Glyn Owen and Gwyn Walters?

2

Exciting Background

The background to the establishment of the Ministers' Conference in 1955 was evangelism and the need for fellowship and co-operation. Examples are now provided.

Effective
This gospel-centred evangelism saw significant numbers of conversions in colleges and churches over several years. By the late 1940s and 1950s some converts had become church ministers with a passion to evangelise.

Remarkable period
Before describing the beginnings of the Conference, we pause to provide examples of such evangelism. Conversions were prayed for and expected.

2 Exciting Background

Glyn Owen with other students like Gwyn Walters were involved in evangelistic campaigns during summer vacations in the Rhondda Valley (1941), Carmarthen (1944) and Llanelli (1945). In the Rhondda campaign, three churches worked with forty students from three different University Christian Unions. People were converted and local Christians encouraged. The 1944 Carmarthen campaign was staffed mostly by Cardiff students and Leith Samuel came from England to preach.

Llanelli 1945

The Llanelli campaign in 1945 impacted the town and churches. Many became Christians, some of whom became useful preachers like John B. E. Thomas and Hugh D. Morgan. Their girl friends, Eluned and Mari, were converted a day or so later and eventually married John and Hugh respectively.[1] The students preached, except for one evening when a consultant surgeon from Cardiff, Arnold Aldis, preached powerfully, leaving the entire congregation overawed by the gospel message. 'The local church ... holding up to fifteen hundred people ... was packed every night.'

The Llanelli campaign is known also for effective open-air meetings which students conducted. Crowds standing in the streets listened to the students and men flocked out of the pubs to hear their testimonies and preaching. It was reported that 'well over a hundred young people were converted that week' in Llanelli.

The Rev. W. M. George, pastor of Caersalem Welsh Baptist Church, held a monthly prayer meeting to seek the Lord's blessing on the town. Christians were earnestly praying for God to save young people, including students. Their prayers were answered in astonishing ways.

> 'All one can honestly record', writes Mari Morgan, 'is that it was a very special time ... Dare one say it was a mini-revival? ...'

International rugby players

Pastor W. M. George's daughter, Pegi, was a student in Cambridge. Her boyfriend, later her husband, John Gwilliam, often visited her home and supported student evangelism in Wales. A strong Christian, he had the distinction of captaining the Welsh senior rugby side to two Triple Crown successes within a three year period.

Another outstanding rugby player was Wynford Davies who played scrum half for Newport and Wales. He entered Cardiff University in 1945. Converted through his father, I. B. Davies, he influenced the developing Christian witness in Cardiff University and the wider Christian scene. Wynford was ordained as a Presbyterian minister, and helped to establish the Ministers' Conference.

Other Campaigns

News of the Llanelli meetings spread, so another campaign was arranged for the summer of 1946 in the villages around Llanelli followed two weeks later by a campaign in nearby Ammanford. Here the local Presbyterian minister, Rev. J. D. Williams, was converted which became a turning point in his ministry. Others were converted, including Kit Mullett who later married Dr James Packer.

Student-led campaigns continued. In Pontarddulais (1947) there were more conversions and remarkable open-air meetings with many listening avidly to the gospel. Other campaigns were held in Llwynhendy (1948), Abertillery (1951) and Ogmore Vale (1954). Crowds attended the meetings in Abertillery so the cinema was hired for the final meeting.

The Cross Hands meetings in 1952 were also remarkable. God's presence was so real in some meetings that, after the preaching, many people sat on the gravestones outside the church building to ask questions and a good number trusted in Christ.

Idris Davies, the Ammanford teacher and evangelist, reported in 1949:

'... I can say ... that the Lord is blessing generously with men and women coming to the Saviour in several places, especially in Swansea, Tondre, Ystalyfera, Kilgetty—where many came together and numbers gave themselves to Christ.'[2]

North Wales

Some young people in the North felt led to hold a campaign in Bala but first decided to prepare themselves, partly by means of a weekend of fellowship, teaching and prayer.

That weekend, referred to in Welsh as an 'Encil' (Retreat), was held at Dolgellau in early January 1948 and twenty-six attended, mainly students. Most of them were converted that weekend! The final meetings were marked by spiritual reality and power as they were humbled but also overwhelmed with joy in the Lord. Later in January, the Betws Garmon Conference was held for students from Bangor. More students were converted there and also in the Bangor Colleges over the following months.

Bala 1948

Some Bangor students and local young people were involved in the Bala campaign held over Easter 1948 and which was originally intended to last for only four days. The team of students was led initially by the Rev. I. D. E. Thomas,[3] a former Bangor student and minister of a Welsh Baptist church in Glanaman, Carmarthenshire. Other students involved included Elwyn Davies, Arthur Pritchard and Glyndwr Jenkins.

The first two days were hard but on the third evening several became Christians and many more on the fourth evening:

> 'That evening we can never forget and it was midnight before it was possible for us to go home. We saw that it was necessary to have more meetings and so the campaign was extended for a further week. We saw more also coming to the Saviour. And the work continues too ...'[4]

These meetings vividly reminded the older folk of the 1904–05 revival.

It was in this Bala campaign that the Welsh Evangelical Magazine (*Y Cylchgrawn*) was born because young people requested 'sound' but easy to read Christian literature explaining the Christian faith and suitable for their friends.[5] The decision was made to produce the Magazine, though they had no funds.

Hearing of the Bala campaign, young Christians in Caernarfon agreed to meet for prayer each Saturday evening. Others joined them over the following weeks and several young people trusted in Christ in subsequent months.[6]

Elwyn Davies

But God was working apart from campaigns. For example, Elwyn Davies, a Bangor student was a morally-minded young man who was training to be a pastor. God dealt with him unexpectedly.

Elwyn was concerned to relieve poverty in post-war Germany by collecting second-hand clothing from homes in Penygroes, some four miles outside his home in Caernarfon. Cycling home, and with no one near him, Elwyn heard a clear, unusual voice saying: 'Why are you doing this work here?' It was an unfamiliar voice and more 'penetrating' and 'inescapable' than human voices.[7]

He needed no explanation. He understood God had spoken to him and he began to recognise his own sinfulness before a holy God; he saw the emptiness of his religion. A few months later, Easter 1947, he experienced forgiveness after seeing that Christ had died for his sin. We will meet Elwyn again later in the story.

In the next chapter we refer to other locations where there was significant blessing.

Questions for reflection and discussion

Are there lessons to learn from the Llanelli and Bala campaigns? Were the Llanelli meetings (1945) 'a mini-revival'? Suggest reasons for your answer.

3

Further progress

Because this was the context in which the Ministers' Conference was established, we continue the story by referring to more evangelistic meetings.

In 1948 and 1949, for example, campaigns were held in the South in Llwynhendy, Llandybie and Penygroes while in North Wales there were three-day or longer campaigns in Glascoed, Felinheli, Nantperis, Cwm-y-Glo, Tudweiliog, Llansannan, Carrog, Llanymawddwy, Coedpoeth near Wrexham, Mold, Llanfairfechan and Trefor. The latter was extended to three weeks with daily visits to quarry workers to share the gospel message. During this campaign the local Presbyterian minister, Emyr Roberts, was converted.

'The hand of the Lord'

In Swansea, in the late 1940s and early 1950s, the Youth for Christ rallies were used to bring young people to faith. There were also powerful open-air meetings in Neath, especially in the fairs, led by the Rev. I. B. Davies who was the minister at the Neath Presbyterian Mission Hall.[1] Many people, including some notorious characters, were saved through his ministry. A local funeral director encouraged drunkards to listen to this evangelist and get their lives sorted out!

Writing in 1953, Leslie Jones, a theological student in Aberystwyth, reports:

> 'The hand of the Lord has obviously been on Wales during the last six years ... In chapels, in Colleges and in schools in our land, a significant number of young people—and elderly—have come to a personal experience of the saving power that is in the gospel of Jesus Christ ...'[2]

This issue of the Cylchgrawn provided evidence in support of the above claim. For example, there had been an evangelistic mission in Aberystwyth University with the main speaker, Leith Samuel, being used significantly in the meetings.

> 'It was a great joy to see a good number of students come into His sheepfold. Many testified that they had come to a personal knowledge of the Lord Jesus Christ and that their lives—like ours—had been changed completely.'

Glenys Davies, a teacher in Dyffryn Ceiriog, also reported that:

'during the last months a number of young people in Dyffryn Ceiriog came to know the Saviour ...'[3]

A Welsh Presbyterian church, Seion, in Fforest, Aberdulais, near Neath held a week's campaign with Idris Davies preaching 'very powerfully each night'. The number of people present increased each night and believers were encouraged as,

'a number of people who were church members came to know the Lord Jesus Christ as their personal Saviour ...'

A student-led campaign was held for eleven days in the South Wales valley town of Nant-y-Moel during early summer 1954. Open-air and also children's meetings were held alongside evening preaching services when several local people trusted in Christ.[4]

The autumn issue of the Magazine reported fruitful meetings in Pontardawe near Swansea where the local chapel witnessed swelling congregations each evening. On the final evening the local cinema was hired but they still failed to accommodate all the people. More confessed Christ as Saviour and Lord.[5]

Holywell

As a teenage student recently converted, this author during September 1954 assisted in similar evangelistic meetings in Holywell on the North East Wales coast where Glyn Owen preached each evening of the week to crowded congregations.

'By the end, it was necessary to move to an even larger building for the meeting ... Glyn Owen felt that the presence of such large congregations was evidence of the hunger for God amongst the local people ... about sixty people ... accepted Jesus Christ for the first time or re-consecrated themselves to Him. God's presence was amazingly evident in the final meeting ...'[6]

Whether in colleges, schools, churches, cinemas or open-airs, prayers were being answered.

Now we turn to the link being forged spontaneously between the students and Lloyd-Jones.

Lloyd-Jones

J. O. Williams[7] reported concerning the Welsh Magazine's first tent in the National Eisteddfod (a Welsh language cultural festival) in 1949 at Dolgellau. The tent was rented for evangelism and distribution of the Magazine. This annual festival held over a one week period is attended by many thousands of people. On the Thursday evening in early August 1949, Dr Lloyd-Jones, although recovering from illness and holidaying nearby, preached for the students.

That evening an open-air meeting was held first, when 'many people' were present and heard the gospel. Then they moved to Bethel church nearby for a 10.30pm meeting where the ground floor and gallery quickly filled, mostly with young people. After a hymn, prayer and singing by a group of young people accompanied by a harp, Lloyd-Jones was introduced. He read from Philippians chapter four and preached 'powerfully' on the words: 'Rejoice in the Lord always. Again I say, rejoice' (verse 4).[8]

Significant

This meeting is significant for several reasons. First, it was a bold step for Christian students and others to witness, and for the first time, in this prestigious national festival. They made many new contacts and increased the Magazine's circulation. The next day, J. O. Williams spoke on B.B.C. Radio about the Bethel meeting so there was wide publicity. What is important is that these young people felt

> 'a necessity to tell others of their generation of the One who had died for them and given them new life, great joy and hope'.

Second, the meeting is significant for indicating Lloyd-Jones's awareness of what was happening more widely. During his message,

> 'he emphasised the fact that he was certain there was a mysterious but divine stirring taking place in some Colleges in England, Scotland and Wales'.[9]

His intimate involvement in the student work in England coupled with his own recent deep experiences and a prayerful expectancy to see the Lord work powerfully confirmed him in this conviction. It was this fact, too, that encouraged him to agree to continue strengthening the student work in Wales by speaking at their first annual Welsh IVF Conferences 1949–1951.

Third, this further contact with Welsh students served to develop a bond which led him to identify himself closely with the Ministers' Conference from 1955 until 1978. His conviction concerning the importance of the church and a growing unease with para-church groups, together with personal friendships and a burden for revival, inclined him to support this conference in Wales.

Cornwall

Other parts of the United Kingdom were experiencing similar encouragements in evangelism. One example is Cornwall where in 1953–54 two Cliff College evangelists and students were conducting missions in a group of Methodist churches in St Ives, Penzance, Porthleven, Helston and other smaller village churches.[10]

The early meetings were very ordinary but suddenly the preaching became extremely powerful and touched many lives. Many people sought to be right with God; some without church links were unexpectedly overwhelmed by a sense of personal sin. As the meetings proceeded from chapel to chapel, more folk attended and backsliders were also restored. Prayer groups sprung up without prior organisation. One eye witness reported:

> 'many have never known anything like this before, over 40 people acknowledged their need, it was past 10.30pm when a final hymn of thanksgiving was sung and brought the service to a close'.

And the blessing was not confined to the mission period. One witness reports:

> 'the missions came to an end, but the meetings continued. I organized a coach load of nineteen people from our village to go to Helston. It was a large gathering, and many more people came to the Lord.'

While another reports: 'I remember the powerful prayer meetings and atmosphere at the time ....'

In various parts of the United Kingdom, as well as in Wales, in churches, universities and colleges, there was extensive reaping in evangelism.

It was in this dynamic context of evangelism that our Conference story begins.

Questions for reflection and discussion

Do you agree with Lloyd-Jones that a 'divine stirring' was taking place in the UK colleges during these early years?

'Extremely 'powerful' and 'fruitful' preaching. Discuss this in relation to evangelistic meetings in this period. Can we know such preaching and success today? If so, how?

4

An important diversion

Lloyd-Jones's Early Relationship with Evangelicals in Wales

I do not like them. Nor do other people. They prolong the journey. Motorists can become frustrated. I am referring to a diversion when you are directed by signs, or police, on to an alternative route through a busy town or along country lanes.

This chapter is a diversion within the main story. However, there are good reasons for the diversion.

First, without it we would miss some fascinating details in the story, especially concerning the 1940s and 1950s. That would be a loss. Second, our diversion concerns the relationship of Dr Lloyd-Jones with Christian students in Wales in the 1940s and 1950s. Near the end of the book, this diversion will help you understand more about his relationship with those students who attended the Conference.

Dr Lloyd-Jones

Lloyd-Jones was a powerful preacher, well known in the United Kingdom from the late 1920s. In the 1940s and 1950s he was exercising an influential ministry in Westminster Chapel, London, and was being internationally acclaimed as an outstanding preacher. Between 1927 and 1938 he had also ministered in the Presbyterian Church at Sandfields, Aberavon. That ministry was exceptional, with hundreds of conversions.

There were additional reasons endearing him to Welsh students in the 1940s onwards as a close bond was developing between them. He preached for Welsh-language students at the National Eisteddfod in 1949 and before that in the Bangor College, but he was also the main speaker in the first three Welsh IVF[1] student Conferences held in Borth, Aberystwyth in 1949–1951. Some students were converted there under his ministry while others were challenged to see the glory of the Triune God.

Pre-war period

Lloyd-Jones's relationship with Welsh students and later with the Bala Conference pastors stands in sharp contrast to his relationship with evangelical pastors in Wales during the pre-war period. The former was a dynamic, warm and open relationship while the latter was a more distant one. Lloyd-Jones explains why he had kept aloof from pre-war evangelicals in Wales:

> 'I had no links with the Bible Institute[2] or with any part of the Convention Movement[3] nor 'Nantlais'[4] nor the Magazine.[5] I have

always regarded Keswickism as an attempt to implant English Arminianism in Wales—an attempt which did not take. The Faith Mission to Wales,[6] an imitation of the Faith Mission to Scotland,[7] also failed. I can remember the two lady evangelists at frigid Llangeitho trying to teach children to sing a chorus in the Lushai dialect'.

Considering the demise of the Evangelical faith during this period, his response appears surprising. However, he explains:

> 'Their preachers were primarily evangelists and not enough discrimination was shown when evangelising. After 1929, R. B. Jones[8] started denouncing people as false to their vows whereas in reality these people had always been unregenerate. Under the bad influence of Dr T. T. Shields[9] who was strongly anti-catholic, R. B. Jones went into the attack with his Three Rotten Apples speech, using personal names in accusations. The whole 1925–1930 phase was negative, harsh and almost barren.'[10]

These alien influences coupled with a harsh, negative approach were unacceptable to Lloyd-Jones. But there was more that troubled him:

> 'I deplored the calling in of popular style preachers such as Jack Troup, Peter Connolly, John McNeill and W. P. Nicholson. Indeed I had debates with R. B. and W. S.[11] who insisted on the new method whereas I was saying—Go back to the real preachers. One strand in Keswick preaching was the Brethren technique of drawing together a number of scriptural references into a topic address (not sermon). This humble gathering of Scriptures was regarded as a cure for

carnal, over-emotional preaching but it ran right against the Welsh tradition'.

Underlying the unease he felt, therefore, was not only Arminianism but the adoption of 'new methods' involving a changed attitude to preaching. The latter, he thought, 'ran right against the Welsh tradition' of proclamation and exposition with its prayerful dependence on God for power and fruitfulness.

1930

This background also throws further light on Lloyd-Jones's convening of an Evangelical Presbyterian Ministers' Fellowship in Sandfields Presbyterian Church on 30 December 1930. The timing is significant. Here was a positive response on his part to the '1925–1930 phase' which he regarded as 'negative, harsh and almost barren'. It also represents an even stronger Calvinistic direction on his part and one intended to steer a path outside the Conventions in Wales and the popular Keswick teaching and influence.

Only seven ministers and four church elders attended the December meeting but they felt the need to co-operate with

> 'those who believe and preach the Evangelical truths of the gospel'

who were burdened about revival. They promised to pray for one another, for revival and to emphasise regeneration and conversion in their congregations as well as the assurance of salvation and holiness of life. Unlike the Prayer-Union[12] early in the century, this fellowship functioned apart from the

Conventions, Keswick-in-Wales and the 'new methods' approach; rather it had a strong Welsh emphasis with the traditional view of preaching and revival.

This new Fellowship of pastors/elders was an encouragement to Lloyd-Jones and others. There was also considerable blessing on Lloyd-Jones's ministry in Sandfields, especially in 1931/32 when the numbers of people 'from the world' added to the church peaked.

Contrast
In contrast to pre-war evangelicals in Wales, what happened amongst students in the Welsh Colleges in the 1940s and 1950s was radically different. For example, it was not imported from England nor was it linked to the 'Convention' movement. The work amongst students was indigenous, involving a significant number of Welsh language students; it was spontaneous and fruitful.[13] In contrast to the 'barren' 1925–1930 period in Wales, hundreds of students were being converted and enlivened.

Tracing the Relationship
Some historians[14] major on the late 1940s in tracing the deepening relationship between Lloyd-Jones and students in Wales but it is important to look much earlier for the burgeoning of the relationship.

For example, it was in 1941 at the annual IVF Conference in Cambridge that J. Russell-Jones with four other Cardiff students introduced themselves to the Conference speaker, Lloyd-Jones. Isaac D. E. Thomas from the Bangor Christian Union was also present. They arranged to meet 'the Doctor' for coffee and reported to him what was happening in the Colleges in Wales. He was delighted to hear of gospel success.

Later that year, J. Russell-Jones wrote to Lloyd-Jones suggesting a separate national IVF Conference in Wales as he felt more students would attend from the Welsh Colleges. The correspondent was surprised when Lloyd-Jones advised against such a development. The fact that many young people going to University were now 'unchurched' troubled Russell-Jones and he recognised that the role of Christian students in colleges was crucial in witnessing to their peers. This point was made to 'the Doctor' but nine years elapsed before

> 'I came to see that the churches were so mixed that such a movement standing for evangelical truth was justifiable.'[15]

It was Glyn Owen and Gwyn Walters who led twelve students to Cambridge for the 1942 IVF Conference when Lloyd-Jones gave the presidential address; he was again in contact with the Welsh contingent. For several years leading up to the first Welsh IVF Conference in 1949, students from Wales were attending annual IVF Conferences in England.

At an IVF Leaders' Conference in Swanwick, Derbyshire in 1948, a group of Welsh students met informally to arrange a Wales IVF Conference for the following year. Co-opting Lloyd-Jones's daughter, Elisabeth, also gave weight to their invitation for her father to become the main speaker in the first Welsh IVF Conference in 1949. He agreed!

Wynford Davies was 'mainly responsible' for that first

Conference. Like others, he recognised that the growth of witness in Christian Unions in the Welsh Colleges, like the 'immense encouragement' in Bangor in 1949 plus the increase in the number of evangelical theological students, made the Conference a necessity with 'about sixty'[16] attending.

Back in North Wales, as we noted, students and other young people were being saved; some had met with God in 1948 and 1949. Lloyd-Jones himself was given unexpectedly two profound experiences of the Lord in the summer of 1949.

These two parallel paths were converging. It was in the 1949, 1950 and 1951 Welsh student Conferences where Lloyd-Jones

> 'taught a whole generation of Welsh evangelical students, many of whom were candidates for the ministry struggling against the prevailing theological liberalism in their denominations, basic evangelical and reformed doctrine.'[17]

It is too strong to claim he achieved this 'almost single-handedly' as there were Calvinistic pastors like W. M. George (Llanelli), H. H. Williams (Cross Hands), I. B. Davies and Emlyn Jones (Neath), for example, who exerted some influence but Lloyd-Jones was the key player ensuring that

> 'much of Welsh evangelicalism would be both theologically literate and guided in a thoroughly Calvinistic direction.'[18]

This can be illustrated by considering three students who were present and later became leaders in the Ministers' Conference. John Thomas, converted in the 1945 Llanelli mission, then inducted as minister of Lloyd-Jones's first church at Sandfields in 1953, claimed he learned more from these talks given by Lloyd-Jones than he had learned in his theology course over four years. Derek Swann felt deeply indebted to Lloyd-Jones for making divine election 'heart warming stuff', whereas Gwilym Roberts was overwhelmed by the awareness of the glory and sovereign power of God following these Conferences. The three IVF Welsh Conferences, 1949–1951, had a profound effect on many students, though not all 'embraced his reading of the contemporary church situation'.[19] Geraint Fielder confirms that 'the Welsh evangelical ministers' conference grew out of the student one.'[20]

From 1948 Lloyd-Jones preached for a number of students as they began their ministries. This was so when Glyn Owen was inducted into his first pastorate at Heath Presbyterian Church, Cardiff in 1948 and for John Thomas in Bethlehem, Sandfields in 1953.[21] It was natural therefore that Lloyd-Jones should be invited to address the first Ministers' Conference in 1955. During this crucial period of 1955–1961, as more young men were ordained and attended the Conference, their relationship with 'the Doctor' was being cemented.

After this diversion, we return to the main story in the next chapter, tracing the formation of the Evangelical Presbyterian Ministers' Fellowship and its decision to hold an annual Conference.

Questions for reflection and discussion
How should we interpret Lloyd-Jones's relationship with pre-war evangelicals in Wales?

Write down your reflections concerning the developing relationship between 'the Doctor' and students in Wales during the 1940s and 1950s. Can you identify 'key' stages in that relationship?

5

A New Development
The Evangelical Presbyterian
Ministers' Fellowship

On the 15 November 1954, a letter was sent to Presbyterian ministers in South Wales who were known to be evangelical. The term 'evangelical'[1] referred to Christians who believed the Bible to be God's reliable and infallible Word. The Bible was their supreme authority in all areas of faith and practice.

Evangelicals are passionate and clear about the Christian gospel. This glorious gospel, like a golden thread running through the Bible, centres on God's saving action through the virgin birth, sinless life, obedience and sacrificial death of Jesus Christ, the Son of God, on behalf of sinners as well as his physical resurrection from the dead and victorious ascension to heaven where he rules over the universe and the church. The necessity of new birth and conversion, that is, repentance from sin and personal faith in Christ, are emphasised together with the work of the Holy Spirit in believers and in the church. Between such believers there is a deep spiritual unity which runs across denominations.

By the 1970s, the term 'evangelical' had become somewhat elastic in its meaning and has continued to be modified in recent years.

Encouraging

It was an encouraging letter which was sent in November 1954. Reference was made to 'a number of Rallies' held during the previous twelve months and attended by young people mostly from English language Presbyterian churches in South Wales. Only a week before the letter was sent, a rally was held in Sandfields, Aberavon. The numbers of young people present 'were greatly increased'.

And the letter offers a reason for this remarkable increase. It was a result of groups of young converts being formed following the student-led campaigns and other evangelistic efforts in the area. For this reason the letter was sent urgently to ministers for them to discuss and pray over the situation and then to respond.

On 19th November, eighteen Presbyterian ministers responded to the letter and met. Apologies and good wishes were received from seven others. There was a good mix of ages with almost half the number being younger men recently ordained. Key decisions were made like agreeing to plan quarterly preaching rallies with a strong commitment to 'the conservative evangelical position.'

They also decided to form an 'Evangelical Presbyterian Ministers' Fellowship'. Only Presbyterians could belong to the Fellowship which would meet in January, April, June and October. One of these meetings would be a three-day Conference but 'open to Evangelical Ministers of all Denominations'. Dr D. Martyn Lloyd-Jones was chosen unanimously as the main speaker.

> 'No formal advertising of the Conference was to be made but members were encouraged to invite those they knew to be of like mind.'

Quarterly Fellowship Meetings

They met quarterly as planned for prayer and discussion of important doctrines as well as overseeing the rallies for young people in their churches. The following details provide insight into these meetings and the struggles they faced.

By the January 1955 meeting in Neath,

> 'a list of almost one hundred ministers who were being contacted was approved and added to.'[2]

This was an encouraging number especially as care was taken in approving each name. It was also agreed that because

> 'some of the older and retired ministers would be unable to attend ...'

they should receive a newsletter requesting their prayers.

Interestingly, after

'an excellent lunch provided by Mrs. I. B. Davies at the Manse, it was agreed in future that members would provide their own food in order not to burden any one family or church ...'

In the afternoon discussion which followed

'the Rev. Gordon Roberts raised questions concerning the Parable of the Sower and the messages to the churches in Revelation chapters 2-3.' Then 'a most profitable discussion followed in which many problems and difficulties were dealt with. The blessing continued into a period of prayer ...'[3]

Their third meeting was on April 22, 1955 in Station Road Presbyterian Church, Treorchy in the Rhondda valley when changes were reported for the first Evangelical Ministers' Conference planned for June:

'Letters had been received from the leaders of the United Missionary Council of Wales (UMCW)[4] and from the Foreign Missions secretary of the Presbyterian Church of Wales drawing attention to the clash of dates between the popular Barry Missionary Conference organized by the UMCW and the newly proposed ministers' Conference. The Fellowship's chairman and secretary, in consultation with Lloyd-Jones, agreed to postpone the Conference so as not to clash ... and cause unnecessary offence.'

There was agreement that their Conference could be

rearranged, re-locating within Barry from Coleg-y-Fro to Glan-y-Môr

> 'and pleasure was expressed at the reduced costs of the Conference!'

The success of preaching rallies for young people peaked in November 1954 according to this April meeting but

> 'disappointment was felt in the lack of concern shown by some members in the last rally (Nantymoel) in that they had neither attended nor sent word of explanation'.[5]

The morning session in the April meeting included the Rev. J. D. Jones giving

> 'an excellent address on the covenant of redemption as taught in the Denomination Confession of Faith' (1823).

In the afternoon,

> 'the chairman led a lively discussion on the theme of the morning session, and this proved to be most profitable.' As usual, the meeting 'was closed with a session of prayer.'

Their next meeting was at Seion, Aberdulais on 4 November with eleven members present. The meeting expressed appreciation for many encouragements received in their first Conference the previous June. They then proceeded to plan their second Ministers' Conference for June 1956 to which Duncan

Campbell and Lloyd-Jones were invited as speakers. Following lunch, the Rev. Wynford Davies spoke on

> 'the Holy Spirit in the Covenant of Grace. A free and extremely profitable discussion followed.'

Sandfields, Aberavon was the venue for the fifth meeting of the Fellowship on 27 January 1956; fewer members attended and several apologies were received. It was in Trinity, Clydach where the April 1956 meeting was held. Twelve members were present, including for the first time the Revs Vernon Higham and W. R. James. It was reported

> 'that a goodly number had already booked' for the June 1956 Ministers' Conference 'and the final figure should exceed fifty.'[6] Further, 'the Rev. Duncan Campbell was to speak at three sessions, and Dr Lloyd-Jones at one, also leading three discussions.'

Later, the Rev. I. B. Davies

> 'gave an excellent paper on regeneration ... Many questions raised by Mr Davies were examined and the discussion continued after the lunch break at the close of which a short time was spent in prayer.'

After the profitable second Ministers' Conference in June 1956, twenty-three ministers attended the next Fellowship meeting in October 1956 in the home of the Rev. and Mrs Emlyn Jones, Neath. Apologies were received from five regulars. In warmly welcoming new members, the chairman referred to 'the friends from other denominations and to those of the Monmouthshire Prayer group'.

Membership was now no longer exclusively Presbyterian and a decision was made to have a joint meeting of the Evangelical Presbyterian Ministers' Fellowship and the Monmouthshire Ministers' Prayer Fellowship. The latter was interdenominational and the joint meeting was scheduled for January 25 1957 in Central Hall, Newport. After discussing the practical details, the Rev. Emlyn Jones gave 'a provoking paper' on 'Preaching' and a

> 'very full and lively discussion followed which revealed the deep hunger in the hearts of many for a visitation of God's Spirit.'[7] Appropriately, 'prayer followed the discussion'.

Less formal Minutes were recorded for the combined meeting held as scheduled on 25 January 1957 in Newport. A total of thirty ministers attended but disappointingly no details concerning the attendees or the address and discussion are provided. We are simply informed that

> 'an excellent paper was given by the Rev. J. Russell-Jones'; His subject was 'The Holy Spirit and the Ministry'.

And

> 'Many present confessed to have passed through a searching time. Many contributed to the discussion which followed'.[8]

These brief minutes include a small postscript:

'In view of the success of this meeting a second one was held at the home of the Rev. and Mrs W. K. Sharman of Cardiff.'[9]

No date is provided but it represented the Spring quarterly meeting in April that year. The Rev. Wynford Davies, Tonypandy,

'gave an address of a very high standard on the Life of the Minister drawing liberally from Rev. Richard Baxter and others. The high standard of personal discipline in the life of the Minister of God in the past awakened a sense of shame in many present and by general assent the need of reform among Evangelical Ministers was clearly seen'.

A negative note was struck before the end:

'It was clearly seen (from) the small attendance that many ministers did not fully agree with the particular type of meeting'.

Was the unease felt only by Presbyterians? Were there doctrinal differences? Or unease in changing the Fellowship's aim? No answers are provided.

The trend towards further interdenominational co-operation accelerated. This was evident in their June 1957 Ministers' Conference when the Evangelical Presbyterian Ministers' Fellowship handed over responsibility for the Conference to the Evangelical Movement of Wales (EMW). At this Conference Presbyterian representatives like I. B. Davies, Vernon Higham and John Thomas—met with members of the EMW General Committee 'to discuss under the chairmanship of the Rev. Dr Martyn Lloyd-Jones the future of the Ministers Conference'.[10] Following 'a full and free discussion concerning policy, motives, aims and general practice',

it was agreed to make recommendations to Conference members, including:

1. 'That a Sub-Committee of the Evangelical Movement of Wales be formed to care for the Ministers' Conference and Fellowships'.

2. The Officers recommended were I. B. Davies (Chairman), John Thomas (Secretary) and Vernon Higham (Treasurer).

3. 'Ministerial Fellowships for Evangelicals were to be formed in various parts of the country and, if possible, pursue one course of study, culminating with the Annual Conference in which a speaker would be invited to speak upon that subject'.

There were struggles and encouragements in these Quarterly Fellowships but the annual June Conference became the main focus and unifying influence for expressing gospel unity and co-operation amongst evangelical pastors at an interdenominational level.

We major next on the opening Conference in June 1955.

Questions for reflection and discussion
Explain simply what the following key words mean:

1. 'Evangelical'; 2. 'Regeneration'; 3. 'Covenant of Grace'.

Write down what you know about the Holy Spirit.

PART TWO

The Early Years 1955–1961

Chapter 6   The 1955 Conference in context

Chapters 7–8 Revival emphasis

Chapter 9   Unforgettable but with tensions

6

The 1955 Conference in Context

We now major on the Conference which was for these pastors a significant event in 1955. As a result of personal invitations, about fifty ministers attended.

What was the general situation in which this Conference was established?

Situation
The political situation in the United Kingdom in 1955 was tense and turbulent. Sir Winston Churchill had resigned as the British Prime Minister and was succeeded by Sir Anthony Eden who went on to win the General Election. Early in December that year, Clement Atlee, a former post-war Prime Minister, resigned as leader of the Labour Party and Hugh Gaitskell was elected as his successor.

Internationally, the Warsaw Pact was signed, confirming that the 'Cold War' was a reality. This remained the picture for the next fifty years with its military and ideological conflict between Western powers, including America, and those in Eastern Europe led by Russia.

Social

Socially, there was increasing secularisation, consumerism and materialism while concern was expressed in England over the rising numbers of immigrants from the West Indies. London viewers for the first time had an alternative to BBC television with the launch of ITV while Joe Davis, Britain's snooker champion, made the first ever maximum break of 147 to be captured on television!

Religious

In England, scepticism characterised the 1920s followed in the 1930s by an up-turn in the popularity of Anglicanism. Partly disturbed by the prospect and then the realities of war, people became frightened and disillusioned. One expression of this was the emergence of lay apologetics by intellectual and literary folk. Some of the

> 'most influential figures in contemporary culture found "faith" and their collective return to Christianity represents one of the significant characteristics of the 1935/1945 period'.[1]

These apologists included Sherwood Taylor, Alfred Noyes, C. M. Joad, C. S. Lewis and Dorothy Sayers.

Nevertheless, profound religious changes were accelerating,

resulting in a gradual but serious decline in church attendance and allegiance. The most disturbing decrease in church membership figures in the United Kingdom was in Wales where 'a crisis of dissent ... continued in the 1950s'.[2] The situation caused concern to church leaders while pastors in Wales were also concerned that in many local churches the Bible was hardly taught.

To meet this need, from 1948, interdenominational Seiadau ('Fellowship'/'Society' meetings) for Bible-study and prayer were established for believers lacking teaching.[3] These were arranged informally, often on the initiative of a pastor. In Trefor, Caernarfon, for example, Emyr Roberts started such a meeting and then he and Arthur Pritchard encouraged similar Fellowships in Tudweiliog, Pwllheli, Caernarfon, Porthmadog, Bala and even Chester. For Emyr Roberts, the Fellowship meeting reflected more accurately what the Church of Christ should be.[4] To add to the problem some ministers were struggling in pastorates where their Bible teaching was unwelcome.

Ecumenism

Some important dates are included below to help clarify the situation:

> 1948: The establishment of the World Council of Churches (WCC) in Amsterdam, promoting co-operation and unity between all Churches, despite theological differences.

> 1950s–1960s: Church unity gathered momentum at local/national levels, creating problems for evangelical churches and pastors.

1954: Responding to the WCC Evanston Assembly in 1954, the Welsh Ecumenical Society[5] was established.

1956: The Council of Churches for Wales was formed to spearhead the movement for unity by churches, not societies.[6]

1963: Four Protestant denominations in Wales (Presbyterian, Baptist, Congregational and Methodist) published *Towards Union*.

1974: These denominations agreed to covenant to co-operate and seek unity but on a weak doctrinal basis.

Noel Davies affirms that 'the inter-church climate is very different at the beginning of the twenty-first century compared with the 1950s and 1960s' for the aim now is not one visible church but 'rather a pattern of partnership and collaboration' between churches.[7]

1955/1972: 'Conversations' were initiated between the Church of England and the Methodist Church of Great Britain regarding possible Union. An Interim Report in 1958 led to organic unity becoming the official goal. The Scheme in its 1970 revised form was defeated in 1972. Dr James Packer was prominent in opposition to the Scheme in tandem with Anglo-Catholic representatives.

1972: The Presbyterian Church of England and Congregational Union of England and Wales formed the United Reformed Church.

6 The 1955 Conference in Context

These developments constrained Conference pastors to consider three big issues: What is the gospel? What is a Christian? And what is the church?

1954: The Billy Graham, Haringey, London Crusade represented a 'watershed', and 'new trend' when non-Evangelical church leaders were invited to participate, despite rejecting biblical distinctives.

1955–1966: Iain Murray correctly identifies 'a major shift in evangelical opinion'[8] on ecumenism and liberal theology.

Already the clouds were gathering, giving early warnings to those loyal to biblical teaching.

Travel

Within days of assuming office, the new Prime Minister faced a dock strike which disrupted six major seaports. There was also a national rail strike involving seventy thousand train drivers and their firemen who wanted improved pay and working conditions. The UK Government announced a state of emergency as the strike brought British industry to a standstill, and all this coincided with the first Ministers' Conference in Barry in 1955.

Travelling to the Conference, therefore, was more difficult. From North Wales, the Revs. Elwyn Davies and Gwilym Humphreys hitch-hiked and for most of the journey they were given a lift in a Tate & Lyle sugar lorry!

The main speaker, Dr D. Martyn Lloyd-Jones, was late arriving. He had bought a new car so was obliged to travel at a moderate speed. It was Omri Jenkins who drove. Without motorways or a bridge over the Severn estuary into Wales, the tedious journey from London was lengthened by 'the Doctor's' insistence they should stop for afternoon tea!

1955 Conference

The very first Conference address on the Monday evening was by I. B. Davies in his capacity as Conference chairman and chairman of the Fellowship of Evangelical Presbyterian Ministers. His text was 1 Corinthians 2 verse 2 on preaching Christ crucified. He spoke warmly of the great love of God in sending his only-begotten Son into the world to save sinners from the penalty, guilt and power of their sin. The preacher extolled the uniqueness of this one, final sacrifice for sin. On this basis alone, people can be saved when believing on the Lord Jesus. The men were greatly encouraged by the message.

Structure

The structure of the Conference was an historical address with questions following, two sessions devoted to discussion, daily prayer meetings, two or three main Conference addresses and a closing message from Lloyd-Jones. By 1971 the Conference ended on Wednesday afternoon rather than late Thursday morning to enable ministers to return to church meetings. This structure has been retained with minor modifications, commencing after Monday lunch and by 2014 ending with lunch on Wednesday. It is a packed programme but with time for informal fellowship and one free afternoon for relaxation.

Highlight

The highlight of the 1955 Conference, however, was the addresses given by Lloyd-Jones. He spoke twice on the 'Sealing of the Spirit' from Ephesians 1:13–14 and 3:14–19. He described the 'sealing' as often occurring after conversion, alongside the 'ordinary' work of the Holy Spirit in regeneration and sanctification. Here is a God-given 'extra-ordinary' dimension when the Holy Spirit comes upon the believer in greater power, giving deeper assurance and experiences of God's love in Christ. This was not a 'second blessing' for the Holy Spirit indwells each Christian, but there is need for a greater degree of the Spirit's power in believers, especially for witnessing, preaching and having a greater experiential acquaintance with the Lord. He used the term 'revival' to describe what happens when the Holy Spirit comes upon a whole church or on several churches in an area.

Reaction

Reaction from ministers was varied. Some like Dr Gwyn Walters (1922–1993) and I. B. Davies disagreed with Lloyd-Jones. Were the Bible verses expounded properly? It also seemed to Gwyn Walters that Lloyd-Jones's teaching differed from that of the sixteenth-century Geneva theologian and pastor, John Calvin, whom he had studied for a doctoral degree in Edinburgh University. His research subject was the doctrine of the Holy Spirit in Calvin's writings.[9]

The subject was pursued in discussion sessions. James Packer was present and supported Lloyd-Jones's teaching. Derek Swann acknowledged that the talks had opened his mind to the extraordinary work of the Holy Spirit in periods of revival.

Despite disagreement, the profound sense of God's presence following each message meant no one wanted to speak or leave.

Omri Jenkins felt it was a 'new dimension' for him; in that and later Conferences until 1960 he was 'in a new world' of spiritual reality.

Pattern

The 1955 Conference set the pattern for later Conferences with a continuing emphasis on the gospel and on personal/corporate prayer. Lessons and challenges were drawn from preachers and periods of blessing, including the history of Welsh Calvinistic Methodism. Biblical teaching was prized and pervading all the Conferences was the need to know God more.

In the next three chapters, we trace some emphases in the Cilgwyn Conferences from 1956–1961. It is an exciting story with encouragements and tensions.

Questions for reflection and discussion

In contrast to those lacking fellowship/teaching in the 1940s and 1950s, do we value our Bible-teaching churches?

A 'new dimension' and 'a new world' of spiritual reality, is this an exaggeration or a helpful description of their experience in 1955? Discuss.

7

The 1956 Cilgwyn Conference[1]

The 1956 Conference was relocated to Cilgwyn, a Conference Centre in Newcastle Emlyn, a small agricultural town in South West Wales. Cilgwyn remained the location for the Conference until 1961 before moving permanently to Bryn-y-groes, Bala, in North Wales in 1962.

For those attending the early Conferences, Cilgwyn held special memories. Between fifty to sixty ministers in this period attended the Conference which remained interdenominational, although organised by Presbyterians until 1957.

The key themes of the 1955 Conference were continued in 1956. Revival, prayer with a genuine dependence on God alongside fidelity to the biblical gospel and a passion for evangelism were prominent themes, ones that Lloyd-Jones had emphasised the previous year. Discussion and warm fellowship were also highlights, despite disagreement over Calvinism.

Duncan Campbell

In the 1956 Conference Duncan Campbell had been invited to give the main addresses on revival, due to his experiences in the 1949–1953 revival on the Isle of Lewis in the Hebrides, Scotland. Ill-health prevented him from attending and his place was taken by Iain H. Murray. The latter writes:

> 'I was *not* the speaker expected. Duncan Campbell was due to speak, and Lloyd-Jones via John Thomas brought me in'.[2]

Before considering Murray's role, we must consider the invitation to Campbell. There was disappointment that Campbell could not attend for the revival had been reported in the Christian Press extensively and it aroused considerable interest. For example, Campbell had written a forty-four page booklet, The Lewis Awakening, published by the Faith Mission in 1954. Campbell also described the revival in the 1952 Keswick Convention which was published in The Keswick Week that year.[3]

While the revival was in progress, the Welsh language Evangelical Magazine (*Y Cylchgrawn*) in 1952 gave prominence to the theme of revival. An article on the conditions of revival from Glyn Owen was based on Ezekiel 37:1-10 while 'Caerwyn' from Llangefni shared his memories of two revivalists, Richard Owen and Evan Roberts. What is of interest is Herbert Evans's account of the Isle of Lewis revival 'which is going on now at the moment'.[4]

The article was based on meetings in St Paul's, Portman Square, London, where Duncan Campbell spoke on this 'on-going'. After describing the beginnings of the revival and Campbell's early ministry on the island at Barvas, Herbert Evans underlined two major features that Campbell had shared. One was the overwhelming sense of God's presence in numerous places and meetings. Another feature was the deep conviction of sin that many experienced.

How did the revival come about? The answer is uncompromising:

> 'through prayer in the first place, and through proclaiming the whole counsel of God in the second place ... but if all this is true, why do we not have revival in Wales?'

The editorial following this article pleaded with readers to seek the Lord and plead his covenant promises for a similar work in Wales.

Revival was in progress in Barvas before Campbell arrived. Within days of reaching the island, Campbell reported on 21 December 1949:

> 'We are in the midst of revival. Meetings are crowded ... Already about seventy adults have professed; we are dealing with anxious souls in every meeting'.[5]

He insisted:

'I did not bring revival to Lewis ... but God moved in the parish of Barvas before I ever set foot on the island.'[6]

In the background, there had been earnest prevailing prayer and people were becoming Christians in the locality for months prior to Campbell's arrival on the 7 December 1949.

Early in 1954, Campbell visited Cardiff to speak about the revival and lead Sunday services in Heath Presbyterian Church where the Rev. Glyn Owen was still the pastor, prior to moving that year to Trinity Presbyterian Church, Wrexham. He was in Wales again to talk on the subject in the Welsh language Evangelical Movement of Wales annual Conference in 1957 in Rhosllannerchrugog, near Wrexham. And ministers, including Emyr Roberts, seized the opportunity to listen to him.

Criticism

Were the Conference members aware of criticisms levelled against Campbell in Scotland? Lloyd-Jones and a few others in Cilgwyn were aware but what were these criticisms?[7] One was that he belonged to a para-church organisation and did not respect the principles of the Free Church of Scotland leaders nor seek their support or prayers.

Rev. Kenneth Macrae, the godly and influential Free Church of Scotland minister in Stornoway on the Isle of Lewis from 1931–1964 regarded the phenomena in this revival as 'mass hysteria.'[8] Although an opponent of Campbell, Macrae had a burden for revival and knew blessing and growth in his church which had the largest congregation on the island. Campbell's reporting of statistics regularly to the Faith Mission[9] with the

7   The 1956 Cilgwyn Conference   69

number of 'converts' and those attending meetings, also caused unease amongst Free Church ministers. Nevertheless, critics acknowledge the integrity of the testimonies of individuals blessed and converted in this period of 1949-1953 and whose stories were included in a recent account of this revival.[10] A more serious charge against Campbell was that of Arminianism,[11] but whatever our view of Campbell's theology he emphasised the majesty of the Triune God and salvation by grace.

Iain H. Murray

Why choose the young Iain Murray as a substitute speaker in place of Campbell? Murray writes:

> '... when I went to Oxford in May 1955, with time to determine my own studies,' writes Murray, 'Lloyd-Jones urged me to work on "the Calvinism of the English Reformers." Out of that came 60 or so pages which I wrote and sent to him about the time Campbell had to withdraw for some health reason. The Dr wanted me to give this material at Cilgwyn'.[12]

This was a significant change of topic, but it expressed Lloyd-Jones's strong commitment to Calvinism and his perceived need to highlight Calvinistic doctrine. During the 1950s, Iain Murray writes,

> 'his Calvinistic convictions were more to the fore' and 'while his convictions never changed, his emphasis underwent adjustment in changing circumstances',

There is further significance in this choice of speaker and subject which Murray recognises:

'We were young and the Dr's willingness to encourage the young still surprises me! How patient and kind he was!'

What were Murray's first impressions of the 1956 Conference? He writes:

'I recall arriving in the dining room the first night, scarcely knowing anyone, and sitting down at a table of black-coated gentlemen—all CM (Calvinistic Methodist) ministers. One of them asked me quizzically, "are you a Bangor student?"'

The Calvinism of the English Reformers
Iain Murray gave two major addresses on the above subject and the 'gist of them', Murray adds, is available in his 1956 Evangelical Library Lecture.[13]

Murray described the English Reformers like Rowland Taylor, Ridley, Bradford, Tyndale, Frith and Thomas Hancock as

'a remarkable company of men who ... turned the nation upside down in the sixteenth century and profoundly altered the whole course of English history.'[14]

These English Reformers were

'convinced that the truth they held was the truth of God ... and that the faith once delivered to the saints was the very same as the faith they believed. It was in their appeal to Scripture that the whole confidence of the English reformers lay ... They knew that the doctrine was of God and that he was pleased with them. They were deeply persuaded that no weapon formed against the truth could prosper.'[15]

They 'were convinced that their doctrine was of no temporary importance'. The doctrine of predestination was highlighted by Iain Murray as it was

'one foremost doctrinal principle of the Reformers. It was the assertion of this principle more than any other that separated irrevocably the theology of the Reformers from the theology of Rome and the Middle Ages. To this principle the whole system of reformed doctrine was necessarily related'.[16]

Murray adds:

'this belief that He of mere grace distinguishes between men who are all equally involved in sin and guilt, and that he saves men because of His will not because of their own, is the fundamental doctrinal principle ...'

What were the reasons 'that prominently appear for the place they gave to this doctrine ...?' One reason was that its rejection or neglect 'would overthrow all the rest of the gospel system.' For example,

'without the doctrine of predestination they held that justification could not be truly expounded. For justification is wholly God's action.[17]

A second reason for this doctrine's prominence is

'a practical one ... in their preaching, in their evangelism, they asserted this doctrine to be vital and essential'[18] ... But this same doctrine they viewed as even more vital in strengthening, sanctifying and establishing believers.[19]

Controversial

Elwyn Davies emphasised there was controversy in this 1956 Conference as Arminian pastors objected to the emphasis on predestination. Iain Murray confirms 'it was a controversial Conference'. Four interesting details can be included here. One is the fact that the Arminians expressed openly their objections which was encouraging. Two, Iain Murray reports that

'the Dr took the brunt of it (objections) and in the questions he urged 1 Corinthians 2, and the crucial point of regeneration preceding faith from the words—"the natural man receiveth not the things of the Spirit of God, for they are foolishness to him ...".' (v 14).[20]

Three, while Iain Murray acknowledges 'it highly probable that the Dr saw various parties privately at Cilgwyn,'[21] Elwyn Davies claimed that Lloyd-Jones met at least with the Arminian group in an attempt to pastor them concerning their negative response to predestination. Four, did Lloyd-Jones advise Iain Murray to major on the subject of prayer in his second address and not be controversial? That was Elwyn Davies's view but Murray disagrees as 'the Dr was not for any softening (of emphasis) at that Conference'.

The controversy rumbled on even at the level of prayer. For example, when some younger Presbyterian ministers complained to the Conference chairman, I. B. Davies, that Arminians monopolised the Conference prayer meetings, he replied in his inimitable manner:

> 'You miserable men, then get up on your feet and pray!'

Closing message

In the 1956 Conference, the closing message given by Dr Martyn Lloyd-Jones was, 'Why are we where we are?'[22] This indicated 'the Doctor's' careful analysis and understanding of the situation.

His insisted we should ask about the church before discussing reaching outsiders. First, he stressed the importance of right doctrine. 'Revival has always come when basic truths are proclaimed' such as the doctrines of sin, the holiness and wrath of God, salvation by grace through faith alone and the substitutionary atonement of the Lord Jesus for sinners: 'remember that doctrine is important' as God only blesses such doctrines.

Second, Lloyd-Jones insisted we must recognise

> 'our own utter inadequacy and at the same time our total dependency on God.'

It is possible for evangelistic campaigns to be

> 'one of the obstacles to revival ... as our efforts then become too important and we merely ask God to bless OUR efforts ... We must put our dependence alone on the Holy Spirit. Instead of planning

a campaign, we should ask: Why has God left us? We must pray. We must be importunate ...'[23]

In the next chapter we follow the story of the 1957 and 1958 Cilgwyn Conferences.

Questions for reflection and discussion
Explain and discuss the term 'predestination'.

Why was Duncan Campbell criticised over the revival (1950–1953)? Do you agree with these criticisms?

What is your response or that of your group/church to the 1956 Conference closing address?

8

Cilgwyn Conferences 1957 and 1958

The 1957 Conference continued the theme of revival particularly through the addresses of Ivor Davies, a Welsh missionary who, with his brother David, served with the Worldwide Evangelization Crusade (W.E.C.) in the North East of what was then the Belgian Congo. In 1953, both brothers, based at different locations, were eyewitnesses of the revival that broke out in many churches.[1] That is the story ministers heard in this Conference.

Ivor Davies

Ivor Davies and his wife were based in Opienge, working among the Balumbi tribe. But it was in the southern end of their mission field in Lubutu, Congo, where revival first broke out in February 1953. It was the revival's epicentre. During a conference for African evangelists, a profound seriousness came upon one meeting leading them to express deep longings to know the Lord. As the Africans met alone that night in prayer, the Holy Spirit suddenly descended upon them, resulting in weeping, confession, joy and praise. There were also physical manifestations such as violent shaking, jumping and laughter which troubled the missionaries. Over several days, these evangelists were filled with joy and a burning passion to spread the gospel.

News of these happenings reached missionaries in Opienge where some local Africans had a deep desire for the Lord to work powerfully amongst them too. One evangelist came under intense conviction of sin and others were dealt with before the Holy Spirit fell upon a large gathering of believers there. The revival then spread to Bomili, Biboko and other places like Ibambi where Helen Roseveare was a medical missionary.

Ivor Davies drew attention to the reservations of Western missionaries, especially concerning the more unusual and physical manifestations. They were gradually convicted of their hardness of heart and, repenting, experienced the Lord powerfully. In his concluding address, Ivor Davies drew attention to Psalm 24, especially verses 4–6 and described conditions for blessing that served to fuel Conference prayer meetings and discussions.

In the Conference itself, pastors were challenged in different ways and Elwyn Davies shared one example that occurred, he thought, in this 1957 Conference.

Tension

There was a tendency for pastors to stay together with denominational colleagues. One afternoon Elwyn reports[2] he went with others to a café for refreshments. Observing the Presbyterians sitting aloof from those of other denominations he was embarrassed. When they returned in separate groups to the Centre, they all stood talking leisurely in the entrance foyer. Without planning it, a circle was being formed. Suddenly, the informal talking gave way to spontaneous prayer when, within a few minutes, the Holy Spirit unexpectedly fell on them and gave them a great love for one another. Elwyn Davies describes what happened:

> 'The Rev. I. B. Davies came to me and said, "I love you brother" and I returned the same sentiment. Then all the other men also expressed their love for each other personally and genuinely.'

A deeper sense of unity and love between the ministers was experienced.

Lloyd-Jones's message[3]

Lloyd-Jones's closing message in the 1957 Conference was on Mark 9:23; 'why could we not cast him out?' He emphasised the church's ineffectiveness, then referred to the expanding movement within Protestant churches for church unity as 'a pressing problem'. The prior need, he argued, was to safeguard the gospel, as the unity created by the Holy Spirit comes only through this biblical gospel. He argued the point in detail[4] and used the picture of a man lying unconscious on a country road.

'What are we to do? He may be asleep. Or he may have poison in his system. The position in earlier times in Wales such as in 1858–59 was not that people denied the faith, but that they had fallen asleep. Today, however, there is a deadly poison in the system of the church, namely, false and unbiblical doctrine'. 'Can the Holy Spirit bless a people who do not own the truth? No. He cannot. Doctrine is absolutely essential'.

Lloyd-Jones reinforced this by referring to the 'irreducible minimum' of doctrines that must be believed. First, he referred to the doctrine of God the Father, that

> 'He is sovereign and Lord of the universe. The sense of the glory of God has gone from us. We must go back to this doctrine.'

Next he emphasised the doctrine of God the Son and His office as mediator.

> 'The heart of my message is that God laid upon Jesus the condemnation of my sins'.

But the doctrine of Christ the Saviour depends on our concept of sin and justification by faith. He then emphasised the

> 'Doctrine of the Holy Spirit, especially conviction of sin as an agony of conviction was present in all the great revivals of the past. Today, there is an absence of conviction of sin ...

One condition of revival, therefore, is that we hold fast to the Truth. The Holy Spirit will not bless anything else ... What we must do is to preach these doctrines, assent to them and live them ...

> Here the Christian position is paradoxical. The gospel is exclusive and intolerant on the one hand and yet is the manifestation of love. We are never to be hard and harsh. We must preach the truth in love. While there is no fellowship between the two sides of this division caused by these truths, yet we must do everything to promote fellowship amongst ourselves.'

Lloyd-Jones also warned of factors which break this God-given unity, including character defects, carnality, sin, the absence of seriousness/humility and the lack of helplessness and waiting on God.

> 'Nothing but desperation about ourselves and our country will send us to real prayer,

he insisted.[5]

Cilgwyn 1958

Lloyd-Jones was absent from the 1958 Conference and explained to Elwyn Davies:

> 'I am, as you know, going to South Africa and now I have had an additional task thrust upon me by the Christian Medical Fellowship of preparing ... a statement on the Wolfendon Report ... there does not seem to be anybody else to do it. As I was not due to speak at Cilgwyn I feel I am not in any way letting you down ...'[6]

Over fifty attended the Conference, representing 'all the

Protestant churches' and 'age groups' from the North and South of Wales, some less than a year in the ministry and others over fifty years, including the 1904-05 revival men.

Another difference was the mix of men pastoring either in Welsh or English churches and areas.

> 'Despite all these differences', reported Gwilym Roberts, 'perhaps the greatest characteristic of the Conference ... was the deep underlying unity of spirit.'[7]

He added that such unity was based on the acceptance of the Bible as God's Word and also 'a common concern and burden for our beloved land of Wales.'

They longed to reach unbelievers with the gospel. These 'two factors', he emphasised, were 'constantly in evidence' even in the opening meeting when Elwyn Davies 'spoke of the spiritual state of Wales today'. From the times of prayer,

> 'it was clear' that 'above all, there was a yearning that His Holy Spirit should come upon His people again ...'

Scripture

Alongside the emphasis on revival, prayer and evangelism was a strong doctrinal note. James Packer, a regular in the early Conferences, spoke on the 'Authority of Scripture,' showing

> 'we must either accept the right of God's Word to rule, or else ... rely on some form of human authority ...'[8] whether reason, tradition or experience.

This subject was timely. That same year, Packer's *Fundamentalism and The Word of God*[9] had been published. This book was 'widely influential'[10] and a 'classic statement' of the way evangelicals understand the nature and authority of the Scriptures.[11] Because many had struggled with a liberal theological training, Packer's scholarly contribution in Conference as well as in his book was a considerable help to them. They felt more confident afterwards to uphold the doctrine of Scripture in their churches.

Following the Conference, T. J. Russell-Jones reviewed Packer's book in the *Evangelical Magazine of Wales*,[12] describing it as

> 'a constructive re-statement of evangelical principles in the light of the current "Fundamentalism Controversy" ...'

Defining key terms, Packer rebuts charges like 'obscurantist,' 'reactionary', 'superstitious' and 'bibliolatrous', then grappled with themes of 'utmost importance' such as 'Authority', 'Scripture', 'Faith' and 'Reason'. The reviewer rightly regarded Packer's book as 'scholarly, sane' and 'intensely readable' and hoped that critics and evangelicals would read it.

Daniel Rowland

Derek Swann brought a Welsh historical perspective to the Conference with two addresses on the Life and Preaching of Daniel Rowland (1711-1790). Rowland's outstanding preaching in Llangeitho, West Wales, for half a century, often in revival, was exceptionally fruitful with thousands of people converted. People flocked from all over Wales to sit under his remarkable ministry. The Conference Committee wanted the two addresses published, but when the speaker recognised that a thorough study of Rowland demanded a command of the Welsh language, he suggested to Eifion Evans he 'should undertake the task.'[13] It was another stimulating Conference. Two further matters 'heartened' Gwilym Roberts, namely,

> 'that God is raising up so many who are returning to ... the old truths ... and to see so many young men ...'. Even more important was the fact that 'the prayer meetings confirmed for pastors that the Spirit of the Lord was at Cilgwyn'.[14]

In the next chapter, we continue the story with regard to the remaining Cilgwyn Conferences from 1959 to 1961.

Questions for reflection and discussion

What are your observations on the 1953 Congo revival as reported in the 1957 Conference?

In which ways should we 'guard' (Ephesians 4:1-6) the God-created unity amongst Christians?

Suggest ways in which the *authority of the Bible* applies in your personal and church situations.

9

Unforgettable but with tensions Cilgwyn 1959–1961

Cilgwyn 1959 stands out in the history of the Conference. A normal, enjoyable Conference but the final meeting was exceptional.

1859 revival
The main speakers in 1959 were Drs Eifion Evans and Lloyd-Jones. The former gave a moving account of the 1859 revival in Wales.

> 'Between 1762 and 1862', writes Evans,' there were at least fifteen outstanding revivals in Wales.'[1]

There were also 'local' revivals beforehand in places

like Staylittle (1851) in mid-Wales and in other localities like Llanfairfechan in North Wales during April and May 1858. Within three months the membership of the Wesleyan Church in Llanfairfechan increased from 24 to 134. The revival spread quickly to nearby towns and villages.

In June 1858, a Wesleyan minister, Rev. Humphrey Jones returned from America where he had participated in revival. Churches and individuals like the recently ordained Presbyterian minister, Dafydd Morgan, were enlivened through his ministry. And

> 'In 1859 Dafydd Morgan was God's instrument to turn many from unbelief to faith ... Morgan's contribution ... can hardly be overestimated.'[2]

These addresses by Eifion Evans were well received and published under the title: When He is Come.

'Greatly helped'

A much anticipated address was by Lloyd-Jones on *The Strain and Stress in the Christian Ministry*.[3] His concern was to help ministers to distinguish between pastoral and medical problems. A. L. Hughes, a Presbyterian minister in Saltmead, Cardiff, reported:

> 'we were greatly helped as to principles of discernment and methods of treatment by striking and revealing examples from Dr Lloyd-Jones' experience.'[4]

Iain H. Murray agreed, describing it as 'a most valuable address.'[5]

9   Unforgettable but with tensions: Cilgwyn 1959–1961

For Murray, Conference discussions relating to revival in particular

'were searching occasions' and 'took their direction largely from a moving question: "Why ... a godly company of men who had met regularly for years in earnest prayer for Revival ... yet had not seen revival?'[6] Recognising 'ultimately the answer was hid in the Sovereign Will of God, there was great searching of hearts as to motives'.

Lloyd-Jones urged the men

'to begin with ourselves, our own relationship to God and what is wrong there'.

Failure to spend time in prayer, he insisted, is

'because we do not sufficiently desire Him and we do not desire Him because we do not know Him'.[7]

Murray reports

'there was much said at that Conference on revival. The Dr said some things which I am afraid we all did not take in sufficiently. He spoke of direct and indirect approaches to revival ... he spoke also of the difference between urgency and despair in prayer and said our lack of confidence is due to our lack of sight of the victorious Christ.'[8]

It was in this Conference that Lloyd-Jones invited Pastor George Griffiths, Tro'r Glien Mission Hall, Cwmtwrch, Swansea to share his experiences of the Lord. Converted in the 1904 revival, he and others in the village received a powerful experience of the Lord in 1909. In 1945, he felt constrained to urge the church to pray for revival. One answer to prayer was given later in 1958 when there was a 'remarkable time' when 'God visited and dealt' with a number of their young people being converted, then 'baptized with His Spirit ...'[9]

Iain H. Murray spoke on Brownlow North[10] (1810-1875) but felt Pastor Griffiths's contribution was one of the 'memorable' features of the 1959 Conference. The elderly pastor, he reports,

'spoke in high emotion and assurance, 'God is coming. Men will come to Wales again to seek God, "and they shall call them the holy people". At one point, while he was speaking, he turned to someone beside him and said, 'He is coming, Mr. Evans. God is coming!'[11]

Remarkable prayer meeting

The most remarkable prayer meeting in the Conference's history was the final meeting in Cilgwyn 1959. Initially, prayer was slow so Lloyd-Jones intervened after an hour, feeling there was despair in some prayers and a failure to see Christ's glory. Referring to Isaiah 63 verses 1-7, he emphasised their prayers should approximate to those in Scripture. There was need to pray like Moses in Exodus 33 verse 18: '... Show me Your glory'. For Lloyd-Jones the chief need of churches and preachers was to experience the Lord's presence and see the Lord's glory. It was a brief but powerful exhortation.

On restarting the meeting, some older 'revival men' prayed fervently before a young pastor prayed, weeping. Repentance, the desire to know the Lord better and petitions for an outpouring of the Spirit were the chief requests. There was freedom in prayer alongside a deep brokenness and honesty. Each prayer became like a baton being passed on to the next person as Conference members drew closer to the Lord and a breakthrough was felt to be near. For A. L. Hughes,

> 'We were brought with a great sense of guilt in tears to the Saviour's feet ... The last prayers of the Conference were that God would make haste to show us His glory.'[12]

'Foretaste of revival'

Gareth Davies, then pastoring a Welsh Presbyterian church in Pontardawe, West Wales, reported[13] he was not the same after this prayer meeting. For Omri Jenkins, 'this was a foretaste of revival' and he referred to Lloyd-Jones' claim that the Conference had never been nearer to revival than on that evening. He added they did not go to a Conference prayer meeting in earlier years

> 'without being profoundly affected' for men 'opened their hearts in prayer.'[14]

Elwyn Davies confirmed this. Later, Noel Gibbard, a Congregationalist minister in the Merthyr and Llanelli areas of South Wales[15] felt this continuing emphasis on prayer helped to create warm fellowship and encouraged pastors returning to their churches. There was 'great brotherliness' and 'unending prayer' in this and other Conferences in this period and all were

> 'amazed at the way in which people prayed.'

Impact

The impact of the 1959 prayer meeting was felt afterwards. Over the next months Hugh Morgan, a Presbyterian minister in Gelli, Rhondda Valley, wanted to pray daily for hours rather than minutes.[16] By the autumn the Ministers' Fellowship in Castleton, near Newport, South East Wales, experienced exceptional times of prayer, locking the door on one occasion to stop their wives disturbing them!

The 1959 Conference represented a peak in terms of spiritual reality, confession, heart prayer, fellowship and expectancy.

Cilgwyn 1960/61

Cilgwyn 1960 saw Dr James Packer speaking helpfully again and this time on Christian assurance. Emlyn Jones, Neath, expounded Philippians with his usual thoroughness in the 1961 Conference. This was a follow-up to monthly studies on the 'Glory of Christ' in the Ministers' Fellowships during the previous winter. Emyr Roberts delivered the historical address on Robert Roberts, Clynnog (1762–1802). Apart from Daniel Rowland, Roberts was one of the most powerful Calvinistic Methodist preachers in Wales between 1750 and 1850. He was also an outstanding man of prayer.[17]

Tensions

The 1961 Conference marked the end of the early period and foreshadowed tensions as well as raising important questions. This was a watershed in the Conference's history.

For example, in the 1961 Conference brochure, the secretary, John Thomas, wrote:

'... there is an increased need felt ... that the time has come to face realistically the situation in which we find ourselves ... and ask ourselves whether we are in the will of God, being led of Him and doing that which is "good in his sight". It is intended therefore to devote as much time as possible to these discussions without neglecting ... prayer'.

Underlying this ambiguous statement were issues like evangelism, 'Societies', the spiritual condition of churches and the lurking problem of strained relationships between some ministers. Three pastors[18] felt they should bring their 'grievances' to the attention of the 1961 Conference, especially that

'personal relationships within the Movement were not right and actually had got worse'.

One of the pastors visited London to share with Lloyd-Jones prior to Conference. He reported personally to me[19] that Lloyd-Jones was supportive. Another of the three pastors claimed there was no improvement later.

'Disturbing features'

A 'Final Draft'[20] of a Document issued to members of the EMW General Committee for Cilgwyn 26–29, 1961, provides clues as to what was happening more widely in relation to the EMW. For example,

'The Movement has, unhappily, turned in on itself, and may be said to exist purely for its own sake ...'

This was unexpected after the progress made in evangelism in previous years and the 1959 prayer meeting. Further evidence of the problem was that

> 'evangelical ministers are not being utilised' (in evangelism and Bible-teaching) and also 'there is little or no zeal in establishing societies (for teaching, prayer and fellowship), and inadequate oversight ...' So they have 'dwindled in number and strength'.

Questions arise here. Was the spontaneous evangelism by students now weakened? Or was the burden of evangelism left more to 'evangelical ministers'? And was the relationship between students and the EMW marked by continuing consultation? Did the EMW and the Ministers' Fellowships tend to institutionalise what was spontaneous evangelism? Or did cohorts of students lose momentum? These questions need further research.

'Societies'

There are other questions, too, concerning the 'societies'. During the late 1940s and 1950s these Societies emerged largely through a small number of enthusiastic pastors and Welsh Magazine distributors who recognised the need of fellowship for scattered believers.

How important were 'societies' for the EMW by 1960? In principle, they were important and attempts were made to establish them. But the situation was changing. More young men were being ordained and were involved in their churches, often with few believers. More also were becoming aware of the principle espoused by Lloyd-Jones that evangelism and nurture are the responsibilities of local churches, not para-church movements such as the EMW and UCCF. Possibly, a more effective strategy at an earlier stage for expanding the 'societies' could have contributed significantly to gospel work and unity in Wales during the sixties and seventies.

Three further 'disturbing features' were identified:

> 'little or no evangelistic activity ... in the name of the Movement', while 'the content of the Magazines is too highbrow' (that is, unsuitable for evangelism and young converts). Also, 'Children's work monopolises far too much ... time, energy and finance'.

While the first 'feature' above was accurate, nevertheless an increasing amount of evangelism was being undertaken by evangelical pastors through their churches and this developed during the 1960s and 1970s. The second 'feature' concerning the magazines has been challenging but progress has now been made. The third feature remains a challenge although there has been lasting encouragement, particularly through annual Camps where many children/young people have professed conversion and have been integrated into church life.

Lloyd-Jones

Between 1955 and 1961, Lloyd-Jones attended all the Conferences except for 1958. His presence encouraged pastors and the close bond being forged continued during the next period as more young men attended.

Despite encouragements and warm fellowship, Conference members now faced pressing theological and relational questions, already hinted at. That is part of the story in the next period of 1962–1978.

Questions for reflection and discussion

'We do not desire Him' as believers 'because we do not know Him'. Suggest ways of addressing the problem.

Which features challenge you concerning the 1959 prayer meeting?

Are there observations you can make on the 1961 situation?

Summary of Parts One and Two

The Early Years—1955-1961

- The immediate context in which the Conference was established was extensive evangelism in colleges, churches, schools and open-airs, mostly by students, resulting in many conversions and the need for nurturing converts.

- In the background there was a dependence on God with priority given to prayer and the preaching of the gospel.

- The Conference was evangelical and interdenominational and included a few men influenced in or as a result of the 1904-05 revival.

- From the beginning the Conference was Calvinistic although in this period there were several Arminians present. Some tensions surfaced, despite underlying unity in the gospel.

- The period ended with tension amongst some pastors but also self-questioning concerning evangelism and the 'societies'.

- Conference members consisted mostly of pastors from Wales with a balance of Welsh and English speakers. Attendance varied from between fifty to sixty and was by personal invitation.

- Conferences were characterised by emphases on the Word-Spirit relationship, prayer, revival, the gospel and important aspects of the pastor's life and ministry.

- Lloyd-Jones's ministry and fellowship were valued. Agreeing on the nature of revival and its need, not all agreed with him concerning the baptism with the Holy Spirit.

PART THREE

Turbulence, Questions and Progress—1962–1978

Chapters 10–12 Relocation and Big Questions
Chapters 13–15 The Story Moves on
Chapter 16   The Last Conference for Lloyd-Jones

10

Relocation to Bala

Bala is an attractive market town with a population of about two thousand people whose first language is predominantly Welsh. The town is located in North Wales in the Snowdonia National Park, a designated area of outstanding beauty with its mountains, rivers and countryside. A popular tourist centre, Bala stands at the head of Wales's largest natural lake and is about one hour's drive from the English border.

Famous
Bala is also famous for its religious history. On the far side of Bala Lake, itinerant Calvinistic Methodist preachers used to travel north along the road from Llanbrynmair and Dinas Mawddwy. Howell Harris, the exhorter, faced violent persecution in the town in the early eighteenth century revival but a 'fellowship' or 'society' ('seiat' is the Welsh word) was established here.

Gradually, in the eighteenth and nineteenth centuries the town became a centre for Calvinistic Methodism. Important leaders like John Evans (1723–1817) and the famous Thomas Charles (1755–1814) were based here. And it was on the famous 'Green,' that the young Ann Griffiths, a gifted hymn writer, danced as she rejoiced in her salvation. It was to Bala that Mary Jones walked a distance of twenty-eight miles alone over the mountains from the western coast for a Welsh language Bible from Thomas Charles. This incident, through Charles's efforts, led to the formation of the British and Foreign Bible Society in London.[1]

In Bala, the Calvinistic Methodists frequently held their Association meetings where their most powerful preachers were used. Vast crowds gathered and many were converted there, often returning home to establish a 'society' or a local church.

On a smaller scale, Bala assumed later significance when some Welsh language students held a remarkable series of preaching meetings over Easter 1948. Many were saved.

In August 1952, the first Welsh language Conference for Evangelicals ('Friends' of *The Evangelical Magazine*) was also held here. Three years later, the Rev. J. Elwyn Davies,[2] who pastored a Welsh Congregational Church nearby in Blaenau Ffestiniog, made Bala his family home as he became General Secretary of the fledgling Evangelical Movement of Wales (EMW).

Answers to prayer

The EMW bought Eryl Aran[3] in 1958 as its main Centre. Very close to Bala Lake, it had an uninterrupted view of the lake and the distant lofty ridges of Aran Fawddwy and Aran Benllyn with the Berwyn range of mountains on the other side. The scenery is breath-taking.

Eryl Aran was a country mansion, later a drinking club and hotel before being bought by Roman Catholics and called 'The Fatima Guest House'. In the entrance hall there was a statue of the Virgin Mary, known as 'Our lady of Fatima'. This name was based on a story that two children in Fatima, Spain, had received a vision of the Virgin Mary. Here was the only shrine in Britain.

The purchase of this mansion, and at an unexpected reduced price, was remarkable though others wanted to purchase it at a higher price. It met a desperate need as the EMW required an office for Mair Jones the secretary, accommodation for the families of Elwyn Davies (General Secretary) and Gwilym Humphreys[4] (Assistant Secretary and Warden), but also to hold youth camps and conferences. There was great relief in being able to use this building. However, it soon became too small for the developing work. Both Gwilym and Elwyn felt burdened to purchase the larger house, Bryn-y-groes, next door, which would be ideal as a conference centre and for camps. After much prayer, in March 1959 Gwilym received assurance that God had answered prayer for the larger house.

But the purchase of Bryn-y-groes looked impossible because the owner was not selling. After a few months, Gwilym heard that several other groups wanted to purchase the property and one obtained planning permission to convert it into flats for men working on the controversial Treweryn Reservoir Scheme[5] near Bala. Roman Catholics wanted to buy Bryn-y-groes and the adjoining field for they believed the well in that field had healing properties and had associations with Fatima. Their purpose in buying was to secure regular pilgrimages from England to the shrine.

Fascinating

When EMW representatives eventually spoke with the owner, she was willing to sell to them at a much lower price, though they had no money at the time. This centre was then used for camps. Many hundreds of young people have become Christians here over the years with some called to the Christian ministry and missionary work.

The annual Evangelical Ministers' Conference was held in Bryn-y-groes from 1962 and remains the current venue. As the majority of ministers attending the Conference by 1962 were pastoring churches in South Wales, they were reluctant to relocate and some tried unsuccessfully to reverse the committee's decision.

Distinctive period: 1962–1978

The 1962 Conference represented the beginning of a distinctive period in the Conference's history; it ended in 1978, the last occasion for Lloyd-Jones to attend.

This period was distinctive. First,

> 'for Wales in the 1960s all aspects of its economic, social and political life were in flux'.[6]

British culture and society were changing significantly with the questioning and jettisoning of traditional values. Joe England captures well 'the swinging decade' of the sixties:

> 'The ending of national service in 1960, rising incomes and the waning influence of religion resulted in a decline of deference, a rise in consumerism and the creation of a youth culture that cut across social classes ... Most voted for the Sunday opening of pubs. A new Wales was in the making'.[7]

One writer[8] argues that this change occurred suddenly rather than slowly from the 1960s onwards. This is questionable but the growing popularity of the Beatles emerged in this era of 'permissiveness', 'flower power' and 'we've never had it so good'. During the sixties and seventies, Britain was becoming more feminized and rebellious in what was now a consumer society. Prime Minister Harold Macmillan's famous reference to 'the wind of change' was true nationally as well as internationally but in 1962 the Cuban missile crisis almost led to a world disaster.

New challenges

Second, the religious and theological contexts were also undergoing change. Eastern mysticism was popularised by the Beatles and packaged within the eclectic New Age teaching with its extensive influence on Western society. Within Christendom, 'The death of God' theology made its brief impact while the Bishop of Woolwich's book, *Honest to God*, became a best-seller. The latter was recycling the critical views of Bonhoeffer, Bultman and Tillich, leading Protestant scholars. Professor R. Tudur Jones observed:

'If Rudolf Bultmann, Paul Tillich, Dietrich Bonhoeffer ..., Dr J. R. Jones and the Bishop of Woolwich are correct, then for twenty centuries Christianity has been built on a lie'.[9]

Professor Jones's critique is correct in that they rejected orthodox teaching in favour of what was new and critical.[10] Professor Jones also affirmed in 1966 that 'we are facing a crisis of belief'.[11] Writing in 1995, Professor D. P. Davies observed that in Wales as a result of this critical approach

> 'ministers are sometimes confused as to what exactly they believe. There is ... a crisis of belief in some circles ...'[12]

These challenges needed to be faced and also those concerning the charismatic movement, the nature of the gospel, evangelism and revival. But it was especially the nature and unity of the church which began to dominate the Conference programme during the sixties, largely at the request of pastors.

Another distinctive factor was that the composition of the Conference changed as more young men attended. Numbers slowly increased to eighty. Although Lloyd-Jones was absent from the 1962, 1968 and 1969 conferences, a distinctive feature of this period is his presence until 1978. A further factor is that the tensions felt by a few pastors continued, partly because of differing attitudes concerning ecclesiology. This became evident by the early 1970s when relationships became more strained, even temporarily severed.

One final feature concerns the interpretation of the impact of Lloyd-Jones's 1966 London address. For Rob Warner, UK evangelicalism was a cohesive unity until this decisive division occurred between Lloyd-Jones and John Stott immediately following the address. Warner argues that the polarisation which occurred in 1966 was not between those emphasising doctrine ('biblicist-crucicentric') and others pursuing ecumenism, but between the first group and 'activist' evangelicals, along with Charismatics, who emphasised both conversion and the changing of society ('conversionist-activists'). The resulting vacuum was filled by a new type of evangelical such as progressive activists like Clive Calver of the Evangelical Alliance, Spring Harvest, and the Alpha movement who rejected an inerrant Scripture and the penal substitutionary death of Jesus Christ as not belonging to 'a timeless and culture-free articulation of gospel truth.'[13] However, the Bala Conference insisted that major biblical doctrines do not evolve but rather are unchanging, despite changing cultures.

The work of the Spirit in the Ministry

A. L. Hughes, Cardiff, spoke in the 1962 Conference on 'The Work of the Spirit in the Christian Ministry'. He based his messages on Isaiah 61 verses 1-3, words which he claimed were fulfilled in Christ but also should be true of all gospel preachers. 'He has anointed me to preach ...' so the fruit and foremost purpose of the anointing is to preach the gospel and do so effectively.

In one address, he referred to Alexander White's advice that every minister should read Isaiah 61 verse 1 every Sunday morning before preaching, to remind himself of the privilege of preaching the gospel and also to be reminded of the condition of those in the congregation. There was a strong experiential emphasis in these addresses and he concluded by calling ministers to devote themselves to prayer and fasting. 'Have we the Spirit of the Lord upon us like the fathers of old?' was a salutary question.

1662

Noel Gibbard's address on 'The Significance of 1662'[14] was appreciated for its clarity and relevance to their different situations. The Ministers' Committee felt the address should 'be published'. There was considerable probing and discussion in attempting to understand the reasons for secession in the seventeenth century. It was a genuine attempt to learn lessons applicable to the contemporary situation. The committee minutes reported that Conference members had met from the summer of 1962 in denominational groupings to discuss church unity and to 'work out a common policy' for the coming years. This was a significant development.

In the next two chapters, we trace how Conference faced this complex situation during the 1960s.

Questions for reflection and discussion

From these examples of answered prayer, how can we be encouraged to expect answers from the Lord?

How can we help each other to pray for preachers and preaching?

11

Digging for Bible Answers to Big Questions

Digging! It certainly felt like it! And it was hard work! In fact, the digging for answers to these big questions spanned at least a five-year period. But I must explain first what was happening in the Conference during the early 1960s.

Question one: what is the gospel?

Late in the 1950s, Lloyd-Jones preached to a crowded South Wales valley church. He preached powerfully, emphasising sin, divine wrath, the uniqueness of Christ and his death as a punishment for our sin. Only Christ, he insisted, can save sinners.

When the church pastor stood to announce the closing hymn

he told the congregation he disagreed with what Lloyd-Jones had said for there were several ways to be saved, apart from Christ.

Following the final hymn, Lloyd-Jones moved forward, as pre-arranged, to close the meeting in prayer. He told the people to sit and then proceeded to contradict the pastor, reiterating there is only one Saviour, Jesus Christ.

No compromise

That pastor was expressing his own unbelieving views yet represented many church leaders in rejecting the gospel.

The first big question to answer, therefore, was: what is the gospel? The related basic question is: what is a Christian? Conference pastors were persuaded from the Bible that the gospel is divine, unique, and unchanging: 'Christ died for our sins according to the Scriptures, and that he was buried, and that he rose again the third day according to the Scriptures ...' (1 Corinthians 15:3-4). A Christian is a person who, born again, trusts personally in Christ. What happened in subsequent years was a refusal by evangelicals to compromise this God-given gospel. This was a gospel issue.

Question two: what is the church?

During the late 1950s and early 1960s this big question surfaced for Conference because churches had moved away in varying degrees from the biblical gospel. And congregations suffered as a result. Questions arose: who belongs to the true church? What is church unity?

What forced evangelicals to think more urgently over the issue of the church? There were several contributory factors.

The immediate factor was evangelism in the 1940s, 1950s and 1960s and how converts could be nurtured in the faith. That was a pressing problem. Elwyn Davies explains that

> 'the years immediately after the Second World war, ... were motivated by a concern for evangelism, but also for the spiritual well-being of those who shared their convictions but found themselves ... in churches ... which, to a very considerable extent, had departed from the main tenets of the Christian faith.[1]

This was a major heartache for Christians throughout Wales. Where could they hear the Word?

Blaenau Ffestiniog

Consider an example in Blaenau Ffestiniog, where members from local churches desired Bible teaching and fellowship:

> 'They felt unwilling as things were in their churches, and they decided that the 'salvation' that the New Testament speaks of is something more and deeper than worshipping once or even twice on a Sunday. As a result, they established an 'Evangelical group' where they could first glorify God and discuss subjects related to spiritual and eternal matters in their lives'.[2]

This was a spontaneous response at grassroots level by Christians dissatisfied in their churches. Within a year, prayers were answered when Elwyn Davies became minister of Jerusalem Congregational church in the town.

One more example confirms the bewilderment of believers. A young housewife in North Wales wrote to the *Cylchgrawn* for advice:

> 'The church members are without the new birth, and know nothing about spiritual life but are religious only ... I did not get anything in the church and it is better for me to stay home on a Sunday ... But should I return to witness and seek to save the members? ...'[3]

She was impatient and censorious. The answer given was wise: return to her church and witness in a loving way. However, this was a temporary answer. After all, biblically the church is a fellowship of believers where the Word is faithfully taught and applied, but the question kept cropping up: what is the church?

One immediate step in 1952 was to invite readers of the Welsh Evangelical Magazine (*Y Cylchgrawn*) to meet regularly in 'evangelical fellowships' and attend the first Welsh-language annual conference.

There was a further urgent dimension:

> 'The hope at the time was that if such believers could be strengthened to witness faithfully to their Lord and saviour, others would be added to their number, and in this way ground which had been lost for decades would be regained'.

This was not an attack on churches but an acknowledgement of their spiritual bankruptcy which had been felt for decades.

There was a further factor forcing Conference to reconsider the question of the church, namely, denominational attempts in the late 1950s and 1960s to establish a United Church. The proposals were ambiguous, so Conference had no choice but to embark on a detailed biblical study of the church to find answers to major questions.

That is why for many months during and after the 1963 Conference, the theme was the nature of the church. They saw that a church consists essentially of born-again believers who ensured the Bible was preached faithfully (1 Corinthians 1:2-3, 1 Thessalonians 1).

In 1964 the Conference continued to study how churches should organise their life to ensure the faithful preaching and practice of the Bible.

Question three: what is Christian unity?

This was another urgent question. Urgent because in 1962 a London-Welsh businessman, Sir David James, offered money to Presbyterian, Congregational, Baptist and Methodist denominations in Wales if they formed a united church in Wales. The plan failed but churches had produced an initial working document suggesting a basis of belief and practice for the proposed united church. That basis of belief was vague.

Many evangelicals could not agree to join any new church which did not honour Bible teaching. In the background, as we have seen, was a growing movement for Christian unity, climaxing in the mid-sixties with the creation of local Councils of Churches in which Roman Catholics and Anglicans participated with Free Churches. There was enormous pressure on evangelicals to co-operate at local and national levels.

Conference members were convinced that Christian unity is spiritual and radical, created by the Holy Spirit through the new birth and trust in the Lord Jesus. Our responsibility is to be 'endeavouring to keep (guard) the unity of the Spirit in the bond of peace'. The biblical gospel must be at the heart of such unity.

Question four: should Christians therefore leave their denominations?

This was a difficult question for pastors from the 1960s onwards. If a denomination compromised biblical teaching, should a Christian remain within it? Underlying this question again is what constitutes a 'church'?

Elwyn Davies reported that while several Anglicans attended the 1964 Conference, some pastors in Presbyterian, Congregational, and Baptist churches were unhappy to remain within denominations where only a tiny minority held to Bible teaching. In 1966, Lloyd-Jones made his famous call in London for evangelicals to express their unity in the gospel and leave 'mixed' denominations where major biblical teachings were denied. This call had a muted response in England and to a large extent in Wales.[4]

Conference members agreed concerning both the gospel and the church. There was also unanimous agreement about the spiritual nature of Christian unity. However, there was division concerning how to apply these principles.

Why division?

In answering this question, I offer some personal observations:

First, the Conference never urged members to leave their denomination. Dr Lloyd-Jones himself never resigned from the Presbyterian Church of Wales.

Second, the Conference agreed it was a personal decision for members to make without pressure from anyone else. One example was the formation of the Welsh Evangelical Church in Aberystwyth in 1967. Some believers from different local churches had met regularly for several years in a 'seiat' for Bible-study and prayer. They lamented the lack of Bible teaching in the churches and saw that doctrines like sin, judgement and the death of Jesus Christ for sinners were denied. This sad condition and the prized fellowship with believers from different churches, coupled with the resignation of a local Wesleyan Methodist pastor, led them to form a new church.[5] Neither the Conference nor Lloyd-Jones influenced the decision.

Third, and sadly, some Conference members, irrespective of their decision, failed to show love and understanding towards others. Some, particularly on the English language side, were perceived as being unwise, hard and critical. As a result, a number of men withdrew from both the Conference and regional Ministers' Fellowships.

Fourth, was there too much emphasis in the 1960s and 1970s on the church rather than on the gospel? In the 1997 Conference, I outlined the history of the Conference and in discussion afterwards, Eurfyl Jones affirmed:

'In the 1950s, the major things were of importance in the Conference, namely, knowing and seeking God ... The church is important', he added, 'but not more important than our relationship with God ... We are not now seeking God as we were in the 1950s'.

It was right to ask the big questions but was their relationship with God neglected? Interestingly, blessing was known and progress made in churches during the 1980s and 1990s alongside increased misunderstanding and division. And yet ecclesiology could not be ignored.

'Why are we failing?'

Conference was regularly reminded of the importance of knowing the Lord. For example, a highlight in the 1964 Conference was Lloyd-Jones's closing message, 'Why are we failing?'[6]

He described the confusion and then asked: 'How do we meet this situation?'[7] He warned against merely blaming the situation and being reactionary or condemnatory, but he felt also that evangelicals were guilty of intellectual arrogance. Regarding preaching, the

> 'golden rule is to preach to your people as they are' and not as they should be.

> 'What is our greatest need? Power ... but our first need is to know Him and His love. I am preaching next Sunday because the love of Christ constrains me. What a difference between knowing about Him and knowing Him! ... Our supreme desire must be to have

communion with Him. Then secondly, the power of the Spirit, but this must be second'.

Men returned to their churches humbled and challenged. There were further blessings as well as tensions in the story which the next chapters relate.

Questions for reflection and discussion

Define the key terms 'Christian' and 'Church'. Provide Bible references to support your answers.

Can we avoid division and broken relationships over church affiliation?

'Why are we failing?' as churches today? Suggest reasons.

12

Another Big Question

Another big question troubled Conference members in the mid-1960s. Some felt they knew the answer. Others were open. The question was: has revival broken out amongst charismatics?[1] If not, what is God doing amongst them? Behind this question were several crucial sub-questions: how should we respond? Were the miraculous and revelatory gifts withdrawn when the apostles died?

Background

The emergence of the charismatic movement is traced to a Sunday service in April 1960 in the diocese of Los Angeles when the rector, Dennis Bennett, informed his congregation he had recently experienced the baptism with the Holy Spirit and speaking in tongues. The people were displeased and within a week he was forced to leave. He then settled in a Seattle parish where his teaching was welcomed and the church prospered numerically.

By 1964, several evangelical Anglican clergy, including Michael Harper, a curate at All Souls, London, claimed a similar experience. Harper founded the Fountain Trust to promote the teaching within the historic Protestant denominations. By 1966, more Baptists were influenced by the movement than any other Free Church in Britain. Harper reported that by 1965 over one hundred ministers claimed the baptism with the Holy Spirit, while in 1979 an estimated 10% of Anglican clergy had received the experience. Roman Catholics began participating in this movement by the late 1960s.

Excitement

There was regular reporting of extra-biblical prophecies, healings, miracles, and tongues-speaking which generated considerable excitement but there were many extravagant claims and excesses. New charismatic churches emerged but some wanted to go further and 'restore' the church to the New Testament pattern of contemporary apostles and prophets. These, too, divided into numerous, often rival, groups with different emphases.

A few evangelical Anglican clergy like Michael Harper and David Watson, shared their experiences with Lloyd-Jones who was initially sympathetic and intrigued to know what the Lord was doing. And that was the attitude of ministers in the Conference. However, they also felt unease and suspected this was not revival.

Many discussion sessions were held in the 1965 and 1966 Conferences. Hefin Elias described 'Trends in Modern Theology' in 1965, while Graham Harrison led discussions on paedo- and credo-baptism in continuing consideration of New Testament teaching concerning the church. He offered a strongly Baptistic approach which resulted in further discussion.

The 1966 Conference largely dealt with the doctrine of the church, including detailed study concerning which offices continued in the church. Are there apostles and prophets today? It was agreed that the original apostles held foundational offices which ended when the New Testament was complete.[2] While some members were 'open but cautious' concerning the continuation of gifts like tongues-speaking, there was no support for the practice.

1966 Re-location

1966 was the only occasion since 1962 when the Conference relocated due to renovations being carried out in Bryn-y-groes, Bala. As a temporary measure, the Conference was held in the Boys' Camp in St Athan, situated between Barry and Bridgend in the Vale of Glamorgan, South Wales.

W. C. Burns

Apart from the main times reserved for corporate prayer and discussion, a biographical paper was given by Derek Swann on the Rev. William Chalmers Burns (1815–1868). The Ministers' Committee requested the speaker to

> 'deal with his devotional life and with any connection he had with revival.'[3]

This decision emphasised the desire to care pastorally for members and encourage experiential Christianity. Burns was an excellent choice.

William Chalmers Burns was a Scottish missionary to China with the English Presbyterian Mission and went to China in 1847. It was Burns who preached at St Peter's Church in Dundee while its famous minister, the Rev. Robert Murray McCheyne, was on a mission to Jews in Palestine. Revival broke out during the period Burns served the church and continued after McCheyne returned in November 1839. While in China, Burns met Hudson Taylor in 1855 and they worked together for a period and both advanced into the interior. Hudson Taylor regarded Burns as one of his spiritual mentors and referred to the depth of Burns' personal prayer life. This was a challenging study.[4]

Different

The final evening meeting of the 1966 Conference has lingered in the memories of those present for mixed reasons. For one thing, the meeting was different. The Ministers' Committee at their January meeting had

> 'agreed that Dr Lloyd-Jones be consulted regarding the possibility of inviting to this year's conference the Revs. V. Higham, Stanley Jebb and Tony Stone along with an "Anglican clergyman" (name unknown as yet) to speak on their experience of the Baptism in the Holy Spirit, to be followed by a discussion led by Dr Lloyd-Jones'.[5]

The 'Anglican clergyman' referred to was the Rev. Norman Meeten, a curate then in a Liverpool parish. From the late 1960s, he became a leader in one of the 'House-Church' groups often referred to as 'the North Circuit'.

This final meeting proved to be a long one with only a short interval, then continuing until midnight when Lloyd-Jones closed the Conference. The four men shared their spiritual experiences but there were probing questions and lively discussions. Some pastors were unhappy with the term 'baptism with the Holy Spirit' attached to their experience. Did it suggest a two-tier grading of Christians?

The author became a personal friend of Norman Meeten who spoke in his church during that period. Theological differences, especially over regeneration and sanctification, emerged and these were handled firmly but amicably and with mutual respect. This friendship is one illustration of the cross-fertilisation occurring between some Conference members and those in 'House Church' or charismatic groups. There was a desire in the 1960s to fellowship widely and learn from others. Professor Densil Morgan exaggerates in claiming that by the mid-1960s the type of evangelicalism gaining dominance in Wales and expressed through the EMW was 'Calvinistic and separatist and strongly judgemental ...'[6] The foregoing examples confirm that there was a catholicity and openness within the Conference in the 1960s which was refreshing and fruitful. While some of these relationships continued, by the late 1970s this catholicity gradually weakened and the issue of secession gave rise to mixed responses and attitudes.

1967 Conference

The challenge to personal prayer was felt again in the 1967

Conference when the Rev. Gwilym Humphreys gave an account of the life and work of John Elias (1774–1841). The main speaker was the Rev. Arthur Neil, a Baptist pastor who was pastoring in Brixham, Devon. His background is interesting, and I confine myself to two details.

Experience

First, in 2012 he shared with close friends an experience he had in 1956 which was foundational to his ministry. In 1956, at the age of thirty, he was a Baptist pastor in Lancashire. Deeply challenged concerning his degree of commitment to the Lord Jesus, for three months he sought the Lord, often with fasting and little sleep. While preaching one Sunday afternoon in a small Baptist church in Darwen, the Lord drew near to him.

> 'I was conscious of His presence and of being aware of His glory. Neither before nor since', he added, 'have I known what I knew then'.

The preacher never lost that intimacy with the Lord and the deep awareness of the glory of Christ. His commitment to prayer and communion with the Lord continued unabated.

Spiritual warfare

The second detail is different. In his two Conference addresses, Arthur Neil sought to describe biblically and from his own experience details concerning spiritual warfare and ways in which the devil was working through the occult. There was an urgent need, he emphasised, for pastors to understand and appropriate the glorious triumph of the Lord in His death, resurrection and ascension. Pastors were urged to use prayerfully the armour of God described in Ephesians chapter six. Discernment was desperately needed.[7] Once again, the Conference had sought to maintain a balance between an in-depth study of the church, and a practical, pastoral emphasis, intended to equip pastors for contemporary ministry.

The next chapter draws attention to some highlights in Conference between 1968 and 1973.

Questions for reflection and discussion

What encouragements have you known recently in seeking a more intimate relationship with the Lord?

Read and apply Ephesians 6 verses 10–18 to your situation.

What aspects of the life and work of W. C. Burns challenge you?

13

A Significant Milestone: 1968–1969

Lloyd-Jones was absent from the 1968 and 1969 Conferences. In 1968 he underwent major surgery while in 1969 he was lecturing on preaching to staff and students at Westminster Theological Seminary, Philadelphia.[1]

The big questions lingered over the following years as pastors grappled with different church situations. This part of the story reflects that development, but the 1969 Conference was a significant milestone in the story and demands more attention here.

1968: Main speaker

Arthur Wallis[2] was invited to speak on biblical principles relating to prayer. In 1951, Wallis and his wife Eileen were praying for revival and as they fasted and prayed, they were filled with the Holy Spirit. This impacted his preaching and prayer life. Encouraged through hearing of Duncan Campbell's ministry in revival on the Isle of Lewis, Wallis went to see what was happening. Their prayers for revival in this early period were based on the 'Lewis', and 'Congo' (1953) models.

Wallis was known for his book on revival, *In the Day of Thy Power* (1956)[3] which pastors had read with profit. However, many were unaware of the spiritual journey Wallis was taking in moving theologically through charismatic influences into a movement demanding the restoration of churches to a New Testament pattern, including contemporary apostles, yet outside traditional church structures. While Wallis received a warm reception regarding his teaching on prayer, there was unease over his modified views of revival (preferring the term 'renewal') and ecclesiology.

1969: A Critical Conference

David Bentley-Taylor (1915–2005) spoke on 'Biblical Principles Relating to Church Founding and Expansion'.[4]

He had served in China, then in Java before ministering with UCCF in the UK colleges and he also helped in the early growth of the International Fellowship of Evangelical Students (IFES) before becoming heavily involved in mission work across the Middle East. No wonder *The Daily Telegraph* described him as

'one of the most influential missionaries of the last century'.[5]

One speaker at his memorial service in Hereford Baptist church in February, 2005, was reported as quoting Lloyd-Jones that David

Bentley-Taylor was 'the finest missionary speaker I ever heard.'[6] There were good reasons why Lloyd-Jones recommended this speaker to the Conference.

Intriguing

A report of this 1969 Conference is intriguing:

> 'After an illuminating and refreshing survey of the Acts of the Apostles, Mr Bentley-Taylor moved on in his second talk to touch on more controversial issues, as he attempted to extract and apply principles relevant to the present situation. Clearly many members of the conference could not go along with him in affirming that our lack of success is not related to our faulty contact with God so much as to our faulty contact with the world. "Involvement" and a tenacious traditionalism that pleases neither God nor man seem to be the twin, if opposite, dangers besetting God's people at this time.'[7]

Observations

Several observations are relevant here. One, Conference members found his first address stimulating. The speaker reported in his diary:

> 'My first talk on Acts was very well received. The men were extremely warm and a great many of them thanked me personally.'[8]

Two, a strong statement is made that 'Clearly many members' disagreed with the speaker's second address; he was perceived as disagreeing with the majority view of Conference and of Lloyd-Jones, namely, that the chief reason for failure in churches concerned a defective relationship with God. Three, having been recommended by Lloyd-Jones, it is doubtful whether the speaker would have disagreed fundamentally with him concerning revival.

Differences

What were these differences between Bentley-Taylor and the 'many members' of Conference? The speaker explains and I identify these differences as being cultural, contextual and theological.

> a. *There were cultural differences.*

Living near the Welsh border in Herefordshire, he explains rather surprisingly that

> 'this was the first time I had ever spent time entirely with the Welsh people ... I was the only Englishman among 65 Welshmen, all of whom were ministers'.

And what were his impressions? He records:

> 'I was amazed at the difference between us. I felt I was a lowlander who had strayed among the highland tribes'.

How did he perceive this 'difference'? One difference was that for nearly half of the men their first language was Welsh. They sometimes broke into their native tongue when praying or conversing but 'always courteously interpreting'. He adds:

> 'They also looked Welsh. I was in appearance quite different ... They were more gushing, emotional, fulsome than a similar group

of Englishmen would have been ... more long-winded in prayer and preaching and chairmanship, slower too, and at times simpler. And of course they sang gloriously ... But their mental range was limited ...'

It is surprising that having worked in many cross-cultural situations overseas he found it difficult to adjust to a Welsh culture within the United Kingdom and so close to home. Although identifying positive features, he is scathing in his description of Conference members. The vast majority were University graduates so to question their 'mental range' is somewhat arrogant. Suggesting that the men were 'extremely insular, or rather provincial, in their outlook' is harsh yet contains an element of truth. These cultural differences are significant when interpreting his description of the 1969 Conference.

b. *There were also the related contextual differences in terms of ministry.* David Bentley-Taylor writes:

> 'Part of the problem was no doubt that they were all ministers in church situations, whereas I live in the student world and am thus exposed to worldly ideas and anti-Christian philosophers in a way they are not ...'

This was partly true but some men had also served as student workers or leaders whereas most of the younger men had only recently left University and were in touch with College Christian Unions. To affirm that these men

> 'were probably not within sound of the modern debate' is unfair.

Another difference concerned church links:

> 'I was struck with the fact that not one of them wore a dog (clerical) collar and that not one of them was an Episcopalian. Nor was anyone from the Brethren with us. They came from Presbyterian, Baptist, Methodist and Congregational churches with a few from the Pentecostal and Apostolic churches, and some who had left the main denominations for Free Evangelical churches'.

One appreciates the surprise felt by the absence of Anglicans as evangelical student work in England was dominated by Evangelical Anglicans. He was also meeting for the first time pastors who were contemplating secession from mainline denominations.

c. There were also theological differences.

From reading his diary, I suggest these theological differences related to Calvinism, ecclesiology and revival.

First, Bentley-Taylor was uncomfortable with their Calvinism:

> 'their thinking was permeated with Calvinism—and there were constant references to Calvin—or the word 'Predestination' which created no shadow of a problem for them, or that they could cheerfully say that "regeneration precedes conversion". Their biblical roots were utterly staunch'.

He then remarked:

A Significant Milestone: 1968–1969

'their mental range was limited and deeply rooted in the past, in the Reformation and in the Welsh revivals'.

These remarks provide insight into the strong Calvinistic emphasis of the Conference and the commitment of pastors to these doctrines. Following the tensions between Calvinists and Arminians in 1956, by 1969 few Arminians attended. Conference members were well versed in Reformation history.

Second, Bentley-Taylor found major differences in ecclesiology, noticing that 'All emphasis fell upon the local church'. That emphasis emerged in Conference discussions and was expressed in the booklet, *The Christian Church*. However, while not entirely happy with the emphasis, Presbyterians embraced this local church emphasis in contrast to the rigid centralization which had occurred in the Presbyterian Church of Wales. Some Presbyterian pastors accepted the emphasis as an interim step towards establishing possibly a more biblical expression of Presbyterianism later.[9]

However, far more serious for Bentley-Taylor was talk of 'secession' and the 'apostasy' of historic denominations. One entire meeting was given over to a discussion of secession which had troubled him. Noel Gibbard[10] describes the context for us. Gibbard explains that due to ill-health, Eifion Evans was unable to speak, as planned, on 'Secession and Schism in the Church'. But the subject was raised for discussion by several members. There was complete agreement on the sad decline of churches. Some felt the need for reform within the denominations; others argued that the situation represented apostasy, so separation was required. The discussion concluded that 'in the situation there are two possible paths, reforming from within or separation and going out'.

Bentley-Taylor's account of the discussion, though exaggerated, is reasonably fair:

'strong feeling that evangelicals ought to separate from these bodies and come together undivided in a new, pure association. The declension of the theological colleges was deeply felt and a new college proposed'.[11]

He had clearly been troubled by the suggestion

'that evangelicals were guilty of schism'

not only by remaining in apostate denominations and separating themselves from evangelicals but also in dividing into their own groups after secession.

Revival emphasis

Third, one cannot avoid concluding that Bentley-Taylor's major difficulty was with the 'revival' emphasis in the Conference. This note dominates his diary account, illustrating his strong reaction and misunderstanding. Nevertheless, his remarks anticipate later criticism of this perceived and unbalanced emphasis on revival. For Bentley-Taylor, these Welsh pastors

'were looking backwards, not forwards.'

The criticism is not entirely unfair. Their living in the past

A Significant Milestone: 1968–1969

'had much to do with the most prominent word in their Christian vocabulary, "revival". To a degree I have never met before they were revival-centred in their thinking and hopes'.

For example, he felt they were regularly referring back to the 1904 Welsh revival, despite its defects. They wanted

'a revival of that kind. This was, almost exclusively, the burden of their prayers in the long sessions we had. The recurring petition was "Come, O Lord "... and carrying the meaning "Come down upon us in revival power as in 1762 and in 1904".

'Jumpers'

There were two other problems he had with the Conference's attitude towards revival. One was the opening address describing the 1762 revival in Llangeitho, West Wales under Daniel Rowland.[12] The lecturer was Dr Geraint Gruffydd of Bangor University, who gave a balanced description and assessment of this revival.

However, for Bentley-Taylor,

'the main point of which was the phenomenon of "jumping" seen at that time. God came down upon his people in Wales and they "jumped". They shouted, they wept, they fell down, but in particular they jumped. They were "the jumpers". The English were "the sleepers"'.

He observed the

'intense sympathy for this' from the pastors 'and with loud interjections they endorsed the speaker's attitude. There was a great longing that such days might be seen in Wales again'.

The visitor was 'much troubled at this' and felt restrained from saying anything critical afterwards for

> 'it was the opening meeting and I felt that as the only Englishman present, I could not dissent without forfeiting the sympathy of the ministers I was to address and appearing to criticise what was of the very essence of their Welshness. Holy laughing and holy dancing also came in for favourable mention.'

Bentley-Taylor misunderstood the subject. 'Jumping' and 'dancing' were features in that revival, but the phenomena were not of the essence of revival or even Welshness, as he suggests. It was preaching which was central and on such preaching, Eifion Evans records, 'the Holy Spirit was poured out in exceptional profusion.'[13] This revival was also characterised by persistent, believing prayer as well as many conversions and the renewed spiritual life of many believers, but Bentley-Taylor ignores these aspects. While allowing for excess by a few, nevertheless

> 'the "jumping" was about the unmixed, fresh, irresistible joy of salvation. Energy, emotion, understanding, memory, natural senses, spiritual desires, all—and more besides—were transposed to hitherto unimaginable heights of reality in the enjoyment of God.'[14]

'Mesmerized'

Another problem Bentley-Taylor had with the Conference emphasis on revival was

> 'they are mesmerized by this revival mirage ... Their theological standpoint discouraged them from plunging' into engagement with the world.

He is not rejecting revival but only the passivity and imbalance on the part of those wanting revival. He explains:

> 'in the second talk I avoided those factors in which they were obviously strong, which would have evoked further strong approval, and concentrated on more challenging and critical emphases'.

That was a brave approach but in doing so he misrepresented their theology. For example, he claims

> 'the idea that we are "workers together with God" (2 Cor. 6:1) and that the Lord works "with" us (Mark 16:20) rather than apart from us, was not welcome to them. No, they felt the church was too activist, with which I disagreed'.

I am unaware of anyone who denied this 2 Corinthians 6:1 principle but Bentley-Taylor qualified himself:

> 'It is however possible that the opposition to what I said came more from a newer English-influenced Pentecostal element, than from the true Welsh'.

Clues

His critique is valuable, providing clues as to the danger of being 'mesmerized' by revival while tending to devalue the ordinary work of the Holy Spirit and neglecting evangelism. This tendency became more prominent in later years. One also detects a more defensive attitude creeping into the Conference by 1969 and a false dichotomy emerging for some between depending on God for revival and active involvement in evangelism.

Were some too eager on this occasion to defend Lloyd-Jones's ministry on revival? Possibly! Were they also in danger of misunderstanding his message for he was always eager to understand the times in which he ministered so that his preaching engaged with people where they were? One final observation! Lloyd-Jones insisted there is something more important than revival, namely, knowing the Lord more intimately.

These criticisms are pursued in later chapters but we turn to the 1970-1973 Conferences in the next chapter.

Questions for reflection and discussion

What are your observations on the 1969 Conference?

How do Christians at times become unbalanced and 'mesmerized' over some of their convictions?

14

1970–1973 Conferences

Unlike the previous year, the 1970 Conference was marked by appreciation of all the addresses, although the question of secession continued to exercise pastors. After a number of guest speakers from outside Wales had addressed the previous three Conferences, in the four Conferences between 1970 and 1973 the main speakers were Conference members.

Derek Swann was asked to deal with the contrasting subjects of Heaven and Hell in the 1970 Conference. Emphasising the importance and glorious nature of the gospel message, he exhorted pastors to be diligent in its proclamation while ensuring that as many unbelievers as possible heard the message.

Supernatural
In 1971, Hywel R. Jones explained biblically the initial work of the

Holy Spirit in believers under the title of 'Regeneration and its Evidences'. Explaining regeneration as an inward, supernatural work by the Holy Spirit, he stressed that sinners then become new persons and 'alive' to God. The evidences are faith, love and obedience.[1] Through gospel preaching, God often performs this supernatural work of new birth. That exciting fact illustrates the 'romance' of preaching.

Error

In the 1972 Conference, Elwyn Davies provided a biblical analysis of error which was intended to guide pastors in church situations. What does Scripture teach about our responsibilities when Christians are at variance in interpreting Scripture? Do we break fellowship? Or do we use a slide rule to determine our response, such as primary and secondary truths?[2]

The 1973 Conference addresses were delivered by Eryl Davies, then pastoring in Maesteg. The subject dealt with contemporary issues in church life. Here the Ministers' Fellowships Sub-Committee gave considerable thought to the subject in order to offer guidelines to the speaker. The Committee

> 'agreed that we concern ourselves with the provision of the ministry and of the church for believers and their responsibility towards unbelievers—the addresses to embrace practical matters, including particularly the multiplicity of meetings, visiting and its purpose, evangelism, departmentalisation (children, young people, women and brotherhoods), the purpose of Sunday School and the responsibility of parents, with particular reference to the basic significance of the teaching about the body of Christ, as found in 1 Corinthians 12.'[3]

The speaker encouraged pastors by suggesting ways to express more clearly the unity of the local church while still ministering to the distinctive needs of the young and other groups.

Howell Harris

Eifion Evans delivered two addresses on Howell Harris (1714–1773) in this 1973 Conference. He traced Harris's early years, his call to the ministry, his conversion, then the deep sense of assurance he felt when his heart melted in love to the Saviour, giving him a longing to be with Christ. Now he knew unmistakeably that God was his Father. Harris often referred to this as the sealing of the Spirit.

Dr Evans described the development of Harris's Christian life and witness, his exhorting and remarkable evangelistic zeal. Pastors were reminded that Harris read widely, especially books by Calvin and other Reformers, Puritans, Jonathan Edwards, David Brainerd and George Whitefield. His disagreement theologically with Daniel Rowland was described along with other contributory factors which led to temporary separation from Rowland. There was much to learn so these addresses resulted in animated discussion.

Humbling

Another stimulating discussion in this Conference related to originality in preaching:

> 'I am opposed to gramophone preaching', Dr Lloyd-Jones said, 'and merely commenting on Bible verses or reproducing what one reads.[4]

Our reading ought only to be a stimulus whereas our ideas should come from the Bible. Originality, not staleness, ought to characterise preaching. Not surprisingly, in informal fellowship afterwards pastors felt challenged to improve their own preaching and reading.

It was the closing message by Lloyd-Jones that gripped Conference members as he applied the lessons regarding Howell Harris by expounding and applying 1 Timothy 4 verse 16.[5] Rather than feeling smug and self-satisfied, Lloyd-Jones challenged pastors to search their hearts and lives for any expressions of pride, complacency, lack of self-discipline and ungodliness.

It was a humbling occasion sitting under that ministry.

We follow the story in the next chapter through the years 1974–1977.

Questions for reflection and discussion
What are the causes of 'error' in churches today?

In view of 1 Timothy 4 verse 16, how can we 'take heed' to ourselves?

15

'Crammed to Capacity': 1974–1977

Did pastors follow Lloyd-Jones slavishly? Was Lloyd-Jones choosing subjects and speakers? Those who make such suggestions have little knowledge of the Conference and its chemistry yet some persist in claiming that ministers accepted uncritically what the great preacher said. That is far removed from the real situation. As this is an aspect of the story not yet detailed, we now refer to the planning of Conferences.

The first Conferences in 1955, 1956 and 1957 were planned by the Fellowship of Evangelical Presbyterian Ministers. In practice, that meant that all Fellowship members, if present, participated in the decision-making. The EMW assumed responsibility for this Conference from the summer of 1957 and appointed a Ministers' Fellowships Sub-Committee to organise it.

Committee

This Committee consisted of pastors from different Protestant denominations, from various parts of Wales who represented regional Evangelical Ministers' Fellowships. In addition to a secretary and treasurer, there was also a chairman. As many as twelve pastors or more met in Committee during the annual Conference to plan the next Conference and monitor the Ministers' Fellowships. They also prepared a syllabus for their meetings. An autumn meeting in mid-Wales became necessary, but it was often less well attended because of distance and church commitments.

Suggestions for subjects and speakers were made by the Committee with occasional recommendations or requests for a change of subject from a regional Fellowship. As a Committee member for several years, I confirm it was Committee members who prayerfully made nearly all the decisions relating to Conferences but advice was sought sometimes.

Advice

Neville Rees was Conference treasurer 1964–65, then Conference secretary between 1965 and 1975. Part of his secretarial responsibilities was to meet and transport Lloyd-Jones to and from the Conference. He reports that

> 'planning the Conferences was always in consultation with him. Many phone calls and correspondence'.

For example, in planning the 1975 Conference, the Committee was unsure which subject to choose for the historical address. Several good suggestions had been made but 'after much discussion, it was decided to consult Dr Lloyd-Jones. The latter 'recommended' Thomas Charles of Bala 'as the most relevant'[1] of those suggested.

John Davies assumed the office of Conference secretary in 1975 until 2009. He reports:

'I would confer during the Conference with Lloyd-Jones re possible subjects for Conference addresses and ... historical addresses ... My dealings with Lloyd-Jones were mainly at the Conference, although I did have occasion to write to him on a few occasions ... mostly to arrange day Conferences occasionally and I would contact him re plans, subjects. I would also arrange for him to preach in the area on the Sunday and the day Conference on the Monday, meeting him and taking him to the train ...'[2]

Lloyd-Jones's advice and knowledge of theology and church history were helpful in exploring subjects the Committee wanted to pursue. For example, the Committee planning the 1979 Conference agreed on the theme of revival. But

'after conferring with Dr D. M. Lloyd-Jones, it was agreed we invite the Rev. Derek Swann' to expound a treatise delivered by Jonathan Edwards entitled, 'An Humble Attempt to Promote ... Extraordinary prayer for revival of Religion and the advancement of Christ's kingdom on earth'.

There was unanimity that this topic

'would cover the thoughts the Committee had expressed, namely, His Coming in revival and His Coming in glory'.

The Committee benefitted from Lloyd-Jones's wide knowledge of history and theology, but he did not 'control' the choice of subjects or speakers.

Survey

We now survey the 1974-1977 Conferences to see how the story unfolds, partly through the eyes of the Ministers' Committee and also of the Evangelical Magazine of Wales.

1974 'Touches of the Lord's Presence'

'Bryn-y-groes was pretty well packed to capacity' for this Conference! And the pastors 'who attended would agree it was a most profitable and encouraging time with touches of the Lord's presence.'[3]

That is a fair assessment. But why was it 'profitable and encouraging'?

There was the challenge to think about 'Modern Bible Translations' (Hywel R. Jones) before being treated to a rich study of William Williams (1717-1791) by Emyr Roberts. The latter spoke 'in a way typical of the speaker' which was informative, pastoral yet fresh and, at times, humorous but with 'much to encourage us in the pursuit of God'.

The main addresses were delivered by Iain Murray on Revival and Prayer. He had been asked to approach the subject

> 'from the standpoints of the lukewarm state of the church; the continuance of zeal; seeking the Lord in the spirit, etc'.[4]

His first address was a careful description of revival and its relationship to prayer before providing

'a most illuminating account of revivals in the States at the end of the eighteenth and the beginning of the nineteenth centuries.'[5]

Were there really 'touches of the Lord's presence' felt? Yes, particularly in hearing about William Williams and then revival. Then there were the discussions led by Lloyd-Jones.

The second discussion evening stands out. The subject was prayer and at times some men opened their hearts, expressing their failures but also their love and deep longings for the Lord. It was not finished yet. Towards the end of the discussion, Lloyd-Jones himself spoke powerfully on our desperate need to have a real awareness of God. Do we believe we can know, and have personal dealings with, the living God in prayer? Have we lost this perspective? He concluded by exhorting men to seek God as a priority in their lives and ministries.

The closing conference address by Lloyd-Jones was a searching exhortation: 'Do not quench the Spirit' (1 Thessalonians 5:19). Iain Murray summarises this address.[6] After emphasising the need for balance, Lloyd-Jones illustrated ways in which the Spirit can be grieved and quenched. Included in this list were restricting the Spirit's extraordinary work to the New Testament period, the claim that Christians receive everything at regeneration, pride of intellect, an overemphasis on the human will, over-reacting to excesses, relying more on our prepared sermons rather than on the Holy Spirit and failure to pray earnestly for the Spirit. *The*

Evangelical Magazine report did not exaggerate: it was 'a timely and humbling Word'.

1975 Highlights

The planning for this Conference was finalised by the Committee in its autumn meeting.[7] For myself, there were two highlights in the '75 Conference.

The first was Elwyn Davies's address under the title, 'The Manifest presence of God'. He referred initially to the omnipresence of God; there is no point where God is not present. Then he described the gracious presence of God with all His people. This is true whether or not we feel His presence. He is always with His people and never forsakes them. But there is also what he referred to as 'the manifest presence of God' in which we become aware in varying degrees of his presence, nearness and reality. There are occasions when the 'manifest' presence of God can be awesome and overwhelming but also delightful for believers. This address

> 'led us into a most profitable discussion of the issue. Indeed the meeting virtually became a seiat (sharing or fellowship) to the benefit of all concerned.'[8]

The other highlight was the main addresses by Paul Cook under the title, 'The Triumph of the Cross'. From the Committee, there was a request for the speaker to

> 'consider the objective and subjective aspects of the Atonement in the light of Colossians 2:13–15'.[9]

These addresses were

> 'biblically profound and delivered with forcefulness and urgency'. No wonder that 'like so many of its predecessors', this Conference 'proved to be an inspiration and encouragement to the large number of ministers who were able to attend.[10]

1976 Stalwarts

Numbers attending 'were greater than any previous year' and all agreed the Conference had been 'very profitable', despite the heat which was 'somewhat distracting'![11] Stalwarts of the Conference like Noel Gibbard, Hywel R. Jones, Luther Rees and Omri Jenkins were among the speakers. The latter preached messages from John 17:3 with the theme 'Communion with God', a subject he claimed was 'given' him by God.

1977 Significant

This Conference was significant in several ways. First, Bryn-y-groes

> 'was crammed to capacity for this' Conference and 'only a few last minute cancellations removed the need for some to pitch a tent in the grounds of the Conference Centre'.[12]

A second significant feature is that a recently converted parish priest in the Roman Catholic Church in Spain

> 'gave his personal testimony in an arresting way to God's grace and how he felt compelled before God to leave Roman Catholicism'. And it was on the 'crunch issue for him of the doctrine of justification by faith alone'.

A third feature was the contribution by a Welsh academic, Dr Bobi Jones who spoke on Ann Griffiths (1776–1805),

> 'a remarkable woman and her hymns are even more remarkable ... Yet we were shown that these point us to what should be the ordinary longing of the Christian for the Saviour.' This address 'forced us to concentrate on the need for an experiential knowledge of God'.

A fourth but unexpected feature of the Conference was Dr Lloyd-Jones's 'insistence' that the Rev. Andrew Davies should deliver the closing Conference address in his place on 'The Moravian revival of 1727'. All that was left for Lloyd-Jones at the end was to

> 'underline the necessary lessons that were there for us to see'.

An earlier Ministers' Committee decided

> 'we ought to reckon with the life of the church in the light of recent trends and publications'.

Consequently,

> 'it was agreed that Ephesians 4:1–16 should be the basis for these addresses and the Rev. Elwyn Davies be the speaker ...'.[13]

His 1977 addresses under the title, 'The Organic Unity and Growth of the Church' were presented with a strong biblical, pastoral emphasis.

While the 1977 Conference was significant, in the next chapter we will see that the 1978 Conference was a watershed in the Conference's history.

Questions for reflection and discussion

What steps can individuals and churches take to nurture personal dealings with the living God?

In which ways do WE 'quench the Spirit'? (1 Thessalonians 5 verse 19).

Identify briefly, if possible, an occasion when the Lord 'manifested' his presence in your life and/or church.

16

The Last Conference for Lloyd-Jones

It was an excellent suggestion. And the Ministers' Committee was unanimous in its response to express 'deep appreciation' to Dr Lloyd-Jones for having 'contributed so freely and readily in terms of time, fellowship and ministry'[1] to the Conference since 1955. To express this appreciation, Brian Higham was commissioned to prepare a painting of Daniel Rowland's statue in Llangeitho. Eventually, the painting was presented by Elwyn Davies to Lloyd-Jones prior to the Tuesday evening discussion on 27 June 1978. Lloyd-Jones was deeply moved by the gift.

No one in the 'capacity crowd of eighty-plus'[2] present, including Committee members or Lloyd-Jones, knew that this would be the last Bala Conference that he would attend and address.

Therefore the presentation was timely and appropriate. This was a satisfying and challenging Conference.

Centenary: Evan Roberts' Birth

The first of two historical addresses commemorating the centenary of the birth of Evan Roberts (1878) was given by Emyr Roberts under the title, 'Thoughts on Revival.'[3] His initial emphasis was on the supernatural and sovereign nature of revival; it is 'extensive, deep and powerful' while the 'continued existence of the church and its very life depend on revival'. However, the difference between the on-going 'ordinary' work of the Holy Spirit in believers and the 'extraordinary' work in revival is quantitative, the difference being one of degree, intensity and extent only. If the church is viewed as an institution, then there is no perceived need of revival.

> 'it is only when we see the church as a supernatural phenomenon that we can rightly conceive of the supernatural power of God in revival.'

In Wales, there have been about sixteen periods of revival between 1785 and 1904/05.

Prayer

Emyr Roberts also emphasised that prayer precedes and accompanies revival. David Morgan, for example, had prayed persistently for revival for ten years prior to 1859, while Richard Owen in North West Wales, a little later, had prayed fervently for revival from his youth. There was also a general spirit of prayer among believers.

Results

Emyr Roberts highlighted two major consequences of revival. One is that many preachers are converted and 'called' in such periods. Another result is the large number of people converted. As many as one million professed faith during the revival in America during 1858/59 and the same number in Britain during that period. In the small town of Denbigh in North Wales in 1884, about 430 folk were 'added' as converts to the Presbyterian Church, while nearby in Rhosllannerchrugog, Wrexham, in 1904, 2241 people joined the churches by profession of faith over a four month period.[4]

Today?

Is revival possible today? The speaker gave a resounding positive answer. God 'is the God of wonders and miracles ...' However, a warning was issued: 'denominations need reformation ...' and the 'old doctrines' of the gospel need to be believed and preached. There should be no compromise with liberal, critical theology which had 'swept' over Wales so that the 1904 converts and those afterwards had 'suffered malnutrition ...'

'Extraordinary Phenomena'

The second historical address marking the centenary of Evan Roberts' birth was given by Lloyd-Jones. His chosen subject was 'The Place of Extraordinary Phenomena in Revival'.[5]

Lloyd-Jones's introductory remarks were compelling. Revival was a 'most important question but also a forgotten dimension' in churches. Underlining the 'sad state of our churches today', he emphasised that 'without the 1904 revival, churches would have been worse'. To emphasise the point, he claimed that when he began his ministry in Aberavon in 1927, then his wider itinerant preaching, most of the 'live' people he met in churches 'were revival converts'. He himself had been 'brought up in a church where revival was frowned on.'[6]

'A number of references' were made

> 'to the experiences of men such as Evan Roberts, whom he had known personally. The direct and familiar dealings of God with men often produced extraordinary physical manifestations, particularly in times of revival. The spontaneity of such manifestations and the overwhelming sense of the presence of God which accompanied them were features which pointed to their authenticity'.[7]

No wonder one discussion turned to the subject of praying for revival and difficulties experienced in prevailing in prayer. Encouragement was needed and

> 'quickly given by way of a word from Dr Lloyd-Jones in which we were also challenged by being asked if we really believed God and if the glory of His name was our greatest concern'.

Graham Daniel, an Apostolic Church pastor, preached on 'The supply of the Spirit' in Philippians 1:19. His message 'was full of "light" and "heat"'. What was the main difference, he asked, between our forefathers and us? It was that

> 'they had known unction upon their ministries and, generally speaking, we did not have that'.

Assurance

The main Conference speaker was Sinclair Ferguson from the Church of Scotland. Reporting for the *Evangelical Magazine of Wales*, Bruce Powell observed that the speaker

> 'was a much younger man than many had expected but his ministry could very well have been that of a man of maturer years'!

For his first subject, 'The Assurance of Salvation', 'taking the verses in an unexpected order', he expounded Romans 8 in four ways:

> 'the reality of assurance, the ground of assurance, hindrances to assurance and the experience of assurance'.

Colossians 1:9-14 was chosen for his second exposition, 'The Assurance of Guidance'. The 'foundations' in verses 11-14 were

> 'to be viewed as the prerequisites of guidance. Verses 9-11 showed the character of guidance, which was described as rational, practical, spiritual and biblical. The emphasis upon seeking the will of God as opposed to seeking that guidance which most appealed to the senses was very pertinent'.

The concluding message by Lloyd-Jones was 'the twenty-first time' for him to give the closing Conference message. His text was 2 Timothy 1:7.[8] It was 'an antidote to discouragement and despair.' To be fearful and discouraged is 'a denial of all we stand for. But what has God given us'?

The Lord has given us 'power', namely, the power of the Holy

Spirit but also 'love' for God himself, for each other and for unbelievers. He has also given us a 'sound mind', that is, self-control. When, therefore, we feel sorry for ourselves and think that 'circumstances are submerging' us, then we must 'preach to ourselves as preachers'. For we have 'a big gospel, a great God and are involved in a great work. Timothy was, therefore, urged to apply the truth to himself.'

The Conference report stated that 'our spirits were stirred as the Word came to our hearts'. Over the years this has been the appeal of the Conference. Beyond 1978, attendances increased with some outstanding Conferences. Lloyd-Jones was missed but pastors needed one another for fellowship and prayer.

Lloyd-Jones's legacy has been retained yet a new chapter began after 1978. It was a watershed.

In the next chapters, we outline briefly the growth and influence of the Conference.

Questions for reflection and discussion

Is revival possible today? Identify reasons in support of your answer.

Think of ways in which 2 Timothy 1 verse 7 is relevant and important for your situation.

Summary of Part Three of the Story 1962–1978

- Prayer was the key in purchasing property for gospel work.

- A distinctive period with many new challenges.

- Major questions and issues in this period include:

What is the gospel? What is a Christian? What is the church?

What is Christian unity?

Should Christians leave their 'mixed' church denominations?

Has genuine revival broken out in charismatic and other circles?

Revival—'A forgotten dimension' in churches.

PART FOUR

Growth, Evangelism and Revival

1979–2009

Chapters 17–18	Evangelism and Revival
Chapter 19	The Wind of Change
Chapter 20	'Complacent and Satisfied?'

17

Evangelism and Revival

It was a moving occasion. I am referring to the 1981 Bala Conference, held nearly four months after the death of Lloyd-Jones on 1 March. In one meeting, the eighty men present were stirred as they listened to a recorded address by Iain Murray on the final months of Lloyd-Jones's life. Following this, several spontaneous tributes were paid to 'the Doctor'; in fact, 'many more could have been given if time permitted'.[1] S. Malcom Jones expressed the sentiment of those present:

> 'I would not have missed this session for anything'.

They all felt

> 'a deep sense of indebtedness to Lloyd-Jones for his invaluable help' together with 'thanksgiving to God for giving him to us ...'

Changes

Only four months before Lloyd-Jones's death, the Ministers' Sub-Committee met in Llandrindod Wells to plan future Conferences acknowledging

> 'The Conference had relied heavily in the past on the Rev. Dr D. M. Lloyd-Jones, but since we would not expect him to be present at future conferences owing to ill-health, some changes would be inevitable.'[2]

New chapter

The period 1979-2009, therefore, represents a new chapter in the Conference's history. Now there was the challenge of the increasing secularization of society, theological fluidity, fragmentation amongst evangelicals and issues relating to unity as well as a perceived tension between revival and evangelism. Nevertheless, the Conference endeavoured to retain its own distinctive features of a warm experiential expression of Reformed theology relevant for pastors and churches. In this chapter, we highlight the 1979, 1980 and 1981 Conferences.

1979

The historical address by Gareth Davies in the 1979 Conference on the life and work of Richard Owen, a Welsh Presbyterian evangelist who died in Anglesey in 1887, was warm and deeply challenging.

Richard Owen

Although a young teenager at the time, the 1859 revival had a powerful impact on Owen when Dafydd Morgan preached in his Anglesey village. A week later, Richard Owen was praying with young people when the Holy Spirit fell on them. Within a short period, about ninety people were saved and became active church members.

Owen was an outstanding man of prayer with a deep love for the Lord. Burdened to preach the gospel, his sense of 'call' to the ministry became unbearable. At first, the Anglesey presbytery refused to recognise him because of his limited education but a second request was approved, particularly after he announced to the deputation,

'I will preach, even if I go into the highways and byways ...!'

Ordained in 1873, churches increasingly desired his preaching ministry. By 1876, he had teamed up with four men preaching in churches without pastors, only asking for free accommodation. He gave himself to this ministry for four years. In one year alone, eight hundred people were added to the churches through him. Owen claimed as many as thirteen thousand people were brought to Christ and joined churches through his ministry. He used the ordinary language of the people and was direct in applying gospel truths. His prayers were abundantly answered.

Discussion

The discussion on the two Conference evenings pursued two practical questions arising from this address. The first was the relationship between preaching and prayer. The second issue was the use of plain, direct language by preachers, in dependence on God. Do we feel an obligation to preach the gospel to sinners and do so for the glory of God? These two discussions, under the chairmanship of Elwyn Davies, were helpful.

'Concert for Prayer'

In this 1979 Conference, Derek Swann gave an address on Jonathan Edwards's 'Concert for Prayer'. Some historical background is necessary for appreciating its impact.

Historical background

In October 1774, several pastors in Scotland were concerned for their churches and nation and agreed to unite in extraordinary prayer for one another and their preaching. This was described by them as a 'Concert for Prayer', agreeing to pray on Saturday evenings and Sunday mornings. They also covenanted to pray privately or corporately for more extensive blessing on the first Tuesday in April, August and November, for part or the whole of the day. This commitment was shared personally in conversation and by correspondence. The agreement was for two years, then renewed for seven years.

Jonathan Edwards heard of this development and in 1776 preached a series of sermons which were published in 1778 under the title of 'An Humble Attempt ...'[3] Here Edwards provides Bible promises and prophecies indicating God's purpose to expand the church worldwide and to consummate history in complete victory. In that context, he exhorted Christians to pray for, and expect, great things in terms of the coming of God's kingdom in power. This would be achieved through the preaching of the Word, prayer and the outpouring of the Holy Spirit. There were startling results as Christians in the English-speaking world responded to Edwards's 'Humble Attempt'.[4]

Derek Swann emphasised that 'These people were given a reason to pray' for revivals and the universal accomplishment of

God's redemptive purpose. Through prayer God accomplishes his purposes.

Impact
Conference members were affected through hearing of Richard Owen and Edwards's 'Humble Attempt'. Some of their churches also benefited and I confine myself to three examples.

Peter Jeffrey, a Welsh exile in Rugby, England, returned, convicted his church should do more in bringing people to hear of Christ. He called the church to pray and evangelise more. Within a year at least thirty people became Christians.

Paul Bassett, in nearby Leicester, also called his church to pray for conversions. Numbers of people accepted Christ over several months and the church was encouraged.

Bob Cotton was also present that year and in the 1981 Conference, he shared what happened in his church in the months following the 1979 Conference. He had been convicted to urge his church to pray and seek God more. It was a young church with a mix of Christians and inevitable tensions.

'Unexpected blessing'
When Bob Cotton shared his conviction with the church, those who stayed for prayer knew the felt presence of God after a couple of hours, but not before confessing sin. This was the beginning of unusual blessing in the church over the following months.

Almost immediately, a married couple from a Hindu

background were converted and then an increasing number of unbelievers with no church links started attending services. Bob's three children were saved too. One Sunday in October 1980 there was unexpected blessing. Several individuals were converted between the morning and evening services. There was more to come. After the evening gospel service the pastor walked into the Church Hall to have coffee and to mix with the people, when he saw several crying and calling out in prayer, 'Lord, help me!' That evening over twenty people came to personal faith in Christ.

On this occasion the pastor's teenage son in his diary wrote: 'Today God came to Bury St Edmunds'. Within five months, over fifty were converted.[5] Other examples could be given of ways in which pastors after attending these Conferences experienced encouragements in their churches.

1980/81 Conferences

A prayerful burden for evangelism dominated discussions in the 1980 Conference. First, they discussed:

> 'What does it mean to have a burden for unbelievers?' 'Why are we not more motivated in seeking their conversion?' 'Have we ourselves forgotten or lost a sense of the wonder of the gospel?' and 'Do we feel the gospel we preach?'

For the second discussion, the emphasis was, 'How do we reach unbelievers?' Many valuable suggestions were made and some experiences shared.

Paul Bassett delivered two passionate addresses on evangelism. He drew extensively on biblical texts while also referring to outstanding Christian leaders like Wycliffe, Luther, Calvin, Bunyan ('a pioneer evangelist' who won his prison guard for Christ), Whitefield, Daniel Rowland and Spurgeon. He concluded by calling for a 'God-given vision' (Matthew 9:36) but also a 'God-given compassion'. The leper in Mark 1:44 knew the Lord cared and we, too, need a 'greater compassion from God' for people. Prayer is crucial for

'a prayerless church will be a compassionless church'.

These addresses were

'a vigorous declaration by a man with the heart of an evangelist'.[6]

The 1981 Conference pursued the subject of evangelism further as Eryl Davies spoke on 'Flee from the Wrath of God'[7] and the responsibility of preachers to proclaim Christ. Other subjects included John Jones, Talsarn, Caernarvonshire, who laboured from 1800–1840 and saw hundreds of people turn to Christ through his powerful preaching. Pastors were realising afresh the inseparable link between evangelism and prayer for revival. The most effective evangelists, we were reminded, have been men given to prayer.

This was reinforced by Elwyn Davies in closing the Conference by preaching from Luke 11 verses 1–11. Here was a reminder to persevere in prayer and wrestle with God ('ask' ... 'seek' ... 'knock' ...) for the Holy Spirit to be poured out on preachers in even greater measure.

We now follow this recurring emphasis in the 1982–1989 Conferences.

Questions for reflection and discussion

How does Richard Owen's life and work impress and challenge you?

Summarise what you now know about the 'Concert for prayer' in the eighteenth century.

Reflect on the links between prayer and evangelism. What relevance does this have today?

18

Covenanting to pray

How do you accommodate the growing number of pastors eager to attend the Conference? That was the encouraging problem, especially in 1982. Bryn-y-groes, Bala had a maximum capacity of eighty, possible only by using bunk beds. And the Conference was already 'full with a waiting list of over twenty.' Six weeks prior to Conference, the Ministers' Sub-Committee[1] approached the Warden at Bala Presbyterian College with the request for twenty men to be accommodated there. The response was favourable. Therefore,

> 'with over one hundred ministers booked in and up to twenty others visiting during the three days of Conference,'[2]

the problem had been solved. An increasing trend since has been for some pastors to prefer private accommodation. Approving the current length of the Conference, Gordon Cooke affirms:

> 'And more than two nights listening to other men snoring would definitely be too long'!

Popular
Happily

> 'ministers from all parts of Wales were present, along with Welsh exiles and the group of English brethren who regularly cross the border to join us at this Conference.'

Since 1982, numbers attending have fluctuated between 'a hundred or so'[3] in 1984, to 'about eighty-five' in 1986, ninety in 1991, 'a hundred plus' in 1999 and 'at least ninety' in 2011.

But it was not just numbers. In 1984, the hundred or so men were 'refreshed and thankful servants returning to battle,'[4] while in 1992 'the Conference remains as popular as ever' and the men 'gather annually with great expectation which is rarely disappointed.'[5] This was confirmed by James Brown in reporting on the 1995 Conference when he emphasised its pastoral dimension. The Conference is

> 'a trysting place where pastors and missionaries come to climb the mountain of God—often with a weariness born of the difficulties of ministry but with a far greater ache to be enlarged in heart and mind in the knowledge of God'.[6]

Two years later, Graham Hind reported that

'Bala after forty years is undoubtedly a valuable institution in many ways ...'[7]

We return to an assessment of the Conference in later chapters.

1982
But why a large attendance in 1982? Despite the loss of Lloyd-Jones and the reluctance of some in Wales to attend because of disagreement on issues like secession, charismata and reformed theology, the trend from 1974 was for increased numbers to attend.[8] There were numerous reasons for this growth. There was its growing reputation and the benefits which churches and men received through the Conference. In addition, more young ministers continued to attend.

The main speaker and his subject was the attraction in 1982. The speaker was the Rev. Professor Douglas MacMillan, Free Church College, Edinburgh. An excellent preacher, his subject was 'The Doctrine of Justification by Faith and How to Preach it'.[9] The men were reminded this is theologically one of the most fundamental and most integrating of doctrines in gospel preaching.

1983–1988
Each of these Conferences, with its own distinctive features was appreciated. Reflecting on the 1983 Conference, the Ministers' Sub-Committee[10] reported that

> 'special reference was made to the sense of God's presence in the Wednesday morning prayer meeting'.

Perceptively, T. David Carey-Jones affirms that

> 'one of the most significant things to come out of 'the 1983' conference was that we entered into a solemn covenant before God to pray for revival for one hour every Saturday evening,'[11]

either privately or with others. The background to this decision was the 1979 address on Jonathan Edwards's 'Humble Attempt'. Derek Swann was the main speaker again but now on 'Revival and Some Modern-day Trends'. He gave

> 'a gracious and valuable analysis of the Charismatic Movement'

before turning in his second address to challenge us

> 'from the Scriptures on our own attitudes, and in particular our prayerlessness, especially with regard to revival'.

During the Conference, the 'need was expressed' in various meetings by numbers of men

> 'to enter into some covenant together before God to pray for revival.'

One pastor noted that in the early Cilgwyn Conferences, no covenant was necessary as pastors felt driven to pray for one another. However, Derek Swann, with the 1983 Conference chairman, Dennis Jenkins, underlined this need. The Ministers' Sub-Committee met briefly on the final morning 'to suggest to the conference that we covenant to pray for revival on Saturday evenings from 9-00pm-10-00pm, and where possible to encourage any in our churches who felt so constrained.'[12]

This covenant to pray is still honoured by a significant number of pastors who join with groups of Christians in their churches in Wales and England.[13]

1984

During the 1984 Conference, 'Heaven came down to earth' in terms of God's felt presence when Andrew Davies gave the first of three addresses on 'The Glory of Christ'.

There were also 'some lively discussions' on practical matters as well as a deeply moving address by Gwilym Humphreys on 'The Prayer Life of John Elias'. Elias exemplified the apostolic priority (Acts 6:4) of prayer and preaching of the Word. He spent many hours and days in earnest prayer so his study chair was wet as a result of his tears. A workman repairing the thatched roof on Elias's house, a task taking him several days, saw Elias on his knees praying each time he climbed the ladder. On completing his work, he enquired, 'does Mr Elias do anything else other than pray?' Not surprisingly, Elias's itinerant preaching was powerful.

For the 1985 Conference, the Ministers' Sub-Committee[14] decided there should be

'an opportunity for questions and discussion arising from the Working Party Paper on Marital Infidelity in the Ministry and related issues'.

The 'Working Party' consisted of four pastors appointed by the Conference and it was further

> 'agreed that the Working party should continue to meet and submit a revised statement to the Ministers' Fellowships prior to the 1985 Conference'.

In 1985 three 'inspiring conference addresses'[15] were given by Vernon Higham on 'Preaching Christ'[16] but it was 'felt that more time for prayer was needed', while in 1986 a Scot, James Hogg, pastoring in Sydney, based his three addresses on 1 Timothy 4:16. His burden was:

> 'to show the task of the minister in preaching, prayer and evangelism. In his view evangelical churches lost their impetus in the 1960s, and this was taken up by the Charismatic Movement.'[17]

His second and third addresses exhorted pastors to persevere in their work and obedience and not be overwhelmed by discouragement.

The emphasis on prayer, preaching and evangelism was re-emphasised in Derek Swann's historical account of the American evangelist, Asahel Nettleton. One discussion gave way to a testimony from a former Sikh which was 'a highlight'. Another discussion turned to the importance of unity amongst evangelicals

> 'and the current need for something positive to be done about this'.

Another challenging but 'thorough address' was on the pastor's communion with God and

'the avoidance of "second hand" knowledge of Christ'.

1987

In reviewing the 1987 Conference, the Ministers' Sub-Committee

'generally agreed that the Conference had been quite an exceptional one, with appreciation expressed of the ministry from the beginning to the close of the Conference'.[18]

No reasons were given but the report on the Conference by Stephen Clark in the *Evangelical Magazine of Wales* throws light on the matter. There were, for example, Graham Harrison's Conference addresses under the title of 'More Than Conquerors' based on 2 Corinthians. He

'diagnosed present causes of discouragement by means of a masterly analysis of current spiritual trends and problems. The God-given remedy was applied by way of a heart-moving overview of 2 Corinthians. Here was meat in due season indeed!'[19]

There was also Eryl Davies's address on 'The Beddgelert Revival: 1817–1821'[20] which

'was a heart-warming reminder of what God can do when He lays bare His arm; it emphasised our need of God to revive His work in our land'.

Keith Mawdsley provided a critical analysis of 'heavy

shepherding' in the contemporary Restoration Movement while also exposing our own weaknesses. Peter Jeffrey gave 'two stirring messages' on the theme of 'he that wins souls is wise'. This was 'solid biblical fare', 'seasoned with quotations from McCheyne and Spurgeon'. Altogether, men felt it was a helpful conference.

1988

As in other years, 'the subjects dealt with' in the 1988 Conference 'were relevant to the work of the gospel in our day'.[21] To commemorate the four hundredth anniversary of the Welsh language Bible, an 'interesting' outline of its writing and history was given by Noel Gibbard. Hywel Jones's Conference addresses dealt mostly

> 'with preaching the doctrine of sin to the unbeliever and the believer respectively. The analysis was profound, and the delivery stirring'.

The Conference members thoroughly enjoyed David Davies's honest and compelling account of the 1953 revival in the Congo which he personally witnessed.[22]

The weather for the 1989 Conference 'was unusually hot' so Philip Eveson reported

> 'some of the brethren were found wearing shorts at the meeting and Tuesday afternoon saw men swimming in the lake and canoeing!'[23]

David Paterson of Perth, Scotland, was the main Conference

speaker that year, dealing with 'The Church in Action'. He distinguished

> 'at least eleven types of evangelism seen in the New Testament, but emphasised that the Bible tells us little on how it is to be done. A church likely to be blessed is one where the fellowship is willing to work, willing to exercise a loving, caring concern, and which communicates godliness to others. With moving personal examples and a pastoral heart he exhorted us to continue in the battle and commit ourselves to a gracious, almighty God "who is able to do exceeding abundantly above all that we ask or think".'

One other address merits mention, namely, Graham Harrison's address on Dr Martyn Lloyd-Jones as he assessed his ministry, answering 'many wrong and misleading' statements made concerning 'the Doctor'. He approached his subject by addressing three main concerns:

> 'the Gospel, the Church and Revival' and it 'brought us all back to the fundamental issues of the day, ones which many of us heard directly from Dr Lloyd-Jones ...

The Conference's message and ethos had not changed during this period but there were challenges ahead and new adjustments needed to be made, as the next two chapters indicate.

Questions for reflection and discussion

There are 'at least eleven types of evangelism in the New Testament'. Can you identify these and provide Bible references? Are you considering covenanting with another believer or other believers to pray for gospel preaching and revival? If so, track your response in a diary.

19

The Wind of Change

Change! That is how sociologists and historians describe the 1990s. It was a new decade marking the end of a century and a millennium. The nineties ushered in the Information Age with its worldwide internet access changing our lives as well as how and where we work and live. There was also the end of the Cold War with the collapse of the USSR in 1991 with its domino effect on satellite countries, including the re-unification of Germany. In a different context, Nelson Mandela, after twenty-seven years in prison for resisting the South African policy of Apartheid, was released. In many respects, the nineties represented a new world.

However, it was a world marked by tragedy, wars and ethnic cleansing. There was the Gulf War in 1990 while in Rwanda, ethnic cleansing resulted in the death of one million Tutsis and moderate Hutus over one hundred days in 1994; the mortality rate represented approximately one-fifth of the population. In Europe, on the 31 August 1997, Diana, Princess of Wales, died in a car crash in Paris and a wave of grief engulfed people in England. There were other significant events and changes.

Professor Densil Morgan describes the religious scene in Wales in the 1990s as

> 'the end of an era ... the old order was drawing to a close'[1]

and this was marked, for example, in the deaths of prominent church leaders in Wales like the Anglican Gwilym O. Williams (1990) and Congregationalists Pennar Davies (1996) and R. Tudur Jones (1998).

Changes

Although minor by comparison, the 1990 Ministers' Conference in Bala saw changes[2] too. For example:

> 'The arrangements for the conference programme had been slightly altered from those of previous years, and many felt that the changes proved beneficial. One of these changes was that the opening session was the first conference address ...'[3]

For the Ministers' Sub-Committee, this Conference

> 'was generally agreed to have been a profitable and encouraging conference. The change in the structure of the conference appeared to have been generally accepted'.[4]

Graham Harrison delivered the main addresses on 'The

relationship between Evangelistic Preaching and the Doctrines of Regeneration, Repentance and Faith' which were ably supplemented by Gareth Davies's historical address on 'The Preaching Ministry of Daniel Rowland' and Paul Cook's recounting of events from 'Revivals in Cornwall'.[5] The latter

> 'firmly challenged us: Are we wasting our time when we pray for revival because we are not dealing honourably with one another, and at the same time slipping in an alarming moral decline?'

It was 'generally agreed' by the Ministers' Sub-Committee that the 1991 Conference[6] had

> 'been a most profitable conference. Appreciation was expressed for the three conference addresses by Eryl Davies, and the closing address on "Seeking God" by David Carey-Jones'.[7]

The Conference addresses had the title of 'Contextualising our Ministry' with regard to the secular, religious and evangelical worlds; these addresses left men with

> 'a deep impression of the task facing us ... and of the need for God to come amongst us once again.'[8]

To mark the two hundredth anniversary of the death of William Williams, Pantycelyn, Dr Robert Rhys spoke of him as the 'Sweet Singer of Wales,'

> 'demonstrating clearly that his hymns were an expression of his deep spirituality and his close walk with God'.

This was followed by Sulwyn Jones who described the way Williams led the 'Experience Meetings' to nourish converts in Calvinistic Methodist societies, established as a result of the eighteenth century revival. The emphasis was on God's dealings with them personally.

The ministry of Maurice Roberts, Scotland, in the 1992 Conference 'had been outstanding'[9] in dealing with the expansive subject of 'God's Supremacy in Preaching'.

Elwyn Davies retired as EMW General Secretary in the summer of 1990 which represented a major loss and created a vacuum in leadership. This emphasised further the changing situation which the EMW and churches were facing. Elwyn Davies addressed the 1992 Conference on the uniqueness of Christ. He majored on John 14, a subject which served as a response to what Peter Cotterell had written in his Mission and Meaninglessness.[10] Conference members were anxious to recognise Elwyn's 'considerable contribution to the ministry in Wales', so they presented Elwyn with a painting of Caernarvon Castle to remind him of his childhood years—not the English conquest!

Appreciation

Over the following years, despite disquiet on the part of some, there was general appreciation of the Conferences. The 1993 Conference was 'challenging and encouraging,'[11] under the ministry of Andrew Anderson while the 1994 Conference 'had been a well-balanced Conference.'[12] In the latter, Professor Douglas Kelly of Reformed Theological Seminary, Jackson,

Mississippi, 'greatly helped and refreshed' pastors by expounding Jeremiah chapters 30–32

> 'on how to respond as preachers when the tide of gospel blessing is out, when it begins to turn, and when in the floodtide of full gospel renewal.'[13]

Gwynn Williams's addresses on 'The Lamb upon His Throne' in the 1995 Conference were well received whereas Professor Edward Donnelly, Northern Ireland, was the main speaker in the 1996 Conference on

> 'Simon Peter—a fellow elder.' Peter's 'example as a disciple, preacher and pastor were brought before us through clear and incisive exposition of the Gospel narratives, Acts and 1 Peter. There was much encouragement ...'[14]

Philip Swann, a young pastor, started attending the Conference in 1990 and found fellowship with pastors and Bible ministry encouraging. The messages on authentic ministry from 2 Corinthians by John Armstrong (Chicago) in 1997 were particularly relevant and needed as he identified himself with the biographical introduction in the text of 2 Corinthians 1 as it was explained. The three addresses by

> 'Dr Armstrong dealt with the issue of our humanity in ministry, taking as an example Paul's humanity as it is primarily displayed in 2 Corinthians. The addresses were thought-provoking and encouraging ...'[15]

Vernon Higham was the main Conference speaker in 1998,

handling the theme of 'The Pastor', covering his relationship to the Lord, his work as a shepherd and the message he preaches. This was followed in 1999 by addresses given by Andrew Davies on the 'The Grace of God'.

Disquiet

While many appreciated the Conference's ministry and fellowship, others expressed disquiet. Some Welsh language speakers no longer attended. One reason was the establishing of a sister Conference under EMW auspices for Welsh-speaking pastors with the need to address the distinctive challenges facing their ministries. This has served as a way of bridging between men inside and outside denominations.

Ethos

With a growing number attending from England, it was perceived by some that the Conference ethos was changing. No longer did some feel free to pray in their first language or choose a Welsh language hymn occasionally, as in the past. This particular aspect of the problem has been resolved by the introduction of a Welsh language Conference yet the Bala Conference is still grappling with its 'Welshness'. However, Philip Eveson, reporting on the 1989 Conference, made 'one plea', namely,

> 'that more of our Welsh-speaking brethren would gather with us. We do miss their valuable contributions, insights and uplifting prayers. It was good to learn over the meal table how Welsh and English pastors are working together to further the gospel of Jesus Christ in North Wales. This is encouraging, for it is more interaction we need, not less ...'[16]

Numbers attending the Conference ranged from 80–100 plus during the 1990s, but the Committee expressed concern

> 'that the number of ministers from Wales was lower'.

Two practical suggestions were made: first the

> 'need to encourage the brethren from our own Fellowships to attend more than we are doing at present'.

The second suggestion was

> 'we should publicise more the private accommodation available in the town'.

Discussions

Continuing disquiet concerned the two discussion evenings. One pastor felt the discussions were 'variable' in quality and some of his 'darkest periods' in the Conferences were in some of these discussions. Underlying the disquiet was criticism concerning the 'sameness of topic,' namely, revival. In October 1989, the Committee had already discussed this in detail when it reviewed the Conferences:

> 'More concern was expressed concerning the benefit derived from the discussion sessions and the 'sameness' of discussion topics.'

There were two official responses: first,

> 'It was emphasised that all members and Ministers' Fellowships should suggest topics for discussion'.

In fairness, regional Fellowships were slow to suggest topics for discussion. Furthermore, ample time was given at the start of a discussion to ascertain which topic men wanted to discuss. It was their choice. Occasionally, there was prior agreement, but the conclusion was that the majority or, at least, the more vocal ones wanted revival as the topic. Were older men making this choice?

A second response was uncompromising:

> it was agreed that 'the emphasis of the Conference is correct, i.e. revival, then we are not to be diverted from it'.

The Committee failed to understand the factors contributing to disquiet over the discussions because questions were still being raised in 1997 concerning these discussions. Graham Hind, for example, asked:

> 'And do the discussion sessions in spite of skilled leadership, really make a valuable contribution to the ministers' time together?'[17]

There was an underlying unease regarding the perceived tension between prayer for revival and the need for evangelism. Did prayer for revival encourage passivity?[18] Not in the earlier years, as earlier Conference addresses until the 1980s at least, often dealt with this relationship between revival and evangelism. But while supporting the need of prayer for revival, this must be with hearts eager to reach unbelievers with the gospel in the contemporary situation. In addition, there are pressing ethical issues which pastors are facing when helping those converted from the 'world.' If these issues are neglected, revival perceived largely through an eighteenth century 'Welsh' grid, will appear irrelevant.

In the next chapter we outline the further changes made in the Conference to adapt to a changing situation.

Questions for reflection and discussion
Note any details/questions needing further explanation.

Is your church maintaining a balance between praying for revival and being prayerfully engaged in evangelism?

20

'Complacent and Satisfied?'

A 'highlight' and a 'precious time' was how one young pastor referred to three addresses by Geoff Thomas in the 2000 Conference. He spoke on 'The Divine Glory of Christ'. Gordon Cooke agreed and reports the addresses 'will live long in my memory'.[1] Pastors found the Conference 'a rich time of fellowship, prayer and discussion.' There was a deep response from those present:

> 'Together we opened our hearts to God that we might know greater blessing in these days and prayed that we might be "Gospel men" ...'[2]

One pastor reports how he found the 2001 Conference helpful:

> 'It certainly was good to have walked these well-known passages of Scripture'

when Stephen Clark gave 'a moving exposition' of Matthew 27:46 and a character study of Caleb. These addresses were ably supplemented by contributions from Gwilym Roberts describing the life and work of Thomas Charles, Bala while Bernard Lewis

> 'spoke warmly about the transition from pastor in the UK to pastor abroad (Papua New Guinea) and a helpful discussion followed this address'.[3]

Derek Swann spoke for the last time, closing the Conference by preaching on Acts 6:1–7. He asked

> 'whether our gospel preaching really was preaching and whether we were really praying'.

Another young pastor, Peter Elward, found the address in 2002 by Geraint Morgan on 'The 1940s and 1950s in Wales' one of several 'which stand out'[4] for him since he started attending in 1986. Encouragingly, and reflecting a trend, 'there were a good number of new, younger men' present in the 2003 Conference. This is underlined by Gordon Cooke:

> 'One helpful recent change has been the encouragement of younger ministers to attend, and the welcome sessions for those coming for the first time.'

Having started attending the Conference in 1996, he continues:

'In my first few conferences, I felt the Conference was a little cliquey with the older ministers tending to keep to themselves. Perhaps that has improved, or maybe I'm getting older!'

Discussion

In his report on the 2003 Conference, Meirion Thomas clearly had younger men in mind when referring to the difficulty of focusing on discussion topics with so many present. In particular, when

'there are seasoned debaters as well as young men starting out on ministry. The need to discuss and debate is not in question but the format and method of discussion needs more thought and attention for it to be profitable'.

Philip Eveson also refers to the discussions:

'I know that many men have been quite frustrated by some of the discussion sessions especially during the latter period of Elwyn's chairmanship' and later ...' But I don't think men appreciate the value of conferring. I have tried to look positively at such gatherings for there are always some gems to take away—people's expectations are sometimes too high, I think, and some just sit back and criticise without contributing'.[5]

Meirion Thomas's report throws further light on the Conference:

'The times of prayer were also a reminder of genuine love and concern as we prayed together for our ministries and churches.

The longing for God-sent power and times of refreshing is still a sustained theme of the prayer times'.[6]

This was not imposed by a Committee but a desire felt deeply by the men. An address on Welsh church history (1800–1830) by John Aaron, a missions overview by Peter Milsom, Stuart Olyott's contribution concerning the use of the Lord's Day, Phil Swann's closing message on 1 Timothy 4:7–12 'did not disappoint', while Hywel Jones delivered three talks on 'the often-neglected epistle of Jude'.

Centenary

To mark the centenary of the 1904/05 revival in Wales, the 2004 Conference included historical addresses on this revival. Geraint Fielder outlined its story in South Wales and Philip Eveson in North Wales. A critical assessment was provided by Dafydd Morris, especially the

> 'lack of emphasis on expository preaching in Evan Roberts' ministry', the 'inadvisable use of young women singers' as well as 'the emotional nature of some revival meetings.'[7]

However,

> 'the consensus of the conference was that the revival was a tremendous move of God, the like of which we have never seen since, and for which we all long and pray'.

Reporting on this Conference, only the second one he attended, Chris Jenkins concluded:

'The prayer meetings and Bible teaching left us all with a godly dissatisfaction regarding our own experience of God in our lives and ministries'.

In 2005, Art Azurdia III (California) provided

'three exhilarating addresses on Spirit empowered preaching from 1 Corinthians 2:1-5. He reminded the men of our message—God's wisdom in providing a crucified Christ'; then the method by which we are to make this message known—a simple proclamation devoid of slick showmanship ... Finally, he reminded us of our means—the Spirit's empowering. The consuming issue for ministers is to know this filling of the Spirit in proclamation, the great hallmark of which is boldness. Art's insistence that we base our expectancy of the Spirit's empowering upon an exegesis of the biblical text as opposed to historic anecdotes was most refreshing ...',[8]

Criticisms of Lloyd-Jones

Iain H. Murray addressed the 2006 Conference on *Dr M. Lloyd-Jones: A Review of Criticisms*.[9] He showed how criticisms focused on the fact that before October 1966 he was the recognised leader of UK evangelicalism but lost that role afterwards.

In exposing misunderstandings of the 1966 address, Murray made three observations. One was Lloyd-Jones's insistence upon the uniqueness of the New Testament gospel. Two, 'the Doctor's commitment to catholicity'. He did not break fellowship with all who disagreed with him. Three, he was not motivated by Welshness or arrogance but the supremacy of scripture. And his priority horizontally was the conversion of the 'lost'.

For Andy Christofides, the 2007 Bala Conference was the first he attended because he had 'received mixed comments on past' Conferences but it is

'something I regret if this year's conference is anything to go by!'[10]

For him, the ministry of the Word was 'awesome', especially as Stuart Olyott

'led us simply, but profoundly through the epistle of Titus—What to do when the Church is in a mess?—We were led to biblical answers—"Fill their minds with great thoughts. Get the right men into leadership. Declare war on false teaching."'

He added:

'What a privilege to spend quality time with quality men! What a blessing to share, to learn, to encourage and be encouraged! ... Everything was excellent!'

Holy Spirit

The guest speaker for the 2008 Conference was Michael Haykin, Professor of Church History and Biblical Spirituality in Southern Baptist Theological Seminary, Louisville, Kentucky, with three addresses on 'The Holy Spirit'.

He described the Protestant Reformation in the sixteenth century as the 're-discovery of the Holy Spirit's work.[11] In the nineteenth century this doctrine became dominated by Methodists, then later by Pentecostals, Charismatics and phenomena like the 'Toronto Blessing'. He warned that John 16:14

is a key which opens up the New Testament, so the dominant theme of the New Testament is Christ, not the Holy Spirit. In his first address, he dealt with 'Holiness and the Holy Spirit's Work in Sanctification.'

His second and third addresses considered the 'Holy Spirit: Spirit's Love for the Church and our Love for one another' and then the 'Holy Spirit: Spirit of Power'. Both messages were expository and applied. There was ample time to discuss in these and other addresses. There was a thought-provoking evening discussion considering 'Christians in a hostile society'. One emphasis was on the positive aspect of such hostility for the gospel but questions remained:

> 'Are Christians complacent and satisfied? Has our love for the Lord grown cold? Is materialism sapping our spiritual life and energies? Have we become single-issue Christians? '

Hearing about 'Africa—Tragedy or Triumph?' from Ian Campbell was also sobering with its unprecedented church growth, prolonged persecution, famine and poverty in many countries. One pastor, probing how best UK pastors could help the African church, was told of the desperate need for godly, instructed leaders because training these leaders in the Word is essential for qualitative church growth.

In the next two chapters we outline the 2009–2014 Conferences.

Questions for reflection and discussion
How can we meet the need for godly, biblical leaders in Africa?

Are materialism and worldliness changing our priorities?

SUMMARY OF PART FOUR
1979–2009

- Pastors were encouraged hearing of gospel success in churches after prayer and evangelism.

- 'God-given compassion' and prayer are required in evangelism.

- Agreement to covenant to pray for revival/preaching and one another.

- A Working Party of pastors, appointed by Conference, reported on the problem of 'Marital Infidelity in the Ministry and related issues'. The 1984/1985 Conferences discussed the issues. Is it still relevant?

- Continuing disquiet was expressed over some church issues and also Conference discussions.

- The wind of change was blowing in the Conference, too.

PART FIVE

Concluding the Story 2009–2014

Chapter 21　Change and encouragement—the 2009–2012 Conferences

Chapter 22　The 2013–2014 Conferences

21

Change and Encouragement: 2009–2013

Change was again in the air. Possibly only a few pastors were aware of the fact. For fifty-one years from 1958 until 2009, the Ministers' Conferences had been planned for EMW by a Sub-Committee of ministers from various church groupings and Ministers' Fellowships throughout Wales. After 2009, that changed.

Structural

This was due largely to a major structural change in the management of EMW. Instead of a large General Committee with numerous sub-committees, a smaller Management Board was introduced with each Board member assuming executive responsibility for one aspect of EMW work such as camps, literature, Welsh language work, evangelism, summer conferences and the Ministers' Conference. While there would be consultation, Philip Swann, Management Board trustee responsible for this Conference, would plan future Conferences. Consequently, the 2009 Conference was a milestone.

All the speakers in 2009 were from Wales, contrasting with the following three Conferences. Appropriately Gwynn Williams, Cardiff, was the main Conference speaker. For several years until 2012 he exercised a leadership role within EMW.

Priorities

He chose to expound and apply 2 Timothy over his three sessions, asking what Timothy's priorities ought to be. From verses 10–17 in chapter three, he demonstrated these should be fundamentally different from those of unbelievers, by continuing to know, speak, believe and obey, as well as meditate, on the Word.

For his final address, he applied 2 Timothy 4 verses 1–5 using the title of 'Paul's Last Words'. Under the imperative to 'preach the Word' (verse 2), he provided a useful checklist for preachers:

> 'What am I saying in these verses? Is there a message? Is my presentation of the message clear and simply profound? Can the congregation digest the message? Do they understand what I am saying? Are there non-essential digressions in the message? And what about the language I use? Am I speaking their language?'[1]

Stimulating discussions followed and Bernard Lewis ('The Blessing of Partnership') and Gwyn Davies ('The 1858–1860

Revival in Wales') further enriched the Conference by their contributions.

The 2010 Conference

This was the first Conference planned by Philip Swann. He reports:

> 'Looking to develop the conference from 2010 it became immediately clear we faced two challenges to its future. Firstly, the notable absence of men ministering in Wales that could attend but were choosing not to.'

This has already been referred to in earlier chapters and the reasons were numerous. What was the second challenge he felt in planning future Conferences? There was

> 'the need to maintain the Biblical and experiential distinctive.'

How did he face these challenges? He explains:

> 'In responding to the first challenge, informal research showed that the conference was suffering from a reputation of being unfriendly and backward looking, among those choosing not to attend. This situation appeared to come from criticisms that the conference promoted revival at the expense of evangelism, historical observation over Bible ministry and was indeed unfriendly. As unity and fellowship in Gospel ministry are vital, these criticisms helped constructively to formulate the thinking behind conference planning since 2010. The second challenge of maintaining a biblical and experiential distinctive has continued to set the agenda for the addresses and we believe is being maintained.

Person of Christ

It is not surprising therefore that the 2010 Conference was different yet satisfying under Philip Swann's leadership. Garry Williams of the John Owen Centre, London, led two sessions on 'Preaching the God-Man'. In his first session, the men in small groups answered questions relating to Christology. Most appreciated the challenge to think through aspects of the Chalcedon definition (AD 451)—a stimulating exercise underlining the need for preachers to grapple with major doctrines.

Islam

Patrick Sookhdeo provided a disturbing account of Islam in Britain. Challenges related to the rise of nationalism in Russia and other countries, ethnicity (most wars are now ethnic/religious in nature), the continuing emergence of extreme 'fundamentalism' in religions like Islam, Hinduism and Buddhism with accompanying violence, the apostasy law and the growing use of Islamic Sharia law in Britain.

He identified global forces heavily influencing churches in the United Kingdom, such as the growing influence of secular humanism which denies absolutes and pedals pluralism, pleasure and other humanist values.

Then there is Islam with its strong politicisation and the trend to develop parallel societies rather than embrace integration. Islamization is occurring also in areas like food and education. Muslims now provide 20,000 UK primary schools with Islamic literature. One final concern was that the Christian church in the United Kingdom is 'weak, insipid, apathetic and bankrupt.' He saw the church in possible 'terminal decline'. As a strategy for hope, he used Nehemiah as a basis for fleshing out this strategy. Questions showed his audience had taken his message seriously.

Contemporary

David Meredith, Scotland, delivered the main Conference addresses, first by considering contemporary preaching which should always have a high God-centred content. The preacher needs to be expository and Christ-exalting. Application is also essential as the preacher 'screws the Word into consciences', using illustrations and being contextualized, using language familiar to people.

In his second address, he discussed 'Contemporary Church' by applying Acts 11, verses 19 and 27–30, emphasising that the church grew because of grassroots evangelism, and key leaders who were 'pace-setters', prepared to take risks, providing quality teaching but also encouraging and pursuing unity and partnership.

Contemporary Evangelism

His third address, 'Contemporary Evangelism', was challenging as he emphasised an evangelism which requires a clear grasp of the doctrines of sin, the necessity of regeneration and the realization of the significance of people created in the image of God. At the heart of this is the understanding that evangelism is all about the gospel and that a response is required from people. He concluded by showing how contemporary evangelism needs a church with a mindset for mission, supported by prayer. The latter involves:

a. Open homes: Acts 28:16. *Christianity Explored* works well in his parish but in homes.

b. Open lives and mixing with all kinds of people in society.

c. Open-air witness but a ban on 'open air idiots'! It must be done well and contextually.

d. Gospel people. We need to talk naturally about the gospel daily.

e. Open faces: we must be warm, loving and united so that people see God is amongst us.

f. Church with a sense of strategy. One example is Nehemiah and also Acts where Paul targeted major key cities. Why are we not growing? Why are there only a few conversions? Is the only stumbling block the cross or something secondary and cultural? We must prioritise on the gospel.

Turning to the 2011 Conference, Professor Don Carson, despite being unwell, spoke on 'The Gospel: Our Priority—Our Pattern—Our Passion'.

Gospel priority

He showed from 2 Timothy 1:3–2:2 what it meant for Timothy to be entrusted with the gospel. This involved six measures:

- As it is easy to 'cool off', Timothy must fan this heritage of teaching, the received faith of parents/grandparents, into a flame (verses 5–6). This involves a 'stirring' and the tests are ethical.

- Maintain a clear grasp of the value of the gospel: verses 8–11.

- Continue to be willing to suffer for the gospel: verses 8, 12 and Chapter 2. We are called to suffer, believe and preach.

- Maintain the mandate to guard the gospel: verse 14. Truth is of first importance.

- Distinguish between supporters and betrayers of the gospel: verses 15–16. Who are your friends? Those passionate for the gospel?

- Work hard at passing on the gospel to others: 2:1–2. In this context, four generations are involved! This is part of Paul's strategy for future evangelism.

Gospel Pattern and Passion

In his second address, he described the gospel as our pattern from Matthew 16:24–28, while in his final address he referred us to Ephesians 1:3–14 to emphasise the gospel as our passion which arises from understanding the glories of the gospel, including being chosen and adopted (verses 4–6), redeemed and forgiven (verses 7–8), shown God's mystery (verses 9–10) and chosen to be God's portion to His glory (verses 11–14).

Invigorating

Paul Kosciecha was late booking but found it was 'a worthwhile conference'; for 2012 he aimed to return his 'booking form a bit more speedily'![2]

Many like Paul found the messages by Paul Mallard on Revelation 4–7 in 2012

> 'insightful as an example of preaching from the book of Revelation as well as fascinating in the explanations that were given'.

Like others, he found it

> 'invigorating to sit under the preaching of the gospel. It was so refreshing and encouraging ...'

Andy Ball, a UFM missionary working with his wife in the Ukraine, traced the church's experience in that country through a period of intense persecution, a time of 'outpouring' and revival but now a period of apathy. There was much to discuss here.

Gospel Co-operation

Stephen Clark described gospel co-operation in Bridgend. In a population of 150,000 people, there are seven gospel churches of different backgrounds and affiliation outside the ecumenical movement. While the churches are united in the gospel, they disagree on secondary issues, including Calvinism/Arminianism. There are 'brotherly disagreements' and areas where they do not co-operate. However, their oneness in the gospel encourages them to express gospel unity.

Their co-operation involves three combined prayer meetings

per year, joint monthly pastors meetings, an evangelistic carol service, a mission, a Bible-ministry weekend, sharing visits to school assemblies, pulpit exchanges as well as sharing pastoral experience and expertise. The fruit of this gospel co-operation has been seen in conversions, the strengthening of believers and clarifying of areas of misunderstanding and theological disagreement on secondary issues. The address was well received and debated.[3]

Questions for reflection and discussion

Note any observations/questions arising from this example of gospel co-operation.

In the light of Professor Carson's application of 2 Timothy chapter 1, verse 1 to chapter 2, verse 2, what does it involve for you and your church to be entrusted with the gospel and to give it priority?

Outline your response to the progress of Islam in the United Kingdom and worldwide.

22

The 2013-2014 Conferences

The 2013 Conference brochure captures the character of the Conference:

> 'The Bala Conference is a place where we look to God to bless us as we share together in prayer, ministry and fellowship with other men from across the UK who believe the Bible, love the Saviour and glory in his Cross'.

Over eighty attended this Conference but some regulars were prevented from attending. One stalwart since 1963, Graham Harrison, died three weeks beforehand.[1] A brief tribute was paid to this faithful pastor and teacher.

Reasons

There are three reasons for devoting this chapter to the 2013 Conference.

One, this Conference provides a further opportunity for comparison. Two, a Wales emphasis re-emerged and all the speakers were from Wales. One younger pastor, Ian Parry, Cardiff, delivered the Conference addresses. This was consistent with the earlier Conference tradition of providing opportunities for younger men to develop by ministering to colleagues. Three, its overall ministry emphases and ethos were reminiscent of early Conferences. It was a helpful Conference.

Speakers

Dr Eifion Evans's title was: 'Calvinistic Methodism (1735–1835): First Century Christianity?' The speaker argued there is a correlation between Calvinistic Methodism in Wales during this period and New Testament teaching and practice. He explained that both were doctrinally orthodox yet also experiential. Regarding the eighteenth century revival, Dr Evans noted its essential features:

- A powerful sense of God's presence.

- Priority given to clear, earnest gospel preaching.

- Dynamic church life, especially prayer and preaching that resulted in unity and zeal for Christ.

- An extensive spiritual harvest with large numbers of people becoming Christians and being enlivened.

- Changed life-styles that conformed more closely to biblical teaching.

He explained that physical manifestations in genuine revival were not of its essence. However, individuals are sometimes deeply, even physically, affected under conviction of sin or on seeing the glory of Christ, His sacrifice for sin and God's amazing grace. When coupled with a greater degree of the Holy Spirit's power, then the physical effect can be overwhelming. But physical manifestations are 'mixed' in that some individuals may not be converted. Even for believers excesses can creep in, highlighting the necessity of discernment and discipline in meetings.

Distinctive features

How do we recognise its kinship with the first century Christian church? Dr Evans identified four distinctives of Calvinistic Methodism:

- Calvinistic orthodoxy.

- Preaching God's law alongside the centrality of Jesus Christ in terms of his person, his life and death with sole reliance on God to save and bless.

- Fellowship regulated by the Word as people were discipled.

- The dimension of revival.

Peter Milsom, former director of UFM International, spoke under the title, 'A Missionary Look at the Mission Field Wales', underlining the enormous challenges and needs facing the church today in reaching the majority of people who are ignorant of the Bible. One searching question was, 'Why do Christians neglect the vast majority of people to concentrate on the very few in churches?'

Pastors were encouraged hearing Meirion Thomas speak of considerable progress being made by churches in China. Bernard Lewis raised the issue of Pastors' Fellowships/Fraternals which had been encouraged and overseen by EMW since the 1950s. Were they needed? Some explained they had been a 'life-line' whereas some younger men felt they were not essential. This needs further reflection.

Tim Gill suggested guidelines from 1 Timothy for 'Developing the Evangelistic Heart and Mind of the Church', but there was little time to discuss the major principles underlined.

Prayer meetings
Times of prayer are jealously guarded in Conference and 2013 was no exception with maximum time given for prayer and preliminaries reduced to a minimum.

'Hosea: our Context, our Gospel and our God' was the theme of the Conference addresses, delivered by Ian Parry, Cardiff.

A. In his first address, he dealt with the context in which we preach.

From Hosea 1:2 and other references, he showed that life is all about our relationship to God and Hosea kept this principle at the centre of his ministry. Question: 'How shall we preach this?'

- First, we are to preach humbly as a sinner to sinners.

- Second, we must preach sin 'up-close' and personal. Sin is the breaking of God's law but also the betrayal of God's love as in chapters ten and eleven.

- Third, sin must be preached as good news that sin can be forgiven by God in Christ.

B. In the second address, he emphasised from Hosea 3:1 that though we have a broken relationship yet we remain objects of God's covenant love. Today, we appear over familiar with God's love but the grace of God should be amazing to us. Here Hosea can help us preach this love of God.

C. For his final address, he opened up Hosea 14:1–2—the fact we must all return to God.

Quoting Tozer, 'You can have as much of God as you like, and you do!' Ian Parry explained how to preach repentance.

- The sinner must be preached home: 'return'. Preaching is incomplete unless people are called back to God.

- God is someone to be pursued but in the right way (chapter 14:1–4) by confessing sin, recognising the breach of trust and love, then appealing for grace and pardon which will result in worship and obedience.

- We are to preach the covenant triune God as THE great prize!

Response

These and other messages were well received by Conference. For John Davies

> 'it was a good Conference. After all the years I have been attending and planning ..., I am invariably blessed. This year was no exception. The ministry was challenging and encouraging'.²

At the end of the final address, a time of sharing, even repentance, then prayer would have been appropriate. One young man declared that his heart

> 'jumped this year hearing Ian opening the Word and speaking so clearly with the authority of God'.

One pastor wanted to be alone afterwards and walked alongside the nearby lake to meditate and pray. The food, fellowship and ministry in this Conference were good and many returned home encouraged.

2014 Conference

The 2014 Conference had an interesting and appealing programme.

Art Azurdia (Portland, USA) dealt with 'Spirit Empowered Mission' in the context of Acts 2 verse 42 as he explored the need for the Spirit's reviving work enabling us to be faithful in fulfilling Christ's ministry on earth. Roger Welch described and assessed the wider contribution of Thomas Charles (1755–1814), a second generation leader of the Welsh Calvinistic Methodists. By contrast, Gordon Stewart described his recent visit to North

Korea, emphasising powerfully the needs/challenges of the persecuted church there. The discussion evening pursued the subject of holiness based on Kevin DeYoung's book, *The Hole in our Holiness: Filling the Gap between Gospel Passion and the Pursuit of Godliness* (Crossway, 2012). Geoff Thomas, Aberystwyth was the main speaker and his theme was Jehovah Saves—Zechariah and the Salvation of Joshua the High Priest in Zechariah 3. Here is 'the central vision of the seven visions of the prophet and the hinge vision. The prophecy all revolves around that vision.'

And Geoff Thomas explains further that here

> 'is the great statement of the gospel in Zechariah and even in the whole Old Testament. I want to remind the brethren of the gospel. That's all. I fear it's getting marginalized. I am going to say this: sometimes people come to us and they say to us, "Brother, what's the secret? How is it that you preach the way you do? How is it that you speak as you do? What's the secret?" CHRIST FOUND ME IN MY SIN. That's my secret ... I was as low as any. And that's what Jesus does. That's my secret. I had nothing to offer him. That's my secret. And ... He saved me ...

> They ask me, "Where did your motivation come from to stay in a small church in a small town for almost fifty years and preach to people? Did you get it from some verse you read, was it in ecstasy, or tongues?" You don't understand. He saved me ... What else needs to be done to motivate us to preach this gospel to everyone in Wales? What else needs to be said? Isn't salvation enough?'

Over eighty men appreciated his contribution as well as the ministry of others.

Progress and challenges
Reflecting on the progress made in the Conferences between 2010 and 2014, Philip Swann writes:

> 'While small cosmetic changes have been made to the running of the Conference, it has been encouraging to see the negative reputation replaced by the development of greater gospel unity as more, particularly younger men have been attending'.

What of the future and the challenges to the Conference? He is in no doubt that:

> 'Challenges to the future development of the Conference remain, such as the need to see men coming from a wider denominational spread and most notably the need to develop our own men in Wales as Conference contributors and we look forward to making good progress with this that the Conference may continue to encourage and bless the cause of Christ in Wales and elsewhere.'

In the next chapters, we attempt an evaluation of the Conference from 1955 and its contemporary role.

Questions for reflection and discussion
Is it legitimate to compare Welsh Calvinistic Methodism with the first century Christian church? Give reasons for your answer.

What are you learning from the Hosea messages?

Have you practical suggestions to make as to how to spend more time in prayer in church and group prayer meetings?

Summary

The story has ended with the 2014 Conference.

- The background and establishing of this Conference has been described in chapters one and two.

- In chapters three to twenty-two the Conference's history was outlined and its main features, emphases and development highlighted.

- To ensure the book is user-friendly, I have refrained from discussing in greater detail some important theological questions. That will be done in the final chapter.

You are now invited to reflect on this story in the following chapters. There is much to think and pray about as well as discuss and act upon.

PART SIX

Conclusion and Assessment

Ministers' Conference: 1955–2014

Chapter 23:   Looking Back and Forward (1)

Chapter 24:   Looking Back and Forward (2)

　　　　　　　Dr Lloyd-Jones's Ministry and Influence in the Conference

Chapter 25:   Lloyd-Jones's pastoral role

Chapter 26:   Lloyd-Jones's piety

Chapter 27:   Lloyd-Jones's highlighting, and preaching of the gospel

Chapter 28:   Lloyd-Jones's emphasis on revival

                Word and Spirit theme in the Conference

Chapter 29:   Word and Spirit (1)

Chapter 30:   Word and Spirit (2)

23

Looking Back and Forward (1)

The situation has changed so we need to look back and learn but also look ahead. In this chapter and the next, we try to assess the Conference over fifty-nine years. That is a difficult but necessary task, especially if it is to serve new generations of pastors. But first we survey the Conference as a phenomenon in Welsh church history.

1. The Conference: a phenomenon in Wales
I establish this fact by underlining four details.

First, the Ministers' Conference has continued in Wales successfully for fifty-nine years since 1955. Numbers have increased from fifty to between eighty and one hundred men. Numbers have been maintained with minimum advertising. Only pastors, missionaries and students near the end of their training can attend.

Second, the Conference has given birth and encouragement to two related but smaller pastors' conferences, both held in Bala in the autumn. One is for Welsh language pastors and the other for those in the first years of ministry.

Third, when established in 1955 this Conference became the first interdenominational Conference held for evangelical pastors in Wales. That is significant. Here is unity expressed across, not between, denominations grounded on firm biblical convictions. The increasing emphasis on Church unity within the denominations from the 1950s, often involving doctrinal ambiguity, stands in contrast to the unity in the gospel enjoyed in Conference over this long period.

Fourth, add to this the presence and role of Dr D. Martyn Lloyd-Jones in the Conference who was for John Macleod,

> 'the eminent London minister ... who was by any measure the greatest preacher of the twentieth century'.[1]

James Packer is also generous in his estimate of Lloyd-Jones:

> 'as, warts and all, one of the greatest Christian men of the twentieth century, a man whom God used powerfully to recall British evangelicals, both individually and corporately, to their true roots in the Bible, in the gospel and in theology ...'[2]

Donald Macleod goes further in describing Lloyd-Jones:

'he would have towered in any age. Indeed he was arguably the greatest British preacher since the Reformation, rivalled only by Whitefield, Spurgeon and Chalmers.'[3]

Lloyd-Jones's support for the Conference and his regular ministry there from the very beginning until 1978 added to its appeal and influence.

Unfortunately, very few details concerning the Conference have been published and that explains partly why it is conspicuous by its absence from church history books covering this period. Even the recent appraisal by academics of Lloyd-Jones's life and legacy[4] barely touch on the subject. One of the editors, David Ceri Jones, acknowledges the Conference was 'perhaps the most important development'[5] with regard to Lloyd-Jones's influence on Welsh evangelicals.

I am not indulging in triumphalism but underlining the fact that this Ministers' Conference was, and remains, an important part of the church history story in Wales. It cannot be ignored. The Conference is worthy of more serious and sympathetic attention, especially with more primary and secondary sources now available in this book.

2. The Conference is a response to the changing religious and theological developments in Wales and beyond

The Conference seeks to understand and respond to radical changes taking place in Christendom and society. The emphasis on conferring and praying together, choosing relevant subjects for addresses, exposition and application of the Word, learning from one another and reflecting on church history are most helpful in this respect. The Conference's response to the changing situation can be described in several ways.

Evangelism

First, the Conference responded by continuing to discuss and engage in evangelism in Wales. As more of the nation became 'unchurched', pastors were often reminded of this need and at local levels endeavoured to engage in outreach. Some local churches experienced encouragements while one pastor led his South Wales valley church in purchasing a tavern to use as an evangelistic centre and haven for the hundreds of young people in the locality. This was well used, enabling the church to reach teenagers in the valley with the gospel and to build good relationships in the community. A significant number of pastors support EMW Youth Camps, Beach missions and, in recent years, missions requested by local churches. Although there was possibly a more spontaneous and prayerful burden for evangelism in earlier years, the focus remains. Whether in prayer meetings, discussions, expositions or major addresses, the concern for evangelism has remained high on the agenda.

Critical Theology

Second, the Conference responded to the spiritual vacuum and critical theology within the denominations.

What happened to the chapels? Without many realising, 'liberal theology,' according to Emyr Roberts, had, at the beginning of the twentieth century,

> 'come in as a strong flood and had in time possessed the land.'[6]

By the 1930s,

> 'the Protestant, evangelical doctrine that had been such a power in our land for nearly two centuries had been laid aside almost completely.'[7]

This fact is also acknowledged by scholars including R. Tudur Jones and Robert Pope. For example, in his chapter on 'Helynt Tom Nefyn yn y Tymbl [Tom Nefyn's Troubles in Tumble]' from 1925 onwards, Pope emphasises that,

> 'Theological Modernism, with its emphasis on the application of the moral principles of the gospel, was common enough by that time.'[8]

He also refers to the effect of liberalism on the beliefs of traditional Protestant denominations:

> '... by 1904, it is clear that the traditional understandings of the Atonement and the substitutionary death of Jesus, and the teaching that his sacrifice was valid in that he was "true God and true man", were moving towards a Christian understanding that considered Jesus in terms of the perfect humanity expressed by his complete obedience to the will of God and his filial awareness of his heavenly Father ... his death was to be understood as a moral self-sacrifice.'[9]

Challenge of Karl Barth

Liberal theology was being challenged by the late 1920s through the theology of the Swiss theologian Karl Barth. This was beginning to influence theologians, initially in Scotland but also in England and Wales, the latter through J. D. Vernon

Lewis, E. Keri Evans but particularly J. E. Daniel (1902–1962) in Bangor. Professor Daniel, like Barth, opposed liberal theology. Consequently,

> 'the whole of Welsh Nonconformity ... was being affected by the Barthian trend.'[10]

Barth's teaching was attractive and perceived initially by evangelicals as an ally in opposing a bankrupt liberal theology. But some evangelicals in Wales were uneasy, including Lloyd-Jones who, after reading Barth, became critical.

I understand why Professor Densil Morgan is unhappy with Lloyd-Jones's negativity with regard to Barth, but the latter's radio broadcast in Welsh in 1947[11] contained positive features. For example, he felt it was time to reconsider the significance of Barth's theology, acknowledging that it challenged the supremacy of reason, and the dependence of theology on philosophy. He was grateful, too, for the emphasis Barth gave to the Word and to theology. There are other valuable features of Barth's work which were not detailed in this address like his work on the Holy Trinity, his upholding of the deity of Christ, the necessity of revelation and many valuable exegetical footnotes in his writings.

Two further comments are necessary in clarifying Lloyd-Jones's response. He concluded rightly that some key theological terms and doctrines were being re-interpreted so that revelation, for example, was conceived in existential, dynamic terms in which the Bible only 'became' the Word of God in moments of 'encounter' with the Living Word, namely Christ himself. This was a significant shift away from traditional teaching which affirms the Bible is the Word of God in all its statements. For Lloyd-Jones that was a major error which led him to oppose

'and curtail 'Barth's 'influence within the conservative constituency.'[12]

A second comment is also important. When Lloyd-Jones advised:

'Don't waste time reading Barth and Brunner'[13]

he had in mind preparation for preaching. In that context, his advice to read Pink is understandable, though inadequate. That Lloyd-Jones discouraged pastors from reading Barth themselves as part of their theological reading is questionable. For example, Lloyd-Jones was encouraging when I shared with him some of the benefits I had derived from my extensive reading of Barth.

Despite Barth's influence, the impact of critical theology on churches remained extensive as we now illustrate.

'Crisis'

A Bangor College lecturer and Presbyterian elder, W. Ambrose Bebb, expressed his concern for churches, especially the Presbyterian Church of Wales in the 'crisis' which faced churches in the mid twentieth century.[14] For Bebb, one major factor contributing to the crisis was liberal theology which had 'controlled' the Presbyterian Church of Wales since the end of the nineteenth century. He felt sad there was now little talk of repentance or new birth with hardly any instruction given to young people preparing them for membership in chapels.[15] That was the situation facing the Conference from 1955 onwards.

No formal or academic response was made by the Conference to liberal theology, but successive Conferences dealt with crucial doctrines like Scripture, Christology, the Atonement, Sin, Regeneration, Justification, Sanctification and experiential Christianity in an attempt to encourage pastors in the contemporary preaching of these truths.

An invitation was extended to Hefin Elias,[16] Cardiff, to address the 1965 Conference on 'Trends in Modern Theology'. Describing the sixteenth century Protestant Reformation as 'a watershed', he referred to 'Liberal' Protestantism as a 'parasite' on the Reformation with a 'common root' in Pelagius but especially Kant's eighteenth century philosophy, which denied revelation and viewed all knowledge as merely relative, with religion reduced to observing moral duties. Others developed and applied Kant's teaching.[17] There was extensive discussion of the subject.

The Conference has played a key role in confirming and encouraging men in their ministries by reaffirming Bible truths, which was also a significant contribution to churches in Wales.

Pastoral Theology

Third, the Conference provided instruction in what is 'in-service training' in the neglected area of pastoral theology. In this respect, many pastors have expressed their appreciation. Gordon Cooke affirms that 'the Bible ministry is much appreciated. It is good for us to sit and listen and be fed ... I think it (the Conference) continues to provide a most helpful resource for men in ministry in Wales ...'[18]

Philip Swann writes similarly:

'the environment with pastors ..., fellowship and Bible ministry are encouraging'.[19]

Peter Elward and Philip Eveson endorsed these sentiments and underlined 'especially the prayer meetings'. Bruce Powell also highlights

'Prayer Meetings as a distinct part of the Conference' together with the opportunity 'to speak to most other attendees, a spirit of unity across a broad range of evangelical ministries, a good balance between Word and Spirit, the historical content, the emphasis on revival and the opportunity to ask questions and discuss issues' together.[20]

For Bob Cotton, the most helpful aspects of the Conference have been

'the historical papers, prayer sessions and evening discussions.'[21]

Sulwyn Jones, Dowlais, Merthyr, began attending the Conference in 1960 and its most helpful features have been

'wide coverage of the needs of ministers—theological trends, lessons from church history, being at the receiving end of the ministry of the Word, fellowship second to none, unity in times of prayer, occasional discussion meetings.'[22]

John Davies started attending the Conference in 1964 as a final year student training for the ministry. For him, the Conference has been invaluable:

> 'For many of my generation the Conference served as a kind of Bible College, only having had University and denominational College training, Bala was an oasis, and to be in the company of the brethren, and sitting under the ministry of these men was a great blessing'.[23]

Sulwyn Jones agrees. The Conference influenced him 'immensely' and he refers to his

> 'considerable debt both to the Conference and "the Doctor" over the years'.

He explains:

> 'early sixties—having fought our way through theological liberalism in College, continuing the same in now evangelical churches and denominational structures, and personally fighting one's way to doctrinal clarity, especially in the doctrine of the church—Bala was a precious oasis among kindred minds. The annual Conference continued to be unmissable for fellowship and as new issues arose.'

For those trained in denominational colleges in Wales, they found little, if any, instruction given concerning pastoral issues, including the life/work of the pastor, so the Conference was a lifeline.

Malcom Denning provides another example. Ordained and inducted into a pastorate of Presbyterian churches in the Vale of Glamorgan in 1964, he moved to Pontarddulais in 1967. His story is typical of what many younger ministers experienced. He felt his training was no preparation for the rigours of the preaching and pastoral ministry but in Conference he benefited from pastoral theology, with a due emphasis on the pastor's prayer life, godliness, study habits, preaching and caring for people. John Davies again comments

> 'the greatest blessings and encouragements I received were ... when our own men were the main speakers ... they could identify with our pastoral situations although men like Douglas Macmillan also identified with us'.

The situation has changed significantly recently with younger pastors having been converted in evangelical churches and trained in evangelical theological colleges.

It is that changing situation facing the Conference we reflect on next.

Questions for reflection and discussion

After reading earlier chapters, do you consider that the Conference has maintained its commitment to, and passion for, evangelism?

In which ways do you think the situation has changed for pastors and churches?

24

Looking Back and Forward (2)

Although instructive, we cannot live in the past. Now we consider the Conference's contemporary role. There are challenges to face, including developing the Conference's strengths.

Changes

Since the first Ministers' Conference in 1955, the situation in Wales and throughout the United Kingdom has changed radically—socially, culturally, politically and religiously. Paul Chambers affirms that

> 'organised religion is declining (in Wales) at a faster rate than anywhere else in the United Kingdom'[1] and it is 'seen as terminally sick' and 'fragmented.'[2]

While the Conference is not in decline, it has changed. For example, nearly all those involved in establishing the Conference have died. Men ordained in the 1960s are now retired and are no longer active in Conference. Again, for the first twenty-three years until 1978, Lloyd-Jones's influence was significant. His legacy remains in terms of a biblically warm and experiential Calvinism but over the past thirty-eight years his influence on Conference has waned. Younger men now attending know little about its early history, pioneers and struggles. Inevitably, earlier attitudes are being re-evaluated in an attempt to be more relevant.

Other changes are apparent. 'Bala' is now one of many good Conferences available to pastors in the United Kingdom and in the United States. The choice of speakers in Conferences or the desire to 'try' a new Conference and engage in new networks of pastors and achieve more cross-fertilization, are some factors attracting pastors. Attendance at Bala can consequently fluctuate between seventy-five to a hundred or more pastors. Some refuse to own loyalty to one Conference as in the past. There are also valuable resources available on the Internet which can stimulate pastors with regard to preaching and understanding theological trends so they may feel less reliant on a Conference.

Attitudes towards accommodation in the Conference have also changed. Shared rooms lacking en-suite facilities are now being increasingly exchanged for accommodation in local hotels. The attraction is comfort and privacy with the opportunity to prepare for the following Sunday ministry. Another question lurking in the background is the future location of the Conference. Is Bala the best location?

Challenges

Just as the Labour Party in Wales faced new and profound challenges from 1970 onwards,[3] this has remained true of the Bala Conference. Some of these challenges are now identified:

1. Relationships

Tensions are not new in the Conference. In 1955 there was, and remains, disagreement concerning Lloyd-Jones's teaching on Spirit baptism.

During the first six years, and despite warm fellowship, there was disagreement between Arminians and Calvinists as the Conference established its clear Calvinistic thrust. Differences to a small degree obtained between Welsh and English speakers but more so over denominational loyalties.[4] By the 1960s, few Arminians attended while in the late 1970s fewer men in Welsh language churches supported the Conference. A new development was the number of pastors in England who attended. The chemistry of the Conference was changing. Regretfully, relationships were damaged in the turbulent 1970s, 1980s and 1990s over secession.

Bill Stead, a Presbyterian minister in Fitzclarence, Aberavon for thirty nine-years, is one example. With his pastor, I. B. Davies, he attended a Cilgwyn Conference as a student and then became a regular after ordination in 1959 until he felt 'unwanted' in the 1970s for not leaving his denomination. Previously, he found the 'fellowship and prayer times extremely helpful' and also benefited from the exposition and historical addresses. 'I used to regard it as a highlight in the year', he explains. Like others, he boycotted the Conference for years because of ungracious attitudes on the part of a few and also a disturbing letter which he and other colleagues received on official EMW paper.

Dafydd Job, Bangor, left the Presbyterian Church in 1985, and confirms

> 'the Conference went through a difficult time, reflecting some of the difficult transitions in churches and Ministers' Fraternals' but it 'has regained direction'[5] and balance.

For Bernard Lewis[6] who started attending in 1984, the Conference

> 'dipped for a while probably in the 90s' but has improved.

Bill Stead reports

> 'the situation between those who left and we who stayed in the Presbyterian Church has healed over later years. I have no bitterness and feel comfortable in our fellowship together.'[7]

Nevertheless, the 1970s and 1980s, represented a painful period in the Conference's history, a period marked by misunderstanding and strained relationships.

Relationships have improved but even more catholicity is required in embracing evangelicals in different church situations such as evangelical Anglican clergy. The Evangelical Fellowship in the Church in Wales (EFCW) was formed in March 1967 for 'purposes of prayer, fellowship and study.'[8] During the 1960s and 1970s a small number of EFCW members attended the

Conference. However, the evangelical movement within the Anglican Church in Wales, according to one member, is

> 'not what it used to be but has become fragmented'.[9]

Encouragingly some younger committed evangelicals have recently been placed in parishes in Wales. More needs to be done in expressing unity and mutual acceptance of one another. For some, Conferences can be lonely occasions but Bernard Lewis feels

> 'the level of care and support is improving'.

Another aspect is the on-going relationship between older and younger men which is generally good. However, older men can be unwise in referring to early Conference leaders and ways of doing things. Sulwyn Jones acknowledges

> 'men of my generation find it very difficult not to refer to Lloyd-Jones constantly still and value his wisdom and balanced judgements'.

But he warns:

> 'We have to be very careful how we speak of him before younger men who never met him for we may create an impression that we idolised him which is not so.'

Has too much respect been given to past leaders so a culture has emerged which refuses to question their statements or actions? While we build on their contribution, commitment to the supreme authority of Scripture must be paramount.

2. 'Revivalitis'

This term does not denote the rejection of genuine revival. Rather it expresses frustration concerning the way in which the subject of revival is handled. Dafydd Job illustrates the point:

> 'There was a danger at times that some of the men talked about revival in a way which was not helpful—they seemed to give the impression that there was nothing which could be done because we were not in revival'.

Was that only a perception gained by younger men? An older pastor[10] disagrees:

> 'There were times in the prayer times and discussions when I was unhappy with an unhealthy Revivalitis, bordering at times on emotionalism. Strangely, Lloyd-Jones never deviated from the vision of our constant need for the work of the Spirit in revival, but in his ministry he maintained a perfect balance, which we lesser mortals have great difficulty with at times'.

On the other hand, the overall teaching concerning revival and prayer was fruitful for Dafydd Job explains that the Conference in the 1980s

> 'helped me sort out my priorities in ministry. It especially helped me clarify my vision regarding revival'.

But some pastors did not attend from the late 1980s and 1990s because of the impression that folk were living in the past and were preoccupied exclusively with revival. Their feedback to Conference organizers confirms that they themselves believed in revival, but they were searching for a biblical pattern for ministering in contemporary situations outside of revival. They found themselves 'up against a wall' on discussion evenings when revival was usually the emphasis.

Immediate challenges

Looking ahead, there are four immediate challenges.

One is to provide a robust exegetical study of revival within the broad sweep of biblical, redemptive history, especially in the light of the fact that

> 'revival as a discrete topic never occurred in the Reformed theology of the sixteenth and seventeenth centuries.'[11]

Considerable attention has been given to historical accounts of revival and more 'pietistic' messages on the subject. It is time to regain ground theologically and to establish a contemporary but rigorously biblical theology of revival. This will also demonstrate that revival is not an exclusively Welsh phenomenon but something given sovereignly by the exalted Christ to his church worldwide.

A second challenge is to continue studying biblically and historically how men can serve appropriately outside of revival with, at the same time, an increasing dependence on God for his help. There is a tension here and a danger of veering exclusively to one or the other.

'Discouragement,' 'disillusionment', 'unbelief'—'Will God really answer prayer for revival?' These are some responses of pastors who have heard much about revival, even prayed for it, yet without answers to their prayers as their church situations worsened. There are lessons to re-learn like trusting God and his Word, while appreciating more the Spirit's 'ordinary' work in believers and the urgency of persevering in prayer, without abusing divine sovereignty by becoming entirely passive.

Third, more important than revival is seeking God himself, enjoying him and cultivating a dynamic, intimate relationship with him.[12] Although this note was struck regularly in earlier Conferences, one detects it may have been neglected in recent years so the 2013 Conference addresses were salutary. Rich exposition of the Word addressed to the mind, but applied, then prayed over together are invaluable in this respect.

Discussions

A fourth challenge for the Conference concerns the discussions. Pastors want to confer and learn from one another in a relaxed and confidential context. Some want more discussion sessions, in addition to discussion after various addresses. This challenge is being wrestled with currently.

Although this subject has been raised in other chapters,[13] some practical suggestions are offered here:

- Doctrinal and ethical/pastoral issues need to be discussed urgently.

- Conferring is important and Bala is one of the very few

Conferences in the UK which has encouraged discussion. However, the quality of discussion needs to improve. Stephen Clark claims that

> 'the quality of discussion at Affinity ... is vastly superior to that at Bala'. In the latter, 'some men wanted to score points (this, I believe, has changed in recent years). People will air a view strongly without recourse to Scripture, and someone will air the opposite view with equally scant regard for the Bible. The best discussions were when (a) one of the subjects was announced in advance with guidelines for how discussion would be chaired; (b) when someone shared a real heart issue ...'[14]

- Sharing 'a real heart issue' is important but not easy to achieve. Perhaps William Williams's model of sharing personal spiritual struggles and joys is one way forward, if pastors are prepared to trust one another while avoiding introspection and triumphalism.[15] Or can pastors sometime share their struggles in thinking through biblically a complex ethical or pastoral issue? Such a 'journey', despite mistakes made, can be extremely stimulating.

Preserving the strengths of the Conference

In a welcoming email urging pastors to attend the 2013 Conference, Steffan Job as EMW Ministries Coordinator, explains:

> 'The Ministers' Conference is for men whose heart and passion are for the gospel. It is a marvellous opportunity to join with other

Bible-believing, cross-centred and Christ-loving men from across Wales and the UK for prayer, ministry and fellowship.'[16]

In the last chapter we noticed how men endorsed those words. It is the emphasis on prayer, fellowship with other pastors and the ministry of the Word that has drawn Keith Plant to the Conference annually since 2009. He finds the teaching relevant and challenging.[17] Steve Carter, Tredegar, reports that the 2013

> 'Conference was very helpful to me in many ways',

but suggests prayer rather than questions following the main addresses, as he himself was left

> 'just wanting time to digest and apply personally its impact'.[18]

Mike Leaves started attending the Conference in 1985 and finds the most helpful features the

> 'prayer meetings, discussions and the informal discussion between meetings.'[19]

Similar sentiments are expressed by John Williams, Gorseinon:

> 'The fellowship with the brethren, times of earnest prayer, stimulating and thought provoking papers and discussions and biblical exposition ...'[20] have been invaluable.

Dafydd Job has been greatly helped in Conference by

'pastors ministering to pastors; younger men seeing senior men at prayer. Fellowship engendered between men of different generations.'[21]

He adds:

'... time for prayer, and enough sessions to challenge the mind, as well as a free afternoon for some relaxation and fellowship. The ethos is probably one of the main strengths of the conference. This is Calvinistic Methodism in practice—the balance of strong theology and experiential life'.

Bernard Lewis finds

'the prayer meetings and discussions' the most helpful features[22]

while for Geoff Thomas,

'The Conference ethos remains one of experiential Calvinism with a longing for revival ... the messages are the bonus, while the fellowship of ministers, the renewal of friendships and the gathering of news the staple of our meetings.'[23]

Graham Harrison, writing three days before his sudden death, views the value of the Conference as a

'recall to fundamentals. Encouragement. Prayer ... Bala is distinctive and must remain so. I am not interested in replicating what is available elsewhere. The prayer times and discussion sessions are vital. What else can call us back to our continuing need of God and revival?'[24]

Jeremy Bailey, Sandfields, Aberavon, began attending in 1998 and shares:

'I was accepted as a minister from England and made welcome ... The prayer times are longer than in most conferences and most uplifting, the ethos is experiential ... Discussions are practical, theological and relevant ... warm and friendly, even when sharp differences of opinion occur!'[25]

The feedback provided by Conference members expresses appreciation and a desire for a vigorous Word-Spirit balance in the Conference's ethos and programme. This balance is characterized by relevant biblical exposition, discussion, opportunities for extended prayer with ample time for informal fellowship.

Concerning this Conference, Meirion Thomas affirms:

'A Conference which majors on prayer and the ministry of the Word is a help to put one's work back in perspective ... There are great strengths in its ministry. May the Lord graciously enable us to build on these strengths and humbly evaluate weaknesses for the future.'[26]

In the next four chapters we consider Lloyd-Jones's influence on the Conference from 1955.

Questions for reflection and discussion

Suggest ways of improving relationships between both Christians and churches.

How can we avoid 'revivalitis'?

In which ways should we encourage each other in fellowship, prayer, and profiting from the preached Word?

Consider taking practical steps to implement your suggestions.

25

Lloyd-Jones's Pastoral Role

Having reflected on the Conference, we now try to understand Lloyd-Jones's role and influence in it. What was Lloyd-Jones's influence on this Conference and consequently on evangelicals in Wales?[1] Emphasis must be placed on his pastoral role which is the theme of this chapter.

1. A pastor to pastors

The Conference has endeavoured to be biblical, theological and pastoral. For Noel Gibbard the Conferences have helped men continue in their ministries, frequently in discouraging situations. Eurfyl Jones had no hesitation in affirming that the Conference had been the means of keeping him and others in the ministry. That in itself points to the Conference's contribution to churches in Wales. Without the Conference, Omri Jenkins insisted he would have been 'impoverished' pastorally and spiritually while Gareth Davies regarded the Conference as an annual 'oasis where I have been fed and refreshed'.

To many Conference members, therefore, Lloyd-Jones was a pastor in the manner he addressed the Conference on different themes, and then led discussions on subjects normally chosen by themselves. These contributions were relevant and informed. In addition, he engaged personally with Conference members.

He corresponded occasionally with Conference men in his distinctively illegible writing style or telephoned them. Whenever possible, he preached in their churches and enjoyed hospitality in their homes. He was a pastor and friend; many personal matters were shared confidentially with him as a relationship of trust and respect developed.

While sharing refreshments with mourners immediately following the burial of Lloyd-Jones in March 1981 in West Wales, I talked briefly with his widow, Mrs Bethan Lloyd-Jones. During the conversation, she pointed to the many younger pastors present, and said:

> 'he referred to you all as "my boys"; he prayed for you all often and was concerned for you.'

Her statement rang true. Like many others, I benefited from his prayers, fellowship and fatherly concern and affection which became increasingly apparent. This was not an exclusive relationship confined to Wales as there were other pastors and networks of pastors elsewhere whom he has also pastored in varying degrees.

This pastoral relationship with 'his boys' has been criticised in different ways. I shall confine myself to two examples.

Criticisms

1. One example is Gaius Davies, a consultant psychiatrist and friend of Lloyd-Jones, who suggests there was something 'more sinister'[2] in that relationship.

The criticism is misguided and cynical. But what does the criticism mean?

Acknowledging that calling these ministers 'his boys' was 'a real mark of affection', he suggests that in such a relationship the ministers would not have been 'allowed ... to challenge effectively' what Lloyd-Jones 'said or did'. He adds: 'It also meant, for a great many, idolising Dr Lloyd-Jones ...'[3]

Referring to those who regarded 'the Doctor' as 'infallible' and 'his conduct always right', Gaius Davies makes this wild claim:

'... I doubt if the true follower of Dr Lloyd-Jones ever attributed any mistake or misjudgement to the hero that they loved and worshipped'.

Underlying this claim is the further statement that

'Dr Lloyd-Jones was very high on the trait of dominance.'[4]

He does not inform us what constitutes 'the true follower' and he may have met a few who attributed infallibility to this great man.

But in the context of the Ministers' Conference in Wales, he misrepresents the relationship pastors had with Lloyd-Jones. Yes, he was respected and valued. He was also missed when it became impossible for him to attend as his ministry and advice were valued. On the other hand, I am unaware of any minister in this Conference who regarded him as 'infallible' and 'always right'.[5]

Numerous examples can be given to answer this criticism. A significant number of Conference men, for example, disagreed with his exegesis of Ephesians 1:13-14 and his understanding of 'the baptism with the Holy Spirit'. They were one with him in an emphasis on, and need for, revival but not in some of the ways he supported that teaching biblically. Disagreement with this aspect of Lloyd-Jones's teaching continues. And some of these were 'his boys'! Numerous other examples can be given. In the early 1940s, J. Russell-Jones felt 'the Doctor' was wrong in advising against establishing an annual Welsh IVF Conference and it was several years before Lloyd-Jones changed his mind.

Personally, I disregarded his advice on at least three important occasions. During 1972 he apologised to me privately, acknowledging he had been wrong in his advice to me four years earlier concerning a personal decision I made. He was pleased I had not listened to him! Consequently, I find Gaius Davies's criticism wide of the mark. 'The Doctor' did not imagine himself to be 'infallible'.

Another example was the 1973 Conference where I delivered the main Conference addresses. Immediately following my first address, Lloyd-Jones was the first to ask a question. He implied I was inconsistent in assuming responsibility for a new Christian

Reading Course introduced by the EMW. He was not impressed by my answer so he invited me to his room for a discussion. I argued there were many believers in denominational and pastorless churches needing help to understand the Bible. He insisted that EMW was a para- church organization and only churches should undertake such a task. Eventually, he was prepared to approve my action and wished me well! We were certainly allowed, perhaps encouraged, to challenge him.

Reflecting on similar situations I concluded that 'the Doctor' wanted assurance I had thought through issues clearly. Only when satisfied on this point would he agree, albeit sometimes grudgingly. Contrary to what some authors claim, he encouraged ministers to think for themselves and not be slaves to their reading or commentaries, or even to individuals, including himself. I am arguing there was nothing 'more sinister' in his relationship with 'his boys' in the Conference. In this context, Wynford Davies recalls 'the Doctor' saying to him after the 1951 IVF Welsh Conference:

> 'I think you are fairly launched. The time has come now when you can move ahead on your own'.[6]

There was no 'control' being exercised by Lloyd-Jones over the young men. His pastoral advice was given freely and humbly.

During my early years in the Conference, I perceived him to be austere, distant and shy. Slowly, through conversations at meals and over coffee, I began to see an ordinariness and tenderness about him as well as a pastoral, fatherly concern. And he was human in so many ways, especially his fondness for desserts, cakes and warmth. When he stayed in our home in February 1973, my wife and I were in awe of him. But we need not have been anxious. He was relaxed and conversed freely as he sat late evening enjoying his supper with his coat on in front of a roaring coal fire! He showed interest in what was happening in our lives and church. When we shared concern over our baby's health, he did not hesitate to examine the child and give his medical opinion which was reassuring. He pastored pastors!

2. A second criticism of this pastoral relationship with 'his boys,' was that Lloyd-Jones had, as Brencher claims, 'a vestry way of speaking and a public way of speaking' so that 'issues could become blurred.'[7]

In other words, privately his advice to pastors would appear to contradict his public teaching. That perception appeared to be true on occasions. But I offer one reason and example why this perception is mistaken. That reason is Lloyd-Jones's careful distinction between biblical principles which are objective and permanently valid and their wise outworking in different situations at different times. He had a high view of divine providence, recognising that pastors were sometimes in different, often complex, church and family situations. This was particularly true of some Welsh language denominational pastors who genuinely felt locked into their situations even though they longed to implement the principle. On the English language side, amongst those who left their denominations there were significant differences in the timing of their decision and actual exodus depending on the circumstances. There was no hesitation on his part acknowledging this and so critics may wrongly perceive him as being inconsistent.

On two occasions, in 1967 and 1968, Lloyd-Jones advised me against withdrawing from my denomination and that, of course, in the immediate wake of his 1966 address. His unsolicited advice surprised me. Although he was unaware, I was not contemplating resigning. I was personally persuaded that such action would have been inappropriate then, as the church I served was enjoying a period of unusual growth and blessing. However, I appreciated his counsel as it gave further confirmation of what I had already decided. There was certainly no 'control' exercised over me by a 'dominant' father-figure. He had clearly recognised the importance of my continuing in that church situation, even though it seemed contrary to his public teaching.

For Brencher to interpret this as an example of Lloyd-Jones contradicting his 1966 public teaching is simplistic. 'The Doctor' was right to emphasise the importance of applying objective biblical principles, but to do so responsibly and wisely within providence.

We consider next Lloyd-Jones's influence upon the Conference in terms of his piety and devotion to the Lord.

Questions for reflection and discussion

Are there circumstances when it is unwise to apply a biblical principle? Or is that an excuse?

Are Christian leaders sometimes 'dominant' and 'controlling'? What are the danger signs?

26

Lloyd-Jones's Piety

Lloyd-Jones's influence in the Conference was considered in the previous chapter in terms of his pastoral role. His piety or godliness is the next area of influence we consider. This is often ignored in assessing his influence.

Piety—The word here describes a person's intimate relationship to the Lord with its transforming effect on a person's affections, values and life-style.

Lloyd-Jones's piety impacted Conference pastors
This will now be described in three ways within the context only of the Conference.

Public ministry
A major way pastors were impacted by his piety was through his

public ministry in the Conference. Noel Gibbard affirms that one of his central subjects in Conference sermons and discussions was 'Life.'[1] This was a central theme, but only one of them. Prayer for revival was another and many of his messages 'ended with a call for more urgent prayer for revival.'[2] David Ceri Jones is right in affirming that

> 'many of these addresses soon came around to some of his favourite topics'.

However, he is wrong in claiming it was 'the need for evangelical unity that pre-dominated' the late 1950s and 1960s. In fact, the one theme standing out in his Conference addresses from 1955–1978 was the need to know the living God intimately. Numerous examples confirm this.

Emphasizing the importance of doctrine and spiritual life in the 1956 Conference, Lloyd-Jones exhorted the men:

> 'Let us ... concentrate on our personal relation with God. Do we realise the presence of God?'[3]

In the 1957 Conference, he observed amongst UK evangelicals

> 'An absence of a sense of helplessness ... An absence of waiting on God ... Nothing matters except our relationship to God ... Nothing but desperation about ourselves and our country will send us to real prayer.'[4]

In the 1959 Conference, he urged pastors

'to begin with ourselves, our own relationship to God and what is wrong there ...'[5]

Failure to pray more is

'because we do not sufficiently desire Him and because we do not know Him.'[6]

In his closing 1964 message, 'Why are we failing?' he insisted:

'My greatest problem is not to prepare my sermons but myself. And the only way to do so is a personal, intimate knowledge of Him ... Our supreme desire must be to have communion with Him'.[7]

For his 1967 Conference address, he reflected on his 1966 London address, then referred to wrong emphases amongst evangelicals before urging 'proper priorities' such as preaching, the dimension of the supernatural and prayer. He added:

'Prayer, however, is first. We cannot, and must not, preach without the preaching being saturated in prayer. And in prayer we come to know Christ better and also His all-sufficiency'.[8]

During his 1971 address on 'The Living God', he complained:

'there is neglect of the living God'

and then he commended an old preacher, W. E. Prothero, he had heard:

'the old preacher talked of a meeting with God.[9]

In 1978, he asked:

'Do we know anything about this dimension—the presence, power and love of God ...? Let us resolve to seek Him our Living God'.[10]

Rarely did he refer to his own experiences or prayer life. One such rare occasion was his 1976 Closing address. Attributing the 'entertainment' and 'personality' approach in evangelism/worship partly to the fact that we do not know God, he maintained that churches need a stimulant to excite themselves,

'we need to preach the living God ... How often do we expect God to break in to our lives and churches?'[11]

Lloyd-Jones here referred to his July 1949 experience in the Bristol Clinic where he was

'tired, overworked, receiving medical treatment and depressed'

but suddenly saw the word 'glory' by his bed.

'Then the whole room was illuminated with glory' and he felt 'transported to the heavens—I have known this a very few times'.[12]

A year later, when Professor Bobi Jones, Aberystwyth University, spoke on the Welsh hymn writer, Ann Griffiths, there was discussion spilling over into two meetings. Acknowledging her experiences of the Lord and profound articulation of theology in poetry, Lloyd-Jones concluded by referring to 1 Peter

1 verse 8, suggesting that such 'inexpressible joy' in the Lord should be true of us 'frequently'.

In his final Conference in 1978, we were given a rare glimpse into his private prayer life. He informed us that in the 1950s and 1960s the Lord often drew near to him as he devoted himself to prayer. The reality of God and His love on such occasions made him wonder whether he was in heaven or on earth. Sometimes he was so unsure that he would go and talk to his wife about lunch or the family. Only then was he satisfied he was not in heaven!

These examples emphasize that his burden in Conference and for himself was a more intimate knowledge of the living God. And there was an appetite for this, expressed especially in prayer meetings as men poured their hearts out in worship, pleading to know the Lord better.

Public praying

Another way his piety impacted pastors was through his praying in a prayer meeting, but more often to end a meeting or Conference.

My outstanding memory of his prayer was the closing of the 1966 Conference. It was a long evening with four pastors sharing their experiences of the Lord and the impact on their ministries.[13] There were questions, disagreement, coupled with a desire to know the Lord more and to exercise more fruitful ministries. It was approaching midnight when Lloyd-Jones decided to end the discussion and Conference. He prayed and then urged us to go to bed. But men felt subdued while some were troubled.

Unexpectedly, Tudor Lloyd, a Presbyterian minister in the Gower, Swansea, broke the silence. He expressed appreciation for the evening but also shared his feelings of nervousness and need for protection from devilish activity. He requested prayer for their ministries and journeys home. It was an awesome moment.

Lloyd-Jones responded at length, praying movingly for divine blessing and protection on their families and ministries. One sensed his own intimacy with God and his experience in intercession. As he pronounced the benediction, many became aware of God's presence. Rather than being idolised, he was respected as a man of prayer who knew God.

Personal

I also saw 'the Doctor's' piety in a different context. The pressures of church work meant my preparation for speaking in the 1973 Conference was limited. I even dreamt I arrived in Bala without notes to be greeted by Lloyd-Jones who asked about my preparation. Hearing my tale of woe, he told me to prepare my notes. In the dream I woke up as I was due to speak but without notes!

On the Conference date, I arrived in Bala and was greeted by Lloyd-Jones. He asked about my preparation but unlike the dream, invited me to have tea with him. I shared details of my dream but he did not smile and remarked:

> 'My boy, that was the devil. I would have told you to trust the Lord and he will give you messages for the Conference.'

I caught another glimpse of his piety. He trusted God. The Bible was precious to him; he believed what God said and that God can 'give' a message, so he rebuked me.

'A man of prayer'

Bethan Lloyd-Jones declared her husband was first

> 'a man of prayer and then an evangelist'.

For her, no one would understand 'the Doctor' apart from this dimension to his life. Conference pastors were influenced both by his piety and encouraging exhortations to know, love, and obey God. Surprisingly, critics fail to highlight this feature.[14]

His piety is an important lens for understanding his influence in this Conference.

Questions for reflection and discussion

How do YOU recognise piety?

Suggest practical steps for allocating more time for prayer and seeking God.

27

Lloyd-Jones and Gospel Preaching

In chapters 25 and 26 we understood 'the Doctor's' influence on Conference pastors by referring to his pastoral approach and personal piety. Now we look at the gospel which was for Lloyd-Jones foundational and priceless.

Highlighting and preaching the gospel
The gospel meant everything to Lloyd-Jones. That point must be grasped.

Background
During medical studies he gradually recognized his sinfulness and guilt before God, then embraced God's grace and forgiveness in Christ. He had found the most valuable treasure of all.

The first text he preached in Sandfields was 1 Corinthians 2:2:

'For I determined not to know anything among you except Jesus Christ and him crucified'. He wanted the text inscribed on his gravestone in West Wales. Each Sunday evening, in Sandfields and Westminster, he preached this gospel of Christ. His itinerant preaching trumpeted the same message.

He insisted that his first Romans commentary to be published should be his exposition of chapters 3:20–4:25, Atonement and Justification.[1] His reasons were predictable. One, the theme of Justification by Faith is worked out in detail there. The passage shows there is only one way of salvation, demonstrating that the gospel belongs entirely to God. It was God who had planned and accomplished salvation in his Son and he was also applying it to sinners.

Its nature

For Lloyd-Jones, it is an *authoritative* gospel. Scripture, not reason, nor science, nor experience, nor the church, are our supreme authority (1 Corinthians 15:3-4). He encouraged pastors to be clear concerning this central question and he was influential in encouraging men to preach this authoritative gospel.

It is also a doctrinal gospel. Lloyd-Jones recognised the desperate need for God-centred doctrinal preaching which was Christo-centric and expository, highlighting the glory of Christ's Person and Work and consequent exaltation. His distinction between primary and secondary truths was intended to safeguard major doctrines like the Trinity, Sin and Justification by Faith. In the 1957 Conference,[2] he referred to these as 'an irreducible minimum', non-negotiable, with unity only possible on this basis. By contrast, 'liberal' or 'modernist' teaching was reductionist, re-interpreting primary truths which strike at the heart of the gospel. For this reason, gospel related doctrines were expounded regularly and discussed over the years in the Conference. His influence in this respect was considerable.

Conference examples

In his first address to the 1955 Conference, Lloyd-Jones emphasised this God-given gospel in the context of Ephesians 1:13-14. The Ephesians had 'heard the word of truth, the gospel of your salvation' from Paul himself. After explaining the nature and glory of 'the gospel', he emphasised that it was such preaching that the Holy Spirit blesses in bringing sinners to salvation.

Again, in closing the 1956 Conference, he stressed

> 'salvation is by grace through faith on the basis of the substitutionary atonement of Jesus Christ ...'[3]

He did not presume this, for in the 1957 Conference he underlined again that the

> 'heart of the message is that God laid upon Jesus the condemnation of my sins'

and he went on to glory in Christ's sacrifice and justification by faith. In a detailed discussion on the Welsh hymn-writer, Ann Griffiths, in 1977, Lloyd-Jones emphasised with the speaker that this young woman 'had no modesty in her love to Christ who had snatched her from the emptiness of her existence ... the central attraction for her was Christ—his birth, life, death, resurrection and glorification. Christ was everything to her ... She wanted to look at him for ever and longed for fellowship with him ...'

Preaching in churches

Regarding the gospel message he preached in Wales, Lloyd-Jones acknowledged it was generally Baptists in Wales who were

'most enthusiastic in my favour and received me with open arms'[4] from 1927.

His 'close relationship' and 'natural rapport' continued with Baptists in Wales and others in the Baptist Union of Great Britain from 1945 until the early 1970s. This 'rapport' and influence waned following his 1966 London address on secession.[5] A significant number of Baptist pastors he preached for were members of the Baptist Revival Fellowship and/or of the Westminster Ministers' Fellowship which met monthly and of which he was Chairman. He continued to preach alternate years for his friend Iorwerth Budge in Park Baptist Church, Merthyr Tydfil, although he remained in the Baptist Union.

Lloyd-Jones frequently preached in North Wales and for successive years, 1963–1966, he preached in the English Presbyterian Church, Holyhead.[6] On each occasion, the building was crowded; several coaches transported people from outlying villages to and from the meetings. They were outstanding occasions and an encouragement to many.

New pattern

A new pattern emerged during the 1960s and 1970s when he began to preach more in Wales for pastors attending the Bala Conference. He often preached in their induction services[7] or annually as in Heath Church, Cardiff, from 1963 until his last visit in March 1979.

These visits were important. That was true for Graham Harrison in Newport when he preached in his Alma Street Baptist Church in 1964, then for the opening of their new building (Emmanuel Evangelical Church) in 1977. For Tudor Lloyd in the Gower, Swansea, in 1963 a large marquee seating six hundred people was hired near his Bury Green Church building, with many standing outside and around the marquee. The church also arranged for three double decker buses to transport people from Swansea to the meetings. It was a memorable occasion for the area but especially for the small Presbyterian churches in the pastorate.

Under the pastoral leadership of Stanley Jebb, Gilgal Baptist church, Porthcawl, was another venue for Lloyd-Jones's gospel preaching in 1965. The 'Doctor' preached helpfully in 1966 for Malcom Jones who pastored the Baptist church in Maesycymmer.

More examples

Lloyd-Jones preached for Gwilym Roberts in his Caergwrle (near Wrexham) Presbyterian Church Anniversary services in 1969 and 1971. The visit gave a boost to the church's ministry.

Neville Rees, pastoring Libanus Congregational Church, Morriston, Swansea, started attending the Conference in 1963. In

May 1973 and February 1976, Lloyd-Jones preached in his church. The influence of his preaching was considerable, including six known conversions on the 1973 occasion and three in 1976. He preached for Bruce Powell in Tredegar in 1971 and 1975. On both occasions the church building was crowded with eight hundred folk.

> 'People in the town noted that something unusual was taking place and this gave some of our people an opportunity for witness. Those who would not come to any other service came to hear "the Doctor". His visits were a great encouragement to me and the church but also to other local churches ...'

A similar response was found in the South Wales Valley town of Maesteg where Eryl Davies pastored. In February 1973 Lloyd-Jones preached in the afternoon and evening to a crowded Town Hall with a capacity of over eight hundred. The weather was bitterly cold with layers of snow on the ground; the visit encouraged the church in its witness.

In 1974, he preached for John Davies at Bethel, Clydach near Swansea. He reports:

> 'we had a public preaching meeting on the Saturday evening, but he strictly asked me not to advertise his presence on the Sunday so he could be free to minister to our own people'. And the church profited immensely from his visit.

Other examples could be given of how Lloyd-Jones influenced pastors and churches through these visits. A number of men indicated it was the Conference and these preaching visits which kept them in the ministry when tempted to leave for secular employment. Neville Rees, for example, shares how

> 'certainly, 1969, 1971 and 1986 were difficult years for me' but he was 'lifted' to continue through the help provided by the Conference and Lloyd-Jones.

Elwyn Davies claims that:

> 'Only for the Doctor being there at the time, the nature of the gospel in Wales would have been very different from what it was in the following years.'

That is an exaggeration. Nevertheless, Lloyd-Jones was often a lone voice between 1927 and the early 1950s in Wales as he preached the gospel powerfully and fearlessly. He challenged contemporary approaches which reduced the gospel to a political, social or moralistic message, often within the framework of an optimistic, critical framework of theology.

We turn to the theme of revival in the next chapter for understanding Lloyd-Jones's influence.

Questions for reflection and discussion

Describe the links between the gospel, church and revival.

Do we appreciate the priceless nature and wonder of the gospel? If not, what is the remedy?

28

Lloyd-Jones and Revival

We have now described Lloyd-Jones's influence on Conference pastors in terms of his pastoral support, his piety, and his glorying in the gospel.

The final aspect of his influence which we are considering is his teaching regarding revival. While this has been discussed already in several chapters, here further analysis is offered followed by principles governing his emphasis on revival. Finally, we briefly consider some examples of the influence of this teaching on pastors in Wales.

Lloyd-Jones and revival[1]
Although it never claimed to be a revival Conference, the theme of revival has permeated its addresses, discussions and prayers since 1955. However, four qualifying remarks are necessary.

First, during the opening twenty-five years, the revival theme dominated, not merely permeated, the Conference largely due to Lloyd-Jones's influence. More specifically, this emphasis was stronger in the first eleven years until 1966. That fact has gone unnoticed.

Weakening of emphasis

Second, an analysis of the period 1979-2009 reveals a discernible weakening of emphasis on revival in terms of the subjects and content of addresses, although three historical talks touched on it as did a few discussions[2] from 1979 onwards. In addition, in 2004, several centenary addresses analysing the 1904 revival were included while Spirit-empowered preaching was the theme in 2005. A year later, addresses were given on the work of the Holy Spirit. No revival subject was handled or discussed in the years 2010, 2011 and 2012. In 2013, the subject was discussed but only in the context of Calvinistic Methodism in Wales from 1735-1835.

Third, the comparison between 1955-1978 and 1979-2009 is significant. The latter period marks the absence of Lloyd-Jones's leadership, and in discussions he was greatly missed.

Unease

Fourth, unease was expressed by some men during the 1980s, 1990s, and later for they felt revival was given too much attention. The criticism met with a firm response from the Ministers' Sub-Committee in 1989 which, under the strong leadership of Graham Harrison, ruled that the emphasis was 'correct'.

I suggest the Committee was unaware of the continuing

weakening of an emphasis on revival and also failed to understand the nature of the complaint.

The complainants were not opposed in principle to revival, but they wanted to explore biblically how to minister outside of revival, while also anticipating this supernatural dimension. For some, discussions on revival from 1979 tended towards introspection with despair and disillusionment creeping in as little had happened to encourage them in their churches. In fact, the major way the Conference handled the revival theme post 1978 was in evening discussions, which only provoked more criticism. Nevertheless, there was, whether intentionally or unintentionally, less emphasis on revival in terms of subjects handled in the main Conference addresses during this period.

We must now assess the influence of Lloyd-Jones through this lens of revival.

Reasons

In assessing his influence on the Conference, I draw attention to five reasons for the Conference's early emphasis on revival.

In the first place, the composition of the Conference in the early period contributed to this emphasis. The 'revival men', for example, welcomed it as did numbers of younger men from different denominations in the 1940s and 1950s. Many of these had enjoyed experiences of the Lord and unusual effectiveness in preaching. They had a story to tell and there was a buzz and sense of expectancy in the Conference. Hearing of Duncan Campbell and meeting Ivor Davies with first-hand experiences of revival confirmed their longings for revival.

Secondly, Lloyd-Jones's role was significant. His profound experiences in 1949, then his powerful ministry to students in the 1949, 1950 and 1951 IVF Welsh Conferences, were providential in preparing younger men for this pastors' Conference. Again, his ministry to pastors, emphasising annually the nature and need of revival, was coupled with constant appeals to seek the Lord and plead divine promises for God to pour the Holy Spirit upon his people. Ian M. Randall observes correctly that Lloyd-Jones 'never wavered' throughout his ministry in preaching this doctrine and its importance.[3] There was a warm response from the Conference to his teaching.

A third reason for the emphasis is that Lloyd-Jones encouraged pastors to study past revivals. He referred frequently to men used in revivals, stimulating pastors to read revival history and share this with their churches. Annually, Conference men were chosen to prepare an historical address, often on a revival subject.

Fourthly, Conference prayer meetings in early years were memorable in terms of honesty, earnestness and reality climaxing in the 1959 Conference prayer meeting which Lloyd-Jones led. He intervened and the result was electrifying. Never before or since, has the Conference felt nearer to revival. His influence here was significant.

Fifthly, Lloyd-Jones's view of the Conference fostered interest in revival for he encouraged pastors to confer and pray together. He was also eager to discern what God was doing nationwide in churches. For that reason, he recommended men who had either participated in revival like Ivor Davies (Congo) or men like James Packer and Iain Murray who, as theologians and historians, were familiar with revival history. Others like Arthur Neil and Norman Meeten were invited to share what had been happening in their lives and ministries. As already noted, the Conference was marked by a significant breadth and openness until the late 1960s.

Some of the above reasons for the revival emphasis, however, no longer apply as it is a different situation with a new generation of pastors.

The revival emphasis of Lloyd-Jones discouraged passivity for he was an evangelist with a burden to reach unbelievers with the gospel. For him, evangelism and prayer for revival were inseparable, but evangelism must be saturated in prayer, expressing complete dependence on God to work powerfully through his gospel.

In that Lloyd-Jones influenced the Conference's emphasis on revival we must ask: was revival an 'over-emphasis' or even a 'form of obsessional thinking'[4] on his part?

I submit that in his Conference ministry to pastors in Wales his biblical answer could be given in terms of seven basic principles which are interrelated.

Principle 1
The Bible is God's revealed, infallible Word, enshrining the glorious gospel with its 'irreducible minimum' of doctrines centred on the Person and Work of Christ. Upon the Lord Jesus, our sin was 'laid by the Father.' That is a foundational principle.

In the 1956 Conference he emphasised that revival comes only 'when these truths are proclaimed' while in 1957 he told Conference:

> 'One condition of revival is we hold fast to the truth. The Holy Spirit will not bless anything else.'

Principle 2

Because we are all sinners and spiritually dead (Ephesians 2:1-5), only the Holy Spirit can give new birth (John 3:3-7). Becoming a Christian is a miracle which only God can work and he does it through the gospel. In revival, many more people become Christians.

Principle 3

A third principle concerns the wonderful works of God, climaxing in the incarnation, life, death, resurrection and ascension of the Lord Jesus Christ, followed by his pouring out of the Holy Spirit at Pentecost. This was the burden Lloyd-Jones shared in the 1971 Conference. 'He is still acting' in making people Christians, strengthening and quickening believers as well as reviving his church. He added:

> '... Our supreme need is to realize God is alive ... cast yourself utterly on this belief that God acts, can act and will act ... Do you believe he can still do it?'

Principle 4

For Lloyd-Jones, revival brings a difference *only* in degree and intensity. That is a major principle for it is the same Holy Spirit working in believers daily who also revives his church.

In revival many people in a church or area become Christians in a short time; also in revival, believers often know and enjoy the Lord more intimately but God decides where and how he works.

Principle 5

Gospel preaching accompanied by the Holy Spirit's power makes it effective. This principle was constantly emphasised by him with frequent reference to Acts chapters 2, 4 and 10 as well as 1 Corinthians 2:1-5 and 1 Thessalonians 1:5 as examples. He saw the principle illustrated in Calvinistic Methodist preaching from 1735-1835 in Wales and in other countries and periods. God acting in revival has kept the church alive over the centuries.

Principle 6

The greatest need of Christians is to know the Lord intimately; this is his most important emphasis.[5]

In the 1967 Conference he urged pastors to maintain right priorities—preaching the gospel with an openness to the supernatural. In the current age of apostasy, he observed that Satanic and occult activity flourishes. He suggested God allows this to remind us of the reality of the supernatural world and of our need to know God and his superior power. Prayer is crucial.

Principle 7

This is prevailing prayer for the living God to work within the church and then society. Amongst his last Conference words (1978) were:

> 'What do we know about such spiritual power? Nothing is impossible with God. Read Acts 4 verse 31 where, in answer to the

united prayer of the church for 'boldness' to preach the Word, God answered. And the answer was remarkable and unexpected ... What do we know of this dimension and of the mighty powers of God in our churches today?

Lloyd-Jones was clear regarding how revival is given.

Revival begins normally with the preacher. For Daniel Rowland, Howell Harris, George Whitefield, John Wesley and others, the Lord dealt with them in power and great reality. This helps us understand his concern for preachers to experience the Lord 'visiting' them. Therefore prayer for preachers is vitally important. While Conference members were always encouraged to pray for preachers, one suspects that Lloyd-Jones's emphasis was blurred somewhat under a more general prayer for revival. For example, when questioned whether he thought a period of blessing and revival would 'make a difference to preaching and preachers', his reply was extremely significant as he rephrased the question:

> 'you will not receive what I have referred to (revival) until something happens to preachers ... This is what happened in the great revivals. Something happened first of all in and to a preacher or minister or a man like Howell Harris. And as a result of this experience',[6] a greater degree of power and blessing came upon the preaching.

Is it 'obsessional' to embrace these biblical principles when God can 'break into our lives and meetings', transforming hopeless church situations and impacting society? If the teaching on revival is biblical and proportional to other doctrines then it is not obsessional.

Why no revival?

Lloyd-Jones did not disparage periods outside revival. Reflecting in 1975 on the period 1950–1975, he suggested reasons why God had not given revival in Wales. One reason is the Lord seeks to bring us to complete dependence upon himself. Preachers and churches have not reached that point yet. A second reason was

> 'there has been an awakening between 1950–1975 in the sense of clearing our minds and getting a grip on the big doctrines of the Faith ... it is still happening. It may lead to revival'.

Third, he insisted

> 'These years have been a great benefit to us. If revival comes, we now have gospel churches ready to receive new people'.[7]

Between the years 1950 and 1975, Lloyd-Jones played a key role preparing, influencing and encouraging new generations of pastors in Wales to adhere to biblical teaching while also striving for holiness and intimacy with the Lord outside of revival.

Response?

What has been the response of pastors to his emphasis on revival? It is not possible to provide a definitive assessment of the ways Conference pastors and churches have been influenced to pray for revival but some continue to do so.

Pastors' prayer meetings for revival have been held since

the 1960s in South Wales, a period when the revival emphasis was dominant in Conference. For example, Luther Rees and I. B. Davies valued the fellowship of Pastor George Griffiths, Cwmtwrch. A weekly prayer meeting for revival on Friday mornings in Cwmtwrch developed, with other pastors like Elwyn Davies, Eryl Davies, Neville Rees and Eurfyl Jones, attending.

Following the 1979 Conference, some pastors initiated prayer meetings for revival in their churches in Wales and England; many of these continue on a Saturday morning or evening.

For years, the EMW has arranged days or half-days of prayer usually twice or three times a year for pastors in North (Bala) and South Wales (Bridgend) with revival as the burden. These were well attended but attendance, especially in the South, has been disappointing in recent years. The South Wales meeting, previously led by Elwyn Davies, then Neville Rees and now Ian Parry, increased its number of meetings in 2013 to six bi-monthly morning prayer meetings. There is a strong conviction that these meetings should continue.

Churches also benefited from Lloyd-Jones's teaching on revival as their pastors regularly shared what they heard in Conference and many of his sermons on the subject have been widely circulated.

The question remains. Are we persuaded we have a warrant from the Bible to seek God for revival? Derek Swann claimed that the early Conferences were a 'bench mark' for measuring what happened in later Conferences. We return to the subject in chapter thirty.

Questions for reflection and discussion

If prayer for revival fluctuates, suggest practical steps you and your church can take to persevere in prayer.

Comment on and discuss the foregoing seven principles regarding revival.

29

Word and Spirit (1)

In these two final chapters we reflect further on Lloyd-Jones's teaching and on the emphases of the main Conference addresses between 1955 and 2014. We are doing this to confirm the predominance of the Word-Spirit theme. We will then interact in more detail with some recent writings and criticisms for the purpose of evaluating and placing the Conference's Word-Spirit emphasis within a wider, contemporary context. There is substantial theological agreement on this subject within Reformed circles, but because there are differences and misunderstandings it is hoped that further dialogue may promote greater clarity and agreement. It is generally agreed that the subject is of major importance for contemporary church life and practice, especially for preaching.

Our reflection initially relates to subjects handled in the main Conference addresses from 1955–2014.

1955–1961

As we saw in earlier chapters, a strong emphasis was placed in this first period on biblical exegesis and Calvinistic doctrines, such as predestination, the effectual call and the supreme authority and inspiration of Scripture. A strong pastoral emphasis characterised all the Conference addresses with the felt need for a greater degree of the Holy Spirit's power in preaching which in turn stimulated prayer for revival. The Word-Spirit theme was central and formative.

1962–1978

A strong link with the first period was made in 1962 when addresses were delivered on the role of the Holy Spirit in the Christian Ministry. However, the historical address in 1962 by Noel Gibbard was significant as he outlined the history of the 1662 Great Ejection. In discussion, pastors continued to express concern over the theological and spiritual condition of the historic denominations. This address anticipated the changing mood in Conference from 1963–1969 when the nature, life, ministry and government of the church were given more attention in the main Conference addresses and discussions. By 1970, these issues relating to ecclesiology faded and the years 1970–1975 saw major doctrines handled; for example, Heaven/Hell, Regeneration and Christ's victory on the Cross. Prayer continued to receive prominence in some addresses as in 1974 with an insistence on the priority of the Word and the need for it to be taught in a Christ-exalting way. A strong pastoral and experiential emphasis again characterized these addresses in

1976–1978 with subjects like Communion with God, Assurance, Prayer and Revival being handled. In 1977 the organic unity and growth of the church was approached but from a pastoral perspective.

Summarizing this period: while ecclesiology was addressed between the years 1963–1969 this was alongside a continued emphasis on the Holy Spirit accompanying the preaching of the Word with a greater degree of power. The need for revival was expressed although the 1904–1905 Wales revival was not regarded as the appropriate model because of the influence of liberal theology, the neglect of preaching often for singing/testimonies and the growing influence of Keswick teaching.

1979–2009
This thirty year period began with renewed emphasis on prayer which immediately impacted a number of Conference pastors and their churches. The subject of evangelism was handled in at least five Conferences when its urgency, motives, message and context were clarified biblically. Key doctrines were also expounded: Justification by Faith, the Wrath of God, the Grace of God, God's Supremacy in Preaching and the Holy Spirit in the Church, with one speaker focusing on Spirit-Empowered Preaching. Conference speakers returned frequently to the glory of Christ's Person and Work.

Reflecting on these subjects, biblical doctrines integral to the Christo-centric Gospel were outlined, biblically exegeted and applied with warmth. The Word-Spirit theme again remained central throughout this period but focused increasingly and more narrowly on the role of the Spirit in preparation for preaching the Word.

2010–2014

This brief period continued the Word-Spirit theme by highlighting in a contemporary and lively manner the Gospel, the Glory of Christ (Revelation 4–7) and the marvellous Grace of God as illustrated in the life and ministry of Hosea the prophet. Exposition of Scripture was prominent and the main speakers illustrated to some degree what it is to preach the Word in the power of the Holy Spirit. For that reason the 2012 and 2013 Conferences were instructive and humbling in highlighting key Gospel doctrines while the 2014 addresses were expository (Zechariah 3), gospel-centred, and encouraged the enjoyment and appreciation of major gospel truths.

Strengths and weaknesses[1]

Over the fifty-nine years of Conference until 2014, a wide range of major biblical doctrines were chosen for the main addresses. The omission of doctrines like the Holy Trinity and providence may appear striking but they were assumed and frequently referred to without sustained attention. All the other major doctrines handled were intended to stimulate personal reading of biblical theology with a view to preaching the Word with greater faithfulness, clarity and effectiveness. Attention was given primarily to the accomplishment and application of redemption so that pneumatology in the context of the Word-Spirit theme surfaced in all the Conferences to varying degrees. Fellowship, quality times of prayer, discussion and absorbing historical papers added to the impact and value of the main Conference addresses.

The Word-Spirit relationship, therefore, was stressed regularly both from a biblical and pastoral perspective with illustrations from history, but the subject was not given extended theological treatment. That is not surprising in that it was a pastoral rather than a theological study Conference. On the other hand, some of the questions being raised by contemporary theologians concerning this relationship were discussed briefly at times but with hindsight, a more sustained theological treatment of the Word-Spirit relationship was required. Possibly this oversight added to the frustration felt by some as they looked for more satisfying treatment of this and related subjects. The subject of revival was over emphasised sometimes and even misunderstood by some of its strongest advocates.

Recent Writings

We are in a position now to identify and evaluate three major features of the Word-Spirit relationship as assumed and taught in this Conference but before proceeding to discuss these three features, we will identify some relevant, contemporary writings on this theme.

In 2003 the Rev. Sung Tae Kim was awarded the degree of PhD for his research at WEST into the role of the Holy Spirit in the act of preaching.[2] This research was innovative and comprehensive, identifying over 50,000 English language books and articles in the USA and UK dealing specifically with the subject of preaching and the work of the Holy Spirit over a fifty year period until AD 2000. Remarkably, less than 0.05% of this material related to the Holy Spirit in the act of preaching. His research revealed that there had only been two books published in that period dealing with this specific subject. One was Pierre-Charles Marcel's *The Relevance of Preaching*.[3] We note here Marcel's conviction that by the Holy Spirit the Word is always in communication with the Lord Jesus Christ and making preaching relevant.[4] The only other relevant book identified by Kim was Ithel Jones's *The Holy Spirit and Christian Preaching*.[5] His concern was the 'lack of power and effectiveness in preaching'[6] but in approaching the subject he urged preachers to recognise the distinct personality and deity of the Holy Spirit. Later he emphasised that proclamation in the Spirit normally takes place in the presence of the 'gathered congregation'.[7]

Ralph Cunnington obtained his ThM on the subject of 'Word and Spirit in Preaching' in 2013.[8] He interacts with some contemporary writings[9] whose authors 'perceive a growing tendency' in evangelical churches in the UK 'to marginalise the role of the Holy Spirit in the work of preaching'.[10] He regards Philip Eveson's article as 'wide-ranging' in introducing the history and contemporary influence of Moore College in Australia[11] and its interpretation of terms like the 'Call', 'Ministry' and 'Revival'. Eveson's major criticisms include the fact that Moore tends to marginalise historical and systematic theology in some key areas with its emphasis on biblical theology while it also under-emphasises the Spirit's activity in the church and the individual.[12] Cunnington challenges Eveson's methodology and his use of limited sources.

However, in fairness to Eveson, the background to his article is important. He was originally invited to address the Westminster Fellowship of Ministers in London on the subject of Moore theology. The reason for the invitation was that 'many pastors were reading the Briefing which contains articles by former students or lecturers of that College. Hence my brief was limited and I confined myself mainly to quotes from that magazine to back up what I was saying ... I was later asked for my paper to be published in Foundations. It is rather unfair ... to accuse me of being narrow in the material I used. I also went out of my way to be conciliatory ...'[13]

Majoring in historical theology, Cunnington attempts to show in his research that writers like Olyott and Strivens misapply the teaching of both Luther and Calvin concerning the Word-Spirit theme. He also evaluates Hywel R. Jones's article briefly but it 'covers much of the same ground'[14] as the others. Robert Letham has also published articles on this important theme which I will interact with in more detail[15] as I now discuss major features of the Word-Spirit theme in the 'Bala' Conference.

The Word-Spirit theme in Conference: major features

There are three major themes to discuss. In the remainder of this chapter the first two aspects of the Word-Spirit theme are considered briefly because there is more agreement concerning them in Reformed circles. The third feature will be discussed in the next chapter.

1. The distinct but inseparable relationship of the Word and Spirit

This principle has been affirmed continually by Conference and in a way consistent with the Reformed tradition. For the Conference, the deity and 'person' of the Holy Spirit were underlined in this affirmation and in a way consistent with the major Confessional standards such as the Westminster Confession of Faith (WCF):

> 'In the unity of the Godhead there be three persons, of one substance, power, eternity: God the Father, God the Son and God the Holy Ghost'.[16]

The relevance of this statement is that the Holy Spirit as God is free and is not in any way imprisoned within the Word; He is the Agent while the Word is the instrument. While the Holy Spirit caused the Scripture to be written and is distinct from the Word, nevertheless he is joined inseparably to the Word and the means of grace, including the proclamation of the Word. The Word is never without the Holy Spirit. Robert Letham correctly affirms that

> 'the Word itself—whether as the text of Scripture or as the message proclaimed by the preacher—does not have power of itself'.[17]

Lloyd-Jones with other Conference speakers like Stuart Olyott articulated this principle strongly, although Ralph Cunnington is right in questioning Olyott's use of Luther in that context.[18] Conference applied the distinct but inseparable relation of Word and Spirit to the means of grace but especially to preaching. Some disagreement exists concerning the nature of the sacraments, but there is agreement between Conference and other Reformed writers concerning the inclusion of preaching, with Letham underlining helpfully its nature and necessity. Preaching is an announcement by heralds of what the Triune

God has done sovereignly to achieve and apply our salvation in Christ.[19] But there is also

> 'an appeal by the preacher to the consciences of the hearers ... an appeal to submit to the Word of God, to trust in Christ, to be obedient to his call ... These appeals are most urgent entreaties to people to get right with God ... the proclamation comes first but without an appeal it is not biblical preaching ...'[20]

There have been passionate and humbling exhortations from Conference speakers over the years for pastors to engage in this kind of preaching[21] which 'is absolutely essential to the being and well-being of the church.'[22] As we saw in earlier chapters, Conference emphasised the importance of preaching being thoroughly biblical whether it is evangelistic, didactic or pastoral. Such preaching accepts the Bible as the Word of God, verbally inspired, reliable,[23] supremely authoritative for faith and practice because God has revealed himself and his purposes in it. The Bible does not 'become' the Word of God only in moments of revelatory encounter as Karl Barth taught for it remains the Word whether we encounter it or not.

2. The Word-Spirit relationship is integral to God's redemptive purposes in Christ

The Westminster Confession provides a helpful framework for understanding the Conference's conviction concerning the *integral* role of the Word-Spirit relationship in God's redemptive purpose. In addition to appointing the elect to eternal glory in Christ and doing so only 'out of his mere free grace and love',[24] it maintains that God also 'foreordained all the means thereunto'.[25] The 'means' by which this 'end' is achieved include redemption by Christ, regeneration and sanctification; consequently, the elect are effectually called to faith in Christ only by the Holy Spirit working through the truth of God's Word.

In this context it is customary to refer to the 'means of grace',[26] namely, the Word of God, the sacraments of baptism and the Lord's Supper and prayer.[27] The phrase, 'means of grace' was coined in the Middle Ages but emphasised by sixteenth century Protestant Reformers to convey the fact that God works corporately in the church and personally in the lives of individuals through specific means. The latter are Bible doctrines and promises read and especially preached when believers meet for public worship, prayer, the Lord's Supper and baptism. While recognising their importance, Conference gave less attention to the sacraments and that possibly for two reasons. One was the strongly held conviction that the Word must 'go before' the sacraments as the Word alone gives them significance. The Word must not be separated from the sacraments but always accompany them as Calvin insisted

'without the Word, the sacrament is but a dumb show; the Word must go before'.[28]

For Conference, secondly, there were the pressing needs of churches where biblical teaching had been neglected for decades. They recognised the urgency of preaching its doctrines, promises and principles for the conversion of unbelievers and the edifying of the church.

Saving faith is one example of how integral the Word-Spirit relationship is in the divine purpose. This grace enables a sinner to discern spiritually the truths of the Gospel and to trust in Christ for salvation, but only as a result of the Holy Spirit's 'work in their hearts' which is 'ordinarily wrought by the ministry of the Word'.[29] This faith is then 'increased and strengthened' through the Word, the sacraments and prayer under the Spirit's ministry. This Word-Spirit relationship is integral to the entire work of grace in the elect and for the life and witness of the church. But as the Word is the great means of grace, it must be diligently used, especially by preachers.

There has been a lack of diligence on the part of some preachers to dig deeply into the Word with the result that congregations can feel dissatisfied over the quality of ministry they receive. Ithel Jones underlines the importance of preparation for preaching in terms of careful exegesis, reflection and prayer.[30] John Murray issues several warnings in this respect to preachers. While the claims of biblical truth are 'paramount', he adds

> 'the battle of the faith is often times focused in the inward travail of soul which the claims of truth demand. There are so many temptations to allow the claims of truth to become secondary.'[31]

But he then proceeds:

> 'Mental laziness is one of these temptations ... It may be surrounded by the halo of sanctity ...'

Harsh words but one suspects that the labour of digging into the Word, wrestling with the text, the diligent use of the biblical languages and available resources such as competent commentaries does not always feature prominently in Wales and beyond as 'the claims of truth demand'. Contrast this, for example, with Lloyd-Jones's thorough preparation for preaching involving many hours of prayer and of grappling with the text as illustrated in his series of addresses on Romans from 1955–1968. He had read all the available commentaries on that famous Epistle before embarking on the series, wrestling with its structure, message and interpretation. He was also familiar with all the Greek variants in the text. Stephen Clark[32] correctly claims that Lloyd-Jones's

> 'emphasis on revival, like Jonathan Edwards, was married to a profound concern for truth and theological understanding ... I think many at Bala wanted their hearts moved but were not quite prepared to have their minds stretched and see that the two go together'.[33]

Discussing 'The Power of the Holy Spirit', Murray refers to the 'Cultivation of the Means'. Here he maintains it is dishonouring for a preacher to acknowledge complete dependence upon God's grace yet 'allow our sense of dependence to be an excuse for sloth.' Our responsibility is to use, read, study and grapple with the Word. Inseparably linked to, and 'correlative' with the power of the Holy Spirit 'will be the blood, sweat, toil and tears of devoted and sustained study of the Word ...'[34] Has the Conference at times over emphasised revival and contributed subtly to a more lax approach to preparation for preaching? I fear it has. Yes, Lloyd-Jones emphasised revival but only in tandem with a passion for the Word and a greater understanding of its sublime doctrines. In this way he understood the implications of maintaining that the Word-Spirit relationship was integral in God's redemptive purpose.

We turn in the next and final chapter to the third feature of the Word-Spirit relationship, namely, its effective and irresistible nature in fulfilling God's purposes in Christ.

Questions for discussion

1. Can you identify any weaknesses and strengths relating to this Conference which you regard as important?

2. Describe in your own words the Word-Spirit relationship and discuss practical ways of safeguarding it in your own life and local church.

30

Word and Spirit (2)

In this chapter we discuss the third aspect of the Word-Spirit theme, namely its *irresistible* nature.

The power to convict, illumine, regenerate and sanctify lies exclusively with the Holy Spirit, as previously emphasised. Ralph Cunnington reminds us of John Calvin's insistence that 'without the illumination of the Holy Spirit, the Word can do nothing'.[1] The Holy Spirit is the inner teacher. Robert Letham adds that

> 'The diligent and faithful preaching is the instrumental cause, while the Holy Spirit is the efficient cause. The two together are indispensable. The Word without the Spirit is ineffective ...'[2]

Criticism
Conference members agree with the above emphasis yet it has

been misunderstood both within and outside the Conference. For example, some attendees tended to feel disillusioned because their ministries appeared ineffective. How did this emphasis relate to them? In hindsight, more attention should have been given to this concern. There was also a perception that the emphasis encouraged passivity, even detachment from societal engagement/evangelism. That perception did not reflect the burden of the main Conference addresses or the responses of most members. Conference organisers continue to address these matters.

We now consider some criticisms of the way this third aspect of the Word-Spirit theme was handled by Lloyd-Jones and preachers associated with him in this Conference. For this purpose I turn to my respected colleague, Robert Letham[3] whose criticisms are contemporary, forceful and representative of the views of others.[4] In conversation with me, my colleague refers to 'a broad brush' approach which he adopted in preparing these articles. His original brief in preparing his paper for the ICRC Conference was 'the necessity of preaching and, following recommendations from the committee, I had a section on preaching and the Holy Spirit.' Acknowledging this background and his 'broad brush' approach, his remarks, nevertheless, are useful in stimulating further reflection and hopefully can promote greater clarity and understanding.

1. 'Revivalist preaching'

Letham refers critically to 'revivalist preaching', regarding Lloyd-Jones as its important representative. The term 'revivalist' used by Letham is extremely ambiguous because of its dominant Arminian history involving 'new' methods.[5] There is also its dubious contemporary significance in many American conservative churches that

> 'reflects the populism, love of novelty and entertainment, fascination with technique, and consumerist orientation ... and has lost most of its links with revivals in the sense that Jonathan Edwards and George Whitefield and the Wesley brothers gave to that word'.[6]

In this context, Packer refers to a 'watershed' and 'a cleavage' over

> 'whether we approve of Whitefield and the other eighteenth-century leaders sending people away from the preaching to pray for a change of heart through new birth, and to keep praying and using the means of grace till they know they have been given what they sought, or whether with Finney and most moderns we opt for the so called "invitation method"'[7] with its semi-Pelagianism.

The latter option was anathema to Lloyd-Jones who with other Conference speakers distinguished carefully between revival[8] and 'revivalism', disassociating themselves from the latter due to their Calvinism. But the breadth of the term 'revivalism' is further illustrated by Keller when he refers to 'unbalanced revivalism' as opposed to 'balanced revivalism'. The former has already been described, but Keller throws light on its background, noting the shift from a 'traditional, highly church-centered (sic) approach' in which a person's faith was influenced by parents and a disciplined church to a more individualistic approach 'which undermines the work of the established church'.[9] In view of the associations attached to the terms 'revivalist' and 'revivalism', clarity is served by abstaining from their use. Concerning revival, Tim Keller explains it is

> 'an especially vigorous season of preaching, gatherings, and evangelistic activity ... an intensification of the normal operations of the Spirit (conviction of sin, regeneration and sanctification, assurance of grace) through the ordinary means of grace (preaching the Word, prayer, and the sacraments)'.[10]

In other words, for Keller, Lloyd-Jones and others, revival is the sovereign and 'surprising' bestowal of a greater degree of life, power and grace on the church by its exalted Head which is often confined to a local church or churches in an area. It is essential to distinguish this from 'revivalism'.

Having understood and defined more carefully some of the terms used, we can now consider Letham's criticism of what he calls a 'revivalist theology of preaching'. Here again Lloyd-Jones is the main representative; such a theology stresses 'the sovereign freedom of the Holy Spirit in which gospel preaching can often be powerless'.[11] He claims there is an Anabaptist[12] tendency within this 'revivalist' theology involving a disjunction between Word and Spirit which is 'not only possible but frequent' in 'that the Word is unaccompanied by the Spirit'.[13] In considering this criticism, we must note that what concerned Conference and Lloyd-Jones was the need for preaching to be accompanied by a greater degree of Holy Spirit power. No disjunction between Word and Spirit was implied, intended or desired. Letham tends to caricature what he considers a 'revivalist theology of preaching' and is guilty of inaccurate and misleading statements in his criticism of preaching as understood by Lloyd-Jones. We now consider this criticism further.

'The sovereign freedom of the Holy Spirit'

While criticising Anabaptists for their

> 'radical separation of the Spirit from the Word of God ... adopted in order to justify claims of special extra-biblical prophetic inspiration',

Letham claims that

> 'under the impact of the revivals of the eighteenth century, a doctrine of preaching has arisen, exemplified by Dr Martyn Lloyd-Jones stressing the sovereign freedom of the Holy Spirit'.

Letham does not explain the phrase 'the sovereign freedom of the Holy Spirit' but assumes that it expresses an Anabaptist tendency to separate Word and Spirit, at least to some degree. We have already indicated Lloyd-Jones's agreement concerning the distinct but inseparable relation of Word and Spirit so what is the significance of the criticism? Letham claims 'the impact of the revivals of the eighteenth century' is responsible for Lloyd-Jones's view of preaching which he suspects has an Anabaptist tendency. As Lloyd-Jones referred to the 'freedom of the Holy Spirit' in a 1967 address,[14] we can find greater clarity here as to what he meant by the phrase and assess Letham's criticism in that light.

Lloyd-Jones's 1967 address was intriguing and radical for he rejected much of what at the time was referred to as preaching. For example, 'preaching is not lecturing'[15] or 'a Running

Commentary'[16] on the biblical text and it must be distinguished from 'the sermon'.[17] Rather 'true preaching' involves something happening between the man who is speaking and the congregation that is listening so that 'the whole man is involved in preaching.'[18] He describes this further as

> 'a unity between preacher and hearers ... a transaction backwards and forwards. That, to me, is true preaching'

so therefore the corporate aspect is essential.

However the relevant section for our purpose is the final part of the address in which he describes 'God in Preaching'.[19] Care is needed in appreciating the three features Lloyd-Jones mentions. He begins by insisting that the preacher is a man whom God has called, gifted and sent to be a herald. He has a God-given authority to declare a message from God's Word so there is no disjunction between Word and Spirit. This is an essential feature which we touched on under the previous point and Letham would support Lloyd-Jones here.

The next feature in preaching for Lloyd-Jones is 'prophesying'. This is not a new and extra-biblical revelation. That cannot be for the preacher 'has been given a message', a 'prophetic utterance'[20] acquired only through diligent study of the Word and after much prayer. True preaching involves declaring this biblical, Christo-centric message so to accuse him of an Anabaptist tendency here is misplaced. In fact, Lloyd-Jones warns:

'Do not misunderstand me; I am not saying that a man has a revelation from God in the sense of receiving some truth; I am not saying that'.

The 'message' is not 'an inspired utterance' in the sense that

'the Scriptures are, but in another sense ... because the Spirit is giving it and using it.'

Here is 'a vital element' in preaching, namely, 'reliance upon the Holy Spirit'.

In preaching, the final feature for Lloyd-Jones is 'freedom' but he struggles to describe it. The preacher 'must be free', 'taken up' by the message and even 'interrupts his own thought'. He is

'possessed and is aware of this ... a spectator, and ... amazed at what is happening',[21] even 'conscious' of 'being used'.

In this Spirit-given 'freedom',

'thoughts are given, and expressions ... ideas ... the imagination is inspired and inflamed ... aware that God is possessing one's whole personality and using every faculty'.

And for Lloyd-Jones, 'that is as near as' he can get to describing what he means by preaching. The content of the 'message' for Lloyd-Jones must be thoroughly biblical and God-centred. However, alongside the content of the message, he is concerned also about its delivery and this is the precise point where 'the sovereign freedom of the Holy Spirit' applies. There is no

Anabaptist tendency here. What Lloyd-Jones admired in the eighteenth century revival preachers was both the biblical, God-centred content in their preaching but also under the Holy Spirit, that they enjoyed this dimension of 'freedom' as well as 'participation' by the congregation. This view of preaching would have been supported and coveted by many in the Conference.

Similarities

I cannot leave the point before indicating similarities between Lloyd-Jones's view of preaching and that of Pierre-Charles Marcel.[22] I have no firm evidence that Lloyd-Jones knew of, or had read, Marcel's book in French from 1951 onwards or that he had obtained a summary or paraphrase or even translation for himself. This is possible of course, because of his travels on the Continent in the 1950s and early 1960s on behalf of IFES.[23] In my own undergraduate studies in the late fifties and early sixties I heard of this book from one of my professors but I did not see an English version. Interestingly however, Lloyd-Jones's close friend from 1942 was Philip Edgcumbe Hughes (1915–1990) an Anglican clergyman and competent New Testament scholar who taught at Tyndale Hall, Bristol from 1947–1953 and went in 1964 to teach at American seminaries. He maintained close contact with Lloyd-Jones for years.[24] This is significant because Hughes was himself competent in French and wrote on the precursors of the reformers like *Lefevre: Pioneer of Ecclesiastical Renewal in France*. What is more significant is that Hughes translated Pierre-Charles Marcel's classic work, *The Biblical Doctrine of Infant Baptism* in 1953[25] so one can assume that Hughes was familiar with Marcel's earlier work of 1951 on *The Relevance of Preaching*. If he was familiar with it, then I cannot imagine him not having shared details with Lloyd-Jones.

But what are the similarities between the two positions? Marcel argues, like Lloyd-Jones, that the Word preached should be characterised by 'opportuness/relevance', 'forcefulness' in commanding repentance, 'simplicity' and 'vitality' under a close relationship with the Spirit. There is even more similarity. Marcel regards the Spirit's 'freedom' as allowing the Word preached to be God's voice heard by the congregation through the activity of the Holy Spirit. This again is reminiscent of Lloyd-Jones but even more so when Marcel affirms that the Spirit 'lifts' and 'stops' the preaching from being a lecture or a meditation. The Spirit can free the preacher from a script and dependence on either intellect or eloquence. In this way the Holy Spirit gives 'a natural freshness and vitality' in preaching.[26] I am only suggesting the possibility that there may have been some dependence by Lloyd-Jones on Marcel in confirming his own understanding of preaching.

We turn now to more issues raised by Letham.

2. 'Ordinary'/'Extraordinary'

Letham is uneasy concerning the distinction made between 'an ordinary ministry' and one 'characterized by an exceptional outpouring of the Spirit ...'[27] I sympathize with his concern for there has been a tendency in Wales to devalue the regular, essential work of the Holy Spirit but this was not encouraged or taught by Conference speakers or Lloyd-Jones. For example, the latter greatly appreciated the 'ordinary ministry' exercised especially from 1950–1975 in Wales[28] and he noted several useful and fruitful benefits of the preaching in the period. Ian M. Randall confirms the fact that 'Lloyd-Jones did not ... minimise the significance of the week-by-week ministries that took place in local churches, although the powerful stress on revival had that danger'.²⁹ Lloyd-Jones recognised the importance of 'the regular use of the means of grace' outside periods of revival. However, Letham may be correct in criticising Lloyd-Jones for giving little attention to teaching on the sacraments.

It is agreed that 'we should not talk disparagingly of "an ordinary ministry" especially in the light of the ascension of the Lord Jesus Christ and his pouring out of the Holy Spirit at Pentecost so the church constantly lives and witnesses in the Age of the Spirit. Nevertheless Lloyd-Jones with those in Conference at Bala believed that the Spirit was not at work in the church to the same degree continuously. And that is not a mere Celtic or Lloyd-Jones conviction but one taught by Reformed theologians and preachers from different countries over a long period of time. They held that there is variation in the degree to which the Holy Spirit is active within the church and there are occasions in the church's history when a larger degree of the Spirit's power and influence are given. On these occasions the means of grace enrich believers even more than normal with significant numbers of unbelievers also being saved. These are 'extra-ordinary' seasons.

Iain Murray offers evidence for the distinction between the 'normal' and the 'extraordinary'. For example, those 'filled with the Holy Spirit' in Acts 2:4 were again 'filled' in 4:31. He finds further support in the Larger Catechism of the Westminster Assembly (Question 182) in that while all believers are indwelt by the Holy Spirit, his working is 'not in all persons, nor at all times, in the same measure'.³⁰ Murray then argues that 'while the Spirit is always present in the church the degrees of his power and influence remain subject to Christ himself,'

so the church is always dependent upon its Head for fresh supplies of the Spirit (Luke 11:13, Acts 4:31, Ephesians 1:17, Philippians 1:19).[31] Murray's final support for the above distinction is his understanding of church history. He regards the sixteenth century Protestant Reformation, for example, as one of the 'extraordinary eras'. John Knox explained the significance of his own situation in Scotland in that period: 'God gave his Holy Spirit to simple men in great abundance.'[32] Similar statements are found with regard to the Cambuslang[33] and Kilsyth[34] revivals in Scotland as well as to Jonathan Edwards in Northampton, America in 1735, while the Great Awakening of 1740 there

'broke upon slumbering churches like a thunderbolt rushing out of a clear blue sky'.[35]

Murray concludes by affirming that

'a revival is an outpouring of the Holy Spirit, brought about by the intercession of Christ, resulting in a new degree of life in the churches and a widespread movement of grace among the unconverted. It is an extraordinary communication of the Spirit of God, a superabundance of the Spirit's operations, an enlargement of his manifest power.'[36]

This is confirmed by Hywel R. Jones who explains that in an 'extraordinary' work the Holy Spirit pursues his regular ministry with 'far more intensity and extensiveness than at other times'.[37]

However, the distinction must be handled with care and the 'ordinary' ministry of the Word respected and safeguarded.

3. Welsh revivals

Another criticism from Letham of 'revivalist preaching' is that Lloyd-Jones is heavily influenced by Welsh revivals and 'to a certain extent' he 'constructs his theology of preaching around these experiences'[38] thereby distorting the Bible's teaching and 'unintentionally undermines the regular use of the means of grace'. Christopher Catherwood is justified in claiming that Lloyd-Jones's 'special affection'[39] was for the eighteenth century revival leaders.[40] As a Welshman reared within the Calvinistic Methodist church in West Wales, his love of Calvinistic Methodist revival leaders like Daniel Rowland, Howell Harris and William Williams was considerable due to their Calvinism but also the place they gave to Christian experience and revival. Calvinistic Methodism became his model for church life. With important qualifications one agrees that Lloyd-Jones 'to a certain extent constructs his theology of preaching around these experiences' of revival. How? I submit that he did so in terms of a 'message' that was thoroughly biblical but also in terms of 'freedom' experienced by the preacher as well as 'participation' by the congregation.

4. Prayer and preaching

Stuart Olyott, regarded as an example of 'revivalist preaching', is criticised for suggesting that 'the preaching of the gospel is often powerless' and therefore believers must 'strive and agonise and prevail in prayer' for God 'to accompany the word to be preached'.[41] In this context Olyott distinguishes between an 'ordinary' ministry and one exercised in revival when large numbers of people are saved and believers are quickened. Letham endorses the importance of prayer yet criticises Olyott and other 'revivalist' preachers for assuming

> 'it not only possible but frequent that the Word is unaccompanied by the Spirit.'[42]

Clarity is required here. Those he criticises agree that preaching is never in vain and that the preaching of the Word 'can cut in both ways',[43] namely in judgement and in blessing, personally and corporately (2 Corinthians 2:1-16). Nor can the preacher know here the extent and manner of the Spirit's working in the minds and hearts of those in the congregation. And many people do not inform the preacher that they have been helped or dealt with through the preaching. Eternity alone will reveal the full significance of a preaching ministry. Behind the statements from Lloyd-Jones, Olyott and others is the desire for a greater degree of the Spirit's influence and power upon the Word preached. That was the burden of Conference as earlier chapters testify. They longed for more conversions and more quickening of believers. The Spirit is not absent from the Word preached but there is a desire for more of the Spirit's power upon the Word being preached. That is the burden behind statements which Letham appears to misunderstand.

Key issue

The relation of prayer to the preaching of the Word is another key issue but Letham does not address this though he assumes its importance. He gives less weight to it than the Bala Conference speakers did. If, as Calvin observes,[44] preaching is both a human and a divine activity with the Holy Spirit working sovereignly through the preacher's words, then the responsibility for prayer on behalf of the preacher and the congregation is of major importance. And that has been the consistent Conference emphasis and the burden of Lloyd-Jones in addressing these pastors.[45] For the success of the Gospel and the church, prayer with the preaching of the Word and the sacraments are the means God has appointed and which the church must major on constantly. No 'special' means are required. George Smeaton expresses the point well:

> 'the church of the present has all the warrant she ever had to wait, expect and pray. The first disciples waited in the youthfulness of simple hope, not for a spirit which they had not, but for more of the Spirit which they had; and Christianity has not outlived itself. The attitude of the church in the first days ... should be the church's still ... the more the church asks the Spirit and waits for His communications, the more she receives'.[46]

Prayer is not an instant 'fix' and it is more than words, a posture or habit. True prayer expresses dependence on God and a heartfelt conviction that only God can save, bless and revive his church for he alone has infinite resources. In a superb treatment of prayer, Calvin describes prayer as

> 'penetrating to those riches which are treasured up for us with our heavenly Father ...' It 'is a kind of intercourse between God and men ... nothing is set before us as an object of expectation from the Lord which we are not enjoined to ask Him in prayer, so ... prayer digs up those treasures which the Gospel of our Lord discovers to the eye of faith.'[47]

Calvin is not suggesting a disjunction of Word-Spirit but rather encouraging people to pray earnestly 'and agonise' in supplication for the exalted Christ to open up these divine treasures and give a greater measure of power upon the preached Word. Calvin exhorts us to

> 'have no hesitation in imploring the aid which he voluntarily offers ... but climbing up by the ladder of the promises ...'[48]

Lloyd-Jones's closing words in the Puritan and Reformed Studies Conference in 1961 were

> 'let us take the phrase of Isaiah and "lay hold upon God" (Isaiah 64:7) ... That is the call to us ... here is the Truth. Yes, but why is it so ineffective?'[49]

There is no suggestion here that the Spirit does not accompany the Word. Rather it expresses a desire for greater degrees of the Spirit's power and effectiveness in preaching with a longing and burden for the advancement of God's kingdom, the beautifying of the church and the salvation of unbelievers. Douglas MacMillan underlines the point historically:

> '... we look back over history and we know of men who were outstanding preachers and through whom many were brought into fellowship with God—men who were used in the transformation of their society. One thing has characterised all great and useful preachers. Whatever their differences in appearance, in presentation and style—all were men of prayer. Prayer is paramount ... prayer is the most important element'.[50]

Prayer is important because it is divinely appointed for the church, expressing the church's dependence on God and involving the graces of believing repentance, love and worship as well as desires to know God experientially and to intercede with child-like trust for the church. Such an emphasis on experience implies no disjunction between Word and Spirit. Nor is this a mere Wales phenomenon; it is a biblical conviction shared by theologians, preachers and churches elsewhere over centuries.[51]

5. Proof-texts

A final serious criticism by Letham is that 'to a certain degree' in constructing his theology around experiences in Welsh revivals, Lloyd-Jones 'distorts the picture presented in the bible ...' and refers to 'a popular proof-text used by this school of thought as determinative'. The proof-text referred to is 1 Thessalonians 1:5 with a reference to 1 Corinthians 2:3–5.

In response, Letham is correct to criticise a 'proof-text' approach. Whether in reference to establishing doctrines like the Trinity, Christology, the Atonement or, as here, the power of the Holy Spirit in preaching, a 'biblo-theological'[52] method is essential. Sinclair Ferguson illustrates how this can be done with regard to the doctrine of the Holy Spirit while James Packer[53] provides a stimulating example of 'digging' and drawing out from John 3 truths concerning the Holy Trinity.[54] A proof-text approach is unacceptable as it often ignores the context and progressive flow of redemptive history.

However, it must be asked, is Lloyd-Jones guilty of proof-texting? Admittedly he referred often to 1 Thessalonians 1:5 and 1 Corinthians 2:3–5 but not exclusively, as a detailed analysis of his final chapter in Preaching and Preachers confirms. For there we find references to Exodus 40 and the Old Testament prophets before confining his attention to the New Testament, particularly John the Baptist, the Lord's own baptism (Luke 3:15–17) and mission (Luke 4:18ff). Acknowledging that he is 'selecting' what he regards 'as the most important passages which deal with the matter,'[55] he turns to Luke 24:46–49 then 'leads on to Acts 1:8', then its fulfilment 'in Acts 2 when the Christian church was ushered in to this dispensation of the Spirit ...'[56] Respecting unique aspects of Pentecost,[57] he underlines this 'accession' and 'effusion of power' on preachers as something which can also be 'repeated many many times'. He makes further references to Acts 3, 4:7 and 31, 6:3–5, 7:55 and 13:9 before turning to 1 Corinthians 2:3–5, 2 Corinthians 4:5–7, 12:9, Colossians 1:28–29 then 1 Thessalonians 1:5 and Revelation 1:10. While the 'biblo-theological' method in this one chapter is inadequate, nevertheless it is not proof-texting, for Lloyd-Jones indicates the progressive development of biblical teaching alongside the important 'rootedness' of biblical texts.

Pursuing the 'biblo-theological' approach further, texts like 1 Corinthians 2:3–5 and 1 Thessalonians 1:5 are often interpreted in terms of Graeco-Roman culture rather than their rich Hebraic Old Testament background which would have been dominant for the apostle Paul, an 'anti-rhetor'.[58] Letham appeals to the former and 'the Greek hankering for rhetoric'[59] but that is only a factor, as Letham may acknowledge. The close connection between Word and Spirit,[60] also Spirit and power in the Old Testament, must be determinative in interpreting these texts as these close connections are carried through into the New Testament (Romans 1:4, 15:13, 19, 2 Timothy 1:7–8). In 1 Thessalonians 1:5, for example, the Spirit and the Word, the Spirit and power are linked inseparably together. God's speaking and working by the Spirit through Judges (3:10, 6:34), prophets and kings (1 Samuel 16:13, 2 Samuel 23:2) was dynamic and often disturbing but always effective in blessing or judgement and finding ultimate fulfilment in the Messiah (Isaiah 11:2, 42:1–4,61:1 and Luke 4:18–21) but also corporately in the church at Pentecost (Joel 2:28, Acts 2) through the exalted Lord.

An examination of Acts demonstrates that in the age of the plenitude of the Spirit, there was a 'commonality'[61] when the Gospel penetrated for the first time into an area. Beyond the more significant Jerusalem (Acts 2), Samaria (Acts 8) and Gentile (Acts 10) moments in redemptive history, when the Gospel entered other areas, especially where there was fierce persecution, the Spirit and the Word were operative in even greater degrees of power. Perhaps the imagery in the prophecy of Joel to 'signs in the earth beneath, the sun turned into darkness …' (Acts 2:19–20) finds partial fulfilment in periods of social upheaval and powerful opposition when the church is under considerable threat as in Acts 4:18, 23–33 and 1 Thessalonians 1. At such times the church was sustained but also enlarged as a result of the Word being ministered in an even greater degree of power in the Spirit. This is repeated in missionary situations in God's sovereign providence.

Conclusion

Despite its weaknesses, for over fifty-nine years the Conference has served to encourage and stimulate many pastors in Wales but increasingly also in England. Its strong emphasis on the Word-Spirit relationship, with the call for pastors to pray in dependence on God and prepare well for preaching, continues to have an urgent relevance in the twenty-first century for churches. A conviction that the living God is always at work in his church and at times works even more powerfully to defend, prosper and enlarge his church remains a major encouragement and stimulus for expectant prayer by Conference members.

Questions for discussion

1. Are 'revivalism' and 'revival' really different?

2. Discuss the view of Lloyd-Jones concerning 'freedom' which can be given by the Holy Spirit to a preacher of the Word. How can we recognise it?

3. If you are able, assess as a group the matter of 'proof' texts. Is this important?

APPENDICES 1–15

Notes of addresses by Dr Lloyd-Jones in the Evangelical Ministers Conference in Wales, 1956–1978 taken by Emyr Roberts and Eryl Davies.

APPENDIX 1

'Why are we where we are?'

Lloyd-Jones's closing message—Cilgwyn 1956

(Emyr Roberts' Notes)

Our first question should be—*Why are we where we are?* We should first ask about the church before facing the problem of reaching outsiders.

The question of the truth

Can we know revival apart from the basis of truth? No. And this truth can be defined. Professor Micklem[1] understands truth to be only a marvellous experience that cannot be put into propositions. That is wrong. Look at Ephesians chapter two, for example, where man is described as being spiritually dead in sin and under the wrath of God. Salvation is by grace through faith on the basis of the substitutionary atonement of Jesus Christ.

Can we expect revival? Revival has always come when these basic truths are proclaimed. But there are people who decry doctrine in favour of a man's devotion or his 'atmosphere.'

One could co-operate with an Arminian. He may fail to explain the way of salvation adequately and yet know that salvation is utterly from God by grace. We must suffer a man's muddle-mindedness and yet remember that doctrine is important. We must agree on our own utter inadequacy and our total dependency on God. Revival follows Calvinism.

Dependence on God alone

Is the holding of evangelistic campaigns one of the obstacles to revival? Our efforts become too important. We ask God to bless our efforts. Before we see a revival, we must realise that we have nothing to do with revival. Campaigns appeared first during the nineteenth century. And since evangelistic campaigns began, revivals have become less frequent.

We must stop asking for 'decisions'. John Wesley had no enquiry room and never asked for a 'decision'. He left it to the Spirit of God. Duncan Campbell stopped 'testing' meetings seven years ago (that is, in 1949). We must put our dependence alone on the Holy Spirit.

Instead of planning a campaign, we should ask: Why has God left us? We must pray. We must be importunate. There must be real agony and concern for our fundamental need.

Again, we have the teaching about taking things (such as victory over sin and the Holy Spirit) by faith as 'non-experiential'.

We have taken so much by faith that we have nothing! When the Holy Spirit comes upon you, you know it. The barrenness of many evangelical churches and the cliché, 'taking it by faith'! We are afraid of emotions and are guilty of sentimentalism. We are so nice ... we are afraid of emotion. But the Holy Spirit influences a whole person. When did you last weep for your sins or exult in sheer joy? We are quenching the Spirit because we are afraid of emotion.

Let us cease from planning this and that and simply concentrate on our personal relation with God. Do we realise the presence of God? How often do we realise his presence?

APPENDIX 2

'why could we not cast him out?'

Lloyd-Jones's closing message—Cilgwyn 25 June 1957

(Emyr Roberts' notes)

Text: Mark 9:28, 'why could we not cast him out?'

The failure of the disciples in Mark chapter 9 and their amazement at the ease with which the Lord Jesus cast out the evil spirit from the young boy! Their helplessness and failure we can identify with. We are having little impact. Our church ministry is ineffective. What are we to do? 'This kind', said the Lord Jesus, 'cometh not out except by prayer and fasting' (verse 29).

What is the peculiar problem facing us? One problem facing us is the ecumenical movement. The problem, they inform us, is the disunity of the church and we cannot evangelise except we unite.

But the whole history of the church is against that thesis. For example, Athanasius stood alone against error and Luther stood against the whole Roman church of that period. We must never proclaim the unity of the church in such a way as to condemn men and movements raised up especially by God.

We must have a right understanding of what we mean by fellowship. A man can have a devotional atmosphere in his home but in his books, as it has happened, deny the faith. We must not confuse a natural fellowship, a fellowship based on natural affinities with the real affinity. Christian fellowship does not depend on 'atmosphere' or natural affinities but on the Truth—the Word.

Christian fellowship does not depend on comprehensiveness or majorities. Think, for example, of Gideon when God did the exact opposite of what our modern leaders wish to do. Rather than marshal the big battalions, God reduced Gideon's army from 32,000 to 300 men! Unity certainly does not mean comprehensiveness.

Then unity does not depend on doing but rather on being. The whole case of the New Testament is that of the 'unity of the Spirit' (Ephesians 4:3) and He has created 'in Himself one new man from the two, thus making peace' (Ephesians 2:15). This is not a coalition between Jews and Gentiles ... but a new creation by the Spirit of God. We cannot create unity. The Holy Spirit alone does that but we are to 'keep' or 'guard' and 'safeguard' the unity He has created.

'This kind ...'—What about our situation today? Why is God withholding His hand? In the nineteenth-century, there were frequent revivals. But why not now? What is there in the present situation? What is wrong?

A man lies unconscious on a country road. 'What are we to do? He may be asleep. Or he may have poison in his system. The position in earlier times in Wales such as in 1858–59 was not that people denied the faith, but that they had fallen asleep. Today, however, there is a deadly poison in the system of the church, namely, false and unbiblical doctrines.

Can the Holy Spirit bless a people who do not own the truth? No. He cannot. And we must never separate the Word and the Spirit ... for they always go together. The Word without the Spirit results in a dead orthodoxy. But the Spirit without the word leads to Quakerism, mysticism and error. In the New Testament the Word and Holy Spirit are always together. We have no right to expect the Lord's blessing unless we own the truth. Doctrine is absolutely essential.

There is an 'irreducible minimum' of doctrines which must be believed. First, the doctrine of God and God the Father. He is sovereign and Lord of the universe. In the last revival there came a tendency to put the Son of God in the place of God the Father. The sense of the glory of God has gone today. We must get back to the doctrine of the glory of the eternal God.

Second, the doctrine of God the Son: 'one Lord ...' (Ephesians 4:5). The heart of the message is that God laid upon Jesus the condemnation of my sins. No fellowship is possible between us and anyone who denies the incarnation and atonement. The history of revivals proves that the men who have been used by God in revivals are always men who have held to these truths.

But the statement, 'Christ is the Saviour', in modern parlance means just a great Pal who stands by one's side. But the doctrine of Christ the Saviour depends on our concept of sin.

John Wesley's ministry did not begin until he saw this doctrine of justification by faith. This was also true of Daniel Rowland.

The Doctrine of the Holy Spirit, especially conviction of sin as an agony of conviction was present in all the great revivals of the past. Today, there is an absence of conviction of sin. '... For I know that in me ... dwelleth no good thing' (Romans 7:18). Have we known this? It is the work of the Holy Spirit to do that.

We need to reconsider our definition of 'faith' for there is an element of feeling in faith. We may be so afraid of Pentecostalism as to 'quench the Spirit'. Sandemanianism claims there is no feeling element in faith but only a mere affirmation; there is a distrust of feelings.

Christmas Evans,[1] the nineteenth-century Baptist preacher in Wales, became spiritually hard and fruitless under the influence of Sandemanianism.[2] One day, he prayed for some time near Cader Idris (a popular and attractive mountain in North West Wales), until he felt his heart being filled by the Holy Spirit.

But Sandemanianism is rampant today. It is the basis of our evangelism ... To get people to declare their faith but without any reference to the heart. But Romans 6:17, 'you obeyed from the heart that form of doctrine to which you were delivered', means the whole person is affected in becoming a Christian so there is believing, feeling and doing. We must never be content with anything less. And there must be agreement on these doctrines ...

One condition of revival, therefore, is that we hold fast to the Truth. The Holy Spirit will not bless anything else. The New Testament teaches that the Holy Spirit at times is poured out by God. Popular evangelistic teaching is that the baptism of the Holy Spirit disappeared once and for all at Pentecost so there is one baptism but many fillings. However, this can rule out revival. While we must remember the 'regular' work of the Holy Spirit, there is also the special or extra-ordinary work of the Holy Spirit. And our doctrine of the Holy Spirit and His work must leave room for this visitation. Are we convinced in our hearts that the Holy Spirit can do again what he has done in the past? Natural, unregenerate hearts cannot receive the things of the Spirit of God—it is the work of God the Holy Spirit to work powerfully.

These are the doctrines that produce union and fellowship among those who believe them and also produce a division—a clear distinction between those who accept them and those who do not. We need a special grace. We must be very careful that we are not drawn into fruitless and endless disputations. Mere argumentation is sterile. What we must do is to preach them (these doctrines), assent to them and live them.

The gospel is exclusive and intolerant on one hand and yet is the manifestation of love. We are never to be hard and harsh. We must preach the truth in love. There is no fellowship between the two sides of the division caused by these truths. But we must do everything to promote fellowship amongst ourselves.

Unity among Christians.

There are things that break this unity:

1. Defects in character, especially absence of lowliness and humility. Spirit of ambition here. Often the modern Evangelical is full of self-confidence.

2. Carnality, that is, thinking of spiritual things in a carnal sense like unbelievers as in 1 Corinthians 3 verse 4 or a show of gifts as in chapter 12. Or putting tradition in the place of the truth. Why should we divide from fellow Christians? Tradition before the truth? Or possibly worldly ideas of leadership. People of wealth, title or distinction ... if you are a general or admiral, therefore a leader. This is pure carnality; see James 2:1-13. Carnality has interest in big names. But the man who should lead in the church is the man who knows God, whoever he may be.

3. Worldliness and sin: 1 Corinthians 5; 2 Corinthians 6 and 2 Peter 2 are examples which divide the fellowship.

4. Our failure to see that we must start with the church. Our first question ought not to be how we can bring these people in but why are they outside the church? There is something in our lives and in our testimony that keeps them outside! In times past, revival started with the church. If the church is

right then the people will come in. Our great campaigns hide this from us, that is, hide from us the need to begin with the church. We need not a method but a live church (We must be busy to pray for the campaigns next March. The assumption was that nothing could happen before then). No such thing as an ordinary Sunday ... if the Spirit of God comes down then the most ordinary man can be used in extraordinary ways.

5. Absence of seriousness. Successful evangelists crack jokes and are often full of self-confidence but contrast Paul ... weakness, fear and trembling. The Rev. Murray McCheyne,[3] (Presbyterian minister in Dundee)—the people wept as he came into the church ... the Spirit of God was upon him ... In the United States, ninety miles from Holywood, people (Christians presumably) were roaring with laughter ... we will show them that we are like them ... that we can enjoy ourselves'. But in the New Testament the Christian is meant to be different.

6. An absence of a sense of helplessness. We still believe in ourselves. The five men who arranged the Billy Graham campaign in Cambridge are today scoffing at the Christian faith. This would not happen if our faith was not in ourselves but in the Lord. We are more concerned in the success of our churches than to know God, to know Christ and to know the power of the Holy Spirit ... This is the start of every revival. We should not desire even sanctity, apart from God.

7. An absence of waiting on God. What we should be asking is: why is my ministry not honouring God? Nothing matters

except our relationship to God. Rather than wait upon God we tend to entertain our people.

8. The testing of meetings, (that is, calling people out to make decisions to trust Christ). Is this a hindrance? That we do not believe in the Holy Ghost, therefore 'we must bring them in tonight in case they do not come again'. John Wesley never tested a meeting. They preached the truth in the strength of the Holy Spirit and left it to God. There is a natural influence of strong personalities ... Hitler had these natural powers so can a highly successful modern evangelist or even the Pope ...

9. Our false believism. We must say, 'believe the truth', but if the man within a year has not felt anything, he is still unregenerate. The apostles did not take it by faith that they had the power of the Holy Spirit. They had it ... and they knew ... If we have taken the fullness of the Spirit by faith all these years, where are the fruit? When men have had it, they knew it and everybody else knows it. This may stand between us and revival.

10. Our fear of emotion. When Jonathan Goforth was invited to speak in the Keswick Convention in 1906, he was given the warning that they did not want in Keswick the scenes that had occurred in China. But we must allow God to do what He likes, even if it means that people will count us fools.

This sleep of death ... Nothing but desperation about ourselves and our country will send us to real prayer. May He deliver us from 'the thing to do' in evangelical churches!

APPENDIX 3

Strain and stress in the Christian ministry

Lloyd-Jones's address—Cilgwyn 23 June 1959

(Emyr Roberts' notes)

A tendency to see everyone as a psychological case. We must protect ourselves from the exhaustion involved in this work.

a. There are mental illnesses. Eventually we do recognise these people, but we must not waste our time. We must honour them and be nice. Let them talk for five minutes and then walk to the door. We cannot help them if we listen to them for three hours.

b. Neurotics are people who think there is something wrong

with them when there is not. As a Doctor, a great many ministers came to see me. Felt 'all ministers are neurotics'! Within nine months, I was a neurotic myself! Tremendous nervous strain. We must be foolish if we do not take account of this. We should see a medical doctor but if we find ourselves going to the doctor again and again, we should know. And we must face it ... talk to ourselves about it.

The neurotic is never really happy if he does not talk about himself. The thing to look for in them is this, that there is this desire to attract interest in themselves. If we find that a person is a neurotic then we must be firm—'Yes, I have heard you say that'. Then turn the conversation to talk about the Faith. And they will then leave you alone.

A neurotic can come under the influence of the gospel but more likely so when we preach in the pulpit rather than privately. But do not talk to them on the level they want to talk but rather bring in the gospel.

How are we to tell whether a person's trouble is spiritual and not psychological? A deputy headmistress came to ask me whether I knew of a Christian psychiatrist. I dealt with her on purely spiritual grounds and she was completely cured. I never treat people who are mentally ill but if I come to the conclusion that they have spiritual needs then I keep them myself.

We need therefore to test:
1. If you have a feeling that you are not making real contact, possibly the person is mentally ill. They are not listening to you and they begin where they left off when you have

spoken. The spiritually ill person's desire is to make contact with you. They cling to your words.

2. If we find that a person is willing to talk of spiritual interest but not put it into practice, then possibly a mental problem. Action follows agreement with you in the case of a spiritually unhealthy person but not for the other.

3. Suicidal threat. People who are spiritually ill will put it like this—'I was so depressed I even thought of ...' There is objectivity there. Those with mental needs are really afraid of suicide. Detachment.

4. The persistence of depression. Send such a person to a medical doctor! Can be striking changes in a person. Suddenly becomes different, withdrawn and silent. Serious trouble. Send to a doctor if someone seems to live in a dream. But if a person who is under depression and you can arouse him from his depression and he is congenial company, he is not mentally ill. It is not serious.

Treatment

If mentally ill, hand the person over to a medical doctor. But if there are spiritual problems, what are we to do?

Handle them in a positive way. A woman came to see me (Lloyd-Jones) and she was terrified of thunderstorms. I asked: 'What have you done?' 'Prayed', she said. 'Then stop praying', I said, 'because you brought it to your mind. Your problem is yourself and morbid self-concern. That is your problem. Pray that God will make you a worthy disciple and that people will be attracted by you'.

The same is true of the homosexual. He will be explained in terms of a disease, physical or psychological. The answer to these people is that there is nothing in their make-up that compels them to sin. Self-concern again. We are to rebuke people. 'Your trouble is ...'; 'you are a very poor Christian. We are all in these troubles and the world, the flesh and the devil. Why should you think that your case is special?'

That is the principle. Treat a Christian as a Christian. We must be much less interested in particular sins. It is sin that matters—our relationship to God. It is not that (particular) sin that matters but your whole relationship with God.

But some practical aids

We must see them as frequent as possible. The case of the man in Sandfields—'I want you to see my father'. He was a serious backslider. For three quarters of an hour I shared texts with him. Fearful. I was back in two days: 'you are suffering because of your backsliding'. Returned in seven days ... he was to recite verses and two he found very helpful.

Every tendency to sit down and think of self is from the devil. Told him: 'You have to talk to the devil. We must stop listening ... If he will not listen to you any more ... You have no business with me ... Go to Christ about me'. It is like taking our case to the solicitor. Do not have any dealings with the devil—talk to Christ about me!

We must not think about ourselves. Think of this example. Will you look after this treasure for me while I am on holiday? Yes ... then a telephone call to ask whether the treasure is alright. But if you have put that treasure in my keeping then you must trust me. You insult me. You must resist the thought of ringing me. Or again—a cure for sea-sickness. Three times a day—look up ... do not look at the waves right in front of you. So too in the spiritual conflict. We must not have direct dealings with the devil. Tell the devil: 'I do not belong to you. I will not have a suspicion or a suggestion'. Look at Christ ... not the waves.

APPENDIX 4

'Why are we failing?'

Lloyd-Jones's Closing Message—Bala June 1964

(Emyr Roberts' notes)

A time of turmoil and confusion. Those who agree must come together. We need to review the situation and strengthen one another.

A note of failure. Why are we failing? We are no more successful than others? Failure in our own churches and in our own work.

How do we meet this situation?
Explanations include:

1. The danger of blaming the times. There are times of

barrenness in the history of the church. But it is wrong to put all the blame on the times. This is the priestly attitude. It may also lead us to a fatalistic approach to the situation. God calls men to break into the situation. The prophetic attitude.

2. One of our greatest dangers is to be in a position of reaction ... Always on the defensive; it becomes a habit of the mind and this is quite wrong. It is a purely negative attitude. We of all people should be positive. We should be leading.

3. Our priorities are not always what they should be. A great danger of being jockeyed into a position where we denounce all others under the conviction that we are always in the right. If we want to win a man we must not knock him on the head. We must have pity; we must love. For example, 'good' evangelical praying is attacking the congregation. Not a single petition for the preacher and he was so annoyed that a large congregation had come to hear Dr Martyn Lloyd-Jones that he prayed against them! We can develop a complex. Why are these people here? Why do they come? An attitude of antagonism to people. We cannot do them any good if we are against them. To use a prayer to attack a congregation is reprehensible as it is in preaching. Are we guilty of intellectual arrogance? Because of our position as a minister we are in danger of reacting in the wrong way—resentment.

4. A puritan scholasticism. This is a kind of intellectualism which becomes a matter of pride ... an unbalanced interest in doctrine and theology can be wrong ... Reading is not food but a stimulus. What we read should become lost in our body and muscles ... A change occurred in the Early

Church. Man wanted to merge the gospel with what he knew, then wanted to present it to others. And because they were persecuted, they emphasised Christianity as a culture. But New Testament Christianity is something very different. Then there was a reaction in the Early Church with Montanus claiming to go back in his preaching and teaching to the primitive pattern. Here was a protest against philosophy. This kind of pattern has continued all down the ages of the church. The Reformation period then changes into expressions of scholasticism until there was a reaction, for example, in the Pietist movement versus the deadness of orthodoxy. In the nineteenth century, too, there was the scholasticism of Charles Hodge ... We must guard against this intellectualism—this puritan scholasticism. However much we know, 'we know only in part ... we see only through a glass darkly ...' (1 Corinthians 13:9-12)

Why is our preaching so ineffective?

We are in great danger of forgetting the object of preaching. A man's business in the pulpit is to preach to people, not as they should be, but as they are. In 1 Corinthians 3:1, Paul says he could not preach to them as to 'spiritual' but 'as to carnal ... to babes ...' Again, in Hebrews 5:12-14 something similar is said. They were preaching to people as they were. We must not appeal merely to the head but also to the heart. The chief end of preaching is to instruct and to persuade.

The golden rule is to preach to your people as they are. And it is not our business so much to say things as to show that they are inevitable. Lloyd-Jones referred to a man who followed his series on Ephesians 2 then wrote a letter complaining that the Doctor had not mentioned Calvinism once. He had been disappointed because the preacher had not actually said, 'This is Calvinism'. But we should try to show the truth as being inevitable and to show from the Scriptures that Arminianism is wrong. But my models are not the Puritans but Jonathan Edwards and George Whitefield and their passion for the glory of God.

What are our greatest needs?

Power? We need power but we need something before that. Our first need is to know Him and to know His love. I am preaching next Sunday because the love of Christ constrains me. What a difference between knowing about him and knowing him!

My greatest problem is not to prepare my sermons but myself. And the only way to do so is a personal, intimate knowledge of Him. Hudson Taylor prayed: 'Lord Jesus, make Thyself to me ... a reality'. Our supreme desire must be to have communion with him.

Then second we need power but this must be second. The Charismatic Movement which started in America by now gives a wrong place to speaking in tongues. Now for them speaking in tongues is the first and foremost thing. At first they emphasised the baptism of the Spirit but now tongues first; they are also teaching a particular method of obtaining this gift. They call an after-meeting and people are told: 'breathe in deeply. You are now breathing in the Holy Spirit' ... then psychologically some speak in tongues. But in the New Testament, tongues-speaking is a gift. If a person can do it at any time it is a psychological phenomenon ... Psychological states and conditions can enable people to speak with tongues. It is all a subjective experience. But there is no power in the preaching!

APPENDIX 5

Looking back on 1966

Lloyd-Jones's Closing message—Bala, June 1967

(Emyr Roberts' notes)

The book of Acts is one of the most exhilarating books in the bible. It is comforting because it is history. And the book of Acts is also comforting because it enables us to see our own situation within an eternal context. The life of the Church has been one of struggle and strife from the beginning. But whatever our difficulties are in Wales, such difficulties are being experienced worldwide by the Church.

Reflection
(Lloyd-Jones referred first of all to the Evangelical Alliance Conference in the Autumn of 1966 in which he gave his now

famous address. He reported that he had been charged with dividing evangelicals because he appealed for evangelical unity.)

I never expected evangelicals to accept my appeal. If Spurgeon failed to get evangelical unity in his day, who amongst us can hope to achieve it?

For the sake of the Anglican/Methodist Union, evangelicals, for the sake of this material unity, are willing to make concessions and accepting that the Anglicans must not be divided. There is also the proposed union of the Congregational Union of England and Wales and the Presbyterian Church of England.[1] Then the 1967 Anglican Evangelical Conference was held at Keele with the Archbishop of Canterbury, a non-evangelical, addressing the Conference.

In all these plans for unity, the one important thing is the unity of the visible church. For example, the Anglican-Methodist Scheme for Union can be interpreted in two radically different ways. We are fighting a mentality. The one thing that matters is the integrity of the denomination whether it is the Anglican or Methodist or Baptist or other churches. Nothing matters more to them than the integrity of the denomination.

At the same time, there is an obvious shift in evangelical teaching on the Bible and the evangelical attitude to the ecumenical movement.

Now this is happening all over the world. One example is in the Presbyterian Church of New Zealand where the Principal of their seminary has denied the physical resurrection of the Lord Jesus

Christ. Presbyteries have protested but error continues. Similarly, the Free University of Amsterdam has stood four square for the Reformed Faith since its foundation by Kuyper yet today there is doctrinal division.

The United Presbyterian Church of America has a new Statement of Faith. This is a formula to keep evangelicals in the denomination so instead of denying the Westminster Confession of Faith, they agree to accept all the great Confessions but for our time this shorter Statement is appropriate.

Evangelical people throughout the world are in these difficulties so what can we do? Can we not see that we must stand on certain broad principles or face extermination?

Wrong emphases

But there is a danger that we put the emphasis on the wrong things, even whether a Confession should be long or short. For some, healing is everything. For others, the whole emphasis is on speaking in tongues or being engrossed in talk about demonology. Our danger is to elevate to prominence things which should not be central and to turn to what is an expedient.

Priorities

We must keep, therefore our priorities right. But what are they?

1. *Preaching*

Preaching is always the first priority. Preaching comes first. And we must hold on to it. We are living in an age which does not believe in preaching at all. But preaching has been God's honoured way of working all down the generations.

There is liberty in preaching and the preacher is a man who does not know what is going to happen in, or as a result of, the preaching. We must stand by this, namely, the priority of preaching. And preaching is truth being mediated through personality.

But we stand by the absolute priority of preaching yet we still continue to preach in the pattern of our denomination. However, we must preach to the people who are in the pews. The apostle Paul preached as a Jew to the Jews. There must be elasticity and we must recognize the idiom. Are we not slaves to a certain pattern of preaching? One can contrast, for example, the preaching of Daniel Rowland and then the later and more 'polished' preaching that began with, and developed after John Jones, Talsarn. Are we too polished in our preaching? We must be more direct and less perfect yet exhorting more. We may be right in our doctrine but slaves in our methods. Preaching is a priority.

2. Supernatural

Pastoral work is secondary and supplementary to the preaching of the Word of God. And demonology is not our first problem either, although it is a problem. Two hundred years ago lethargy was the problem in the churches but today it is apostasy with the denying of God and His truth while Satan is often worshipped. And we can expect more Satanic activity in these days of apostasy.

Why is God allowing these demonic manifestations today? One major reason is in order to remind us of the reality of the supernatural world. Our greatest danger is to be content with doctrinal orthodoxy but know nothing of the spiritual and supernatural world.

Today, Evangelicals in England have little room for revival. They believe in evangelical campaigns or missions but not in revival. For example, the organizers of the Keswick Convention did not want Dr Jonathan Goforth to speak in Keswick unless he understood that he was in Keswick and not overseas. In other words, they did not want to hear of supernatural activity overseas either by God or by the devil. It is as if God says to us: 'if you do not want my Holy Spirit, then I will show you the reality of spiritual powers in this world, and allow these demonic forces to work'.

I recommend to you *The Experience Meeting* written by William Williams, Pantycelyn.[2] How many of you have such a meeting in your church? We are not providing our people with this kind of rich and intimate fellowship in which folk can share their experiences of the Lord or their spiritual needs. All this would be done under the guidance of an experienced exhorter who would apply the Word as appropriate to the needs of individuals.

And remember that we can be orthodox but spiritually cold and hard in our lives and ministries.

3. Prayer

Acts 6 verses 3–4 are key verses. The apostles were determined to give themselves to prayer and to the preaching of the Word. Prayer, however, is first. We cannot, and must not, preach without the preaching being saturated in prayer. In prayer we come to know Christ better and also His all-sufficiency. We can then truly say with Charles Wesley: 'Thou, O Christ, art all I want; More than all in Thee I find.'

We must not allow anything else, and no one else, to be central in our lives.

APPENDIX 6

The next steps

Lloyd-Jones's Address—Bala mid-1960s

(Emyr Roberts' notes)

The position at the moment is this: Can I continue as I am at present or in the proposed United Church? Can I conceive going in to the United Church and consider as brethren those who are 'emissaries of Satan'? If we can say 'yes', then there is nothing more to say. But if not, what do we do?

The Scheme of Union

We should not act individually now. Do not act now.

Steps to Take:

1. We have got to draw up an alternative to this. People will say to us: to what then do you belong? The non-evangelicals

are agreed that certain secondary issues like baptism can be accommodated. Can evangelicals agree? ... We should draw up a scheme of our own at once and publish it.

2. Individual decision. We must begin immediately to discuss this Union Scheme with our local church. And point out the following:

The sheer deception and trickery in their doctrinal position. They all say that they accept their historical statements. Now they say they accept the lot. For example, every branch of the church has believed all the main truths. Now we are going to do it together. But this is meaningless for it is claimed to be a fresh show of an orthodoxy which is not true. These statements are inadequate. This compels us to reassert specific doctrines and specific questions.

3. This new scheme leads to a complete loss of liberty for the individual church. This United Church may proscribe such a gathering as this Ministers' Conference. This puts us back to the uniformity of the Elizabethan Settlement and could lead to union with Anglicanism and Roman Catholicism. All the funds have to be handed over to District Committees. But what liberty would there be to use church funds then?

4. We must tell our people we could not go on with this scheme. They will have to consider the possibility of refusing to join and be willing to form a new evangelical church either with us or with someone else.

5. Are we now where there are no evangelical churches of any

kind? It is part of our duty to gather together God's people in these parts in order to encourage them to form a church.

We must make it clear what kind of church we want. A church worthy of the name is required so that our people may know what alternative there is.

Now we are really at a great turning point in the church. In the country, chapels and churches in many areas, and their numbers have come down to very few. We have to face this, that for many years we will be back to the church in the house. Our thinking should take the form of something radically new.

Major Factors

These are the true doctrines of the church and then the power of the Holy Spirit. In the New Testament there is a balanced combination of these two major factors.

But we are sometimes taunted today when people say: are your churches any better than our churches? But then we can ask ourselves too: why is God not authenticating evangelical truth? Must reformation precede revival? We are much more in line with the beginning of the eighteenth century than 1859 for we need both reformation and revival.

Our need is for the baptism of the Holy Spirit. Is this baptism to be equated with regeneration? In the book of Acts there is a recurrence of the filling of the Holy Spirit as in Acts 3 verses 4–9. Peter was commissioned by the Holy Spirit to heal. In Acts 4 we read again in verse 8 that Peter was 'filled with the Holy Spirit'.

This new emergency produced a new effusion of power and grace. This is the thing we need.

There has been a popular notion since the early twentieth century that all people at regeneration receive the Holy Spirit. Consequently, all that matters afterwards is that they yield themselves to the Holy Spirit. For example, Dr Campbell Morgan could not pray for the Holy Spirit because He was given once and for all at Pentecost. The Holy Spirit, therefore, was present in as much power in Westminster Chapel, London, as on the Day of Pentecost. This belief rules out revival completely.

This was true also of the Keswick leaders in the first part at least of the twentieth century.

But notice four basic points in response to this wrong approach:

1. Christians have been claiming for years that the Holy Spirit is with them and in a way similar to Pentecost but their churches are still lifeless.

2. Church history shows that the Holy Spirit often takes hold of a man and uses him and others in remarkable ways.

3. Our own churches are what they are because we are quenching the Holy Spirit ourselves, namely, by our own yielding and claiming but on the understanding we must not pray for the Holy Spirit to come in power.

4. There is a confusion here with sanctification so the words 'be filled with the Holy Spirit' (Ephesians 5:18) relate to, and

are found in the context of, sanctification. But the baptism of the Holy Spirit is concerned with one thing primarily, namely, the power to witness as in Acts 1 and verses 5 and 8. Here is the promise of power to witness.

5. There is another confusion, namely, that it is the baptism of the Spirit that founded the New Testament church. Here is the birthday of the church. The Baptism of the Spirit ...

(The notes end abruptly at this point)

APPENDIX 7

An affirmation concerning the Nature of the Church

(undated but probably 1966 or 1967)

(Emyr Roberts' notes)

Below are summary notes of two discussion sessions introduced by Graham Harrison who commended an Affirmation concerning the Nature of the Church which had been prepared by him and other Conference members.

There was extensive discussion and analysis of the document by the Conference and Dr Lloyd-Jones also contributed. Brief notes of the contributions from these two men are included below.

Graham Harrison

Within our denominations, whatever they once stood for, they do not stand for it any longer. Confessional standards are a laughing stock ... Evangelicals are written off. The situation is likely to persist ... there is an ecumenical urge for a merger, and even if this scheme fails, others will be brought forward ... They challenge us to produce an alternative ... We need a return to biblical simplicity and also a visitation of the Holy Spirit. The two go together and we need both. Life must take a form but form without life is death.

The present situation is full of opportunity in this twin desire for God to restore and revive the church. We do not assume that a form of church government will necessarily bring life ... But we must stand for the truth in a godly and humble way.

The fact of our essential oneness in Christ. We feel that we belong together. We are brethren in Christ. We are willing to submit our ideas to the Word of God ... We must question our heritage.

This Affirmation is biblical. The biblical church is a spiritual church and a powerful church ... And Scriptures are a sufficient and final revelation. Church traditions may be valuable sometimes but they are all under the judgement of the Word of God.

We are not obsessed with unity but unity is a feature of the N.T. Church. If the time comes, we should be able to ask the people of God in our churches to make up their minds. The honour of God is in question. Should we not be contending for the faith? Is not the gospel an exclusive thing? Have we the right to be silent and tolerant in the face of heresy? Should we not contend for the faith?

Dr Lloyd-Jones

We all agree and are conscious of the fellowship among us today. We are aware of a fundamental agreement in doctrine and spirit. If we do not feel this, we are not evangelical but mainly pseudo-evangelical. True fellowship is impossible without doctrinal agreement.

Why are we evangelicals separated? We are guilty of schism, allowing ourselves to be separated by secondary considerations. Schism is only possible when there is a fundamental agreement on doctrine. Evangelicals are more guilty of schism than anyone. We are already in a sinful position. We have lacked a doctrine of the church; IVF/UCCF and other movements cannot face up to the doctrine of the church ...

The New Testament teaches the visible unity of the church, not invisible only but visible, too.

But we must not be rash. Are we prepared to state that this Affirmation is our position? We need to state it to our churches and put this as a statement of the evangelical doctrine of the church.

If we really believe this is the ideal we put before Christian people, is it not right that we meet together, keep together in this rapidly moving situation?

Can we justify the 'one-man ministry'? Everyone seems to say so. 'Everything is in the melting pot'. We evangelicals must be ready to do this. It is sinful to divide on Calvinism and Arminianism, Baptism, points of interpretation of prophecy, tongues, etc. The primacy of the gospel ... then we cannot divide on these secondary matters.

We must be clear about the goal and then seek the way to the goal.

a. Can we agree on this Affirmation?

b. Do we agree that we must go out of our way to come together again and keep in touch with one another?

APPENDIX 8

Some fundamental questions

Lloyd-Jones's Address—Bala 1970

(Emyr Roberts' notes)

There is a danger in exegetical preaching to become mechanical. We must always be ready to receive a present message from God. Howell Harris was exhorting and gave an appropriate word.

A book by two Anglo-Catholics and two Evangelical Anglicans, including Dr James Packer,[1] has just been published and forces us to face some fundamental questions. Dr Packer is regarded rightly as an evangelical leader and stands behind the published book, as do the other three authors.

What are these divisive issues raised by this book?

The first main issue is the view of Scripture and its relation to tradition.

The book has been written in reply to a challenge from the Archbishop that the Anglo-Catholics and Evangelicals produce their own scheme of union. The latter had criticised the Scheme of Union for the Methodists and Anglicans in that it took no account of doctrine. These four authors met together to consider their differences as Anglo-Catholics and Evangelicals, and the four subscribe to the contents of their book. We are concerned with the doctrinal section of the book.

a. *How do we view Scripture and Tradition?*

This is a difficult chapter reflecting typical Anglo-Catholic thinking with its philosophical reasoning. What is our authority?

b. *What is our view of grace?* These authors claim that they agree.

c. Sacraments. There is the important question of baptismal regeneration but they do not use the term. But the book raises the question: Can an evangelical hold the view of baptismal regeneration?

d. The Nature of the church. They come out against the idea of a congregation of believers.

e. The government of the church.

They hold that bishops are essential to the essence and structure of the church.

Is this evangelicalism? Do we agree? People will quote their leaders and we must be able to say why we are against their book. What is an evangelical? We will have to fight over some of the central issues of the Christian faith. We often feel nearer to the Roman Catholics and Anglo-Catholics than to those who are liberal in theology. Our differences with the former often come in terms of their extras and plus.

As there will be a real division among evangelicals—some will agree (with the authors) and this will be a great diminution in our strength. The 1967 Keele Conference has already decided that there should be one territorial church but on episcopal lines. This book will be the death knell of all evangelical interdenominational movements. We cannot confess together if we do not agree on the basics.

Unity and the Holy Spirit

What are we going to say in response to this book? Shall we be indifferent? But if we stand, and stand we should, we shall become a much smaller minority, especially in England.

We must be careful not to fight one another. We are to 'love the brethren'. Therefore, we need to be careful not to wound one another. It is stressed throughout the New Testament, namely, the unity of believers. We have not been placed in the ministry merely to state doctrine correctly but to bring people to Christ. If we do not do that, then what good are our controversies? As one example I refer to Dr T. T. Shields in North America whose ministry was spoiled by his bitterness. First of all, we are Christians and we must bear with one another. As we are going to be reduced in numbers, we must love one another.

Now there is nothing more dangerous than a pure intellectual interest in the truth. But you can be a Calvinist and a Thomist philosopher without being a Christian. If the truth has not humbled us and broken us we should examine ourselves.

The only thing that will authenticate us is an outpouring of the Spirit of God. This is our most hopeful point. Everything else is institutionalism. The greatest enemy of spiritual religion is institutionalism. But do we really believe in revival? Why is it we forget so easily this dimension of revival?

Can revival happen now? if not, then God has changed and we deny the power of God.

Then why is He not doing it today? We must believe that God can do it. Doctrine alone is not enough—there must be authentication from God. And we are the only people who can claim the authentication of God ... And the only proof of our teaching that God is the God of revival is that He sends revival.

We must realize that our hope lies only in God—the God who breaks in to bring us to a realization of Himself. The whole category of revival is missing. Let us remind our people, and keep it before their minds, the need and prospect of revival.

APPENDIX 9

Religious life in Wales since the turn of the Twentieth Century

Lloyd-Jones's Address—Bala 1970

(Emyr Roberts' notes)

My only qualification to speak on this subject is my age! But I have known personally some men prominent in the religious life of Wales. My objective is not to indulge in personal criticism. I may say things which some will not like, but I do so in the interest of truth.

Why consider this period?
1. Because there are many misconceptions about the 1904-05 revival in Wales.

The subject of revival in itself is misunderstood. People imagine that because there is revival everybody concerned with it is sanctified and has a complete understanding of Christian truth. That is quite wrong. See the letter of 1 Corinthians.

2. Some claim that this Evangelical Movement of Wales[1] was a child of the 1904–05 revival. No, nothing of the kind and there is only a very slight connection.

3. I entered into the situation in Wales as pastor in Sandfields in 1927.

It is profitable for us to study this history and heed the lessons and warnings.

We must come to an assessment of the 1904–05 revival

Both the 1859 and 1904–05 revivals in Wales were under the influence to some degree of the teaching of Charles Finney. Others criticize the 1904–05 revival because it was so evanescent for immediately afterwards modernism developed. This has happened before. For example, Williston Walker in his *History of Congregationalism in America* asserts that the years 1750–1785 formed the lowest period in the religious life of America and that was immediately after the Great Awakening. However, these facts do not invalidate the revival.

Others again criticize the revival for its mystical trends. But there has never been a revival where there are no excesses. For example, James Davenport by 1741 in North America, and following the revival there, was involved in excesses and fanaticism largely because of his conviction that the Holy Spirit was giving him and other believers immediate and 'special' guidance. He referred to this as being given strong 'impressions'. Quite soon afterwards he retired almost completely from public life. What is of interest to us is that Jonathan Edwards still claimed there was an element of truth behind the excesses.

Psychic elements came in especially in the case of Evan Roberts in the 1904-05 Welsh revival. He crossed the line but he would not take any step without a direct leading of the Holy Spirit. This led to his over-strain. There is nothing new in this. In the 1859 revival in Wales, Humphrey Jones was guilty of excess too. There was genuine revival but there were excesses and sometimes physical manifestations also present as in 1859 and 1904-05. There was true revival in spite of excesses.

Positive

Look at it from the positive side. There were two main strands and a third one we note.

1. There was an old Welsh strand. We see this in much of what happened to Evan Roberts before the 1904-05 revival and much of the preparation was in line with Protestant Church history in Wales, especially from the eighteenth century. It is illustrated too in Dr Joseph Jenkins, Newquay, Cardiganshire where the 1904-05 revival actually started. Jenkins is a difficult man to interpret for there were mystical and theological elements in him. He and Evan Roberts represented in the beginning the old Welsh tradition of seeking God for revival. They searched themselves, confessed sin and sought God.

2. The influence of Dr F. B. Meyer and the Keswick Movement was the second strand. Soon Joseph Jenkins, John Thickens, R. B. Jones and W. W. Lewis were influenced in this way and were not then concerned with revival but with the deepening of the spiritual life. Joseph Jenkins did not belong to this strand originally but was drawn into it. Evan Roberts did not belong to this strand either. It is vital to remember these two distinct strands when thinking about the 1904–05 revival in Wales.

When the 1904–05 revival broke out in Wales, all were carried along with it except John Thickens and Joseph Jenkins. Jenkins used to tell me he became aware of a blue flame moving ... before the revival broke out.

A climactic meeting in Blaenannerch ... John Thickens in his account of the meeting keeps on referring to Evan Roberts as 'this neurotic young man'. Both he and Jenkins realized that something wrong came into the revival with Evan Roberts. But they were wrong. Jenkins kept on preaching throughout the revival. R. B. Jones again was disturbed about the mystical and psychical elements, especially in Evan Roberts.

And this division was true in the revival itself. But tremendous things happened when the Spirit of God had come down in revival. My wife can recall things in the meetings. Her father kept her in Castell Newydd Emlyn for many weeks to see and experience the revival for he felt she and her brother could have their education again but not the revival!

Appendix 9: Religious Life in Wales since 1901

What followed? The effects of the revival were tremendous. But note:

a. The vast majority remained in the churches to which they belonged and they were the mainstay of the churches. These 'plant y diwygiad' ('children of the revival') were the people who kept things going. They could pray and they had experiences to relate. They were the salt of the churches. They put up with modernist preaching because they did not understand it. This was true about many ministers—liberal or non-descript in theology—but once you touched on the revival with them, they were different people. They had an authentic experience of God. A revival is not a guarantee of sanctification or of correct theology but only a manifestation of the power of God. It is not a guarantee of doctrinal purity. These members of the churches had great experience but were children themselves in understanding. They had reverence for a minister and were in awe of scholarship. But were it not for 'plant y diwygiad' the churches would have been shattered (much earlier).

b. The Keswick type. Some of these remained in the churches but they were a distinct group, including R. B. Jones, W. W. Lewis, Keri Evans and Nantlais Williams. They had a great concern for sanctification and attended Conventions; these adopted many ideas which were false and under the influence of F. B. Meyer, Keswick and Llandrindod Wells (Keswick in Wales venue). There were later two Bible Colleges established in Swansea and in Porth, the latter under R. B. Jones. R. B. Jones also imitated the Faith Mission of Scotland, sending out women two by two and holding evangelistic campaigns. All these steps are strange elements in the true Welsh tradition. Some of these even left the churches and started churches of their own. These believed in movements, both before and after the revival.

Then division came between the followers of Rees Howells (W. W. Lewis, W. S. Jones and Keri Evans) and those of R. B. Jones. Keri Evans criticised R. B. Jones for his fundamentalism. R. B. Jones was a great man but too ready to borrow other men's ideas as, for example, with regard to Dr T. T. Shields, Toronto and his tirade. He attacked people by name. R. B. Jones began to do the same and his sermons attacked Roman Catholicism and Modernism.

But these people were activists. They had the *Cylchgrawn Efengylaidd* ('Evangelical Magazine') and in 1927 when I came to pastor Sandfields church, Aberavon, these men welcomed me. But I could not join them as I disagreed with movements, including the Holiness Movement. This is the work of the church, not movements.

Then these folk tended towards self-righteousness and Pharisaism. Two women in R. B. Jones's church were asked, 'Do I understand you do not believe in prayer meetings?' So they were like spiritual detectives!

c. Those people who became leaders of the Pentecostal churches mistakenly thought revival was a continuous state to go on for ever. But the true representatives of revival were those who stayed in the churches.

This Pentecostal movement is new and it is not a Holiness Movement for it is more theological. We must not be bound, according to them, by the past and we must be willing to be led by God to a new thing.

However, (in response), we know that nothing will authenticate us but a genuine revival. We contend for the faith but not in the way of T. T. Shields. But we also realize that without the authentication of the Spirit of God on us, the movement will come to nothing.

APPENDIX 10

The Living God

Lloyd-Jones's closing address—Bala 1971

(Emyr Roberts' notes)

There is a lack of life amongst us. What is the cause? It is due to a lack of a realization that God is a living God. There is neglect of the living God.

Through the Bible, we can review what God has done. Stephen does that in Acts 7. Paul in Antioch Pisidia in Acts 13. The importance of seeing the big picture. Our greatest danger is to lose the big picture in the details but the greatest sin of all is to forget that God ACTS in the world. We forget this in some of the following ways:

a. Religion in itself.

The greatest danger here to the Christian faith. Religion is dangerous because it emphasizes what WE do—the practice of religion.

b. We become too immersed in our own activity that we have no time to think what is the meaning of it all—a professionalism and we have no realization of the living God.

c. False evangelism. This is a type of evangelism which conceives its main work as organising a campaign. But we are dependent on God but if we are not, then God is offended with us. Prayer is needed as well as humiliation and pleading which is the background of most of us. It is often an 'after thought' to look for prayer backing as God is remembered only at the end.

Then the appeal. Those who want to believe (gospel statements) then decide there and then. Such 'decision-making' involves merely agreeing with a number of statements about God, ourselves and salvation but there is no meeting with the living God. John Bunyan, by contrast, was under conviction of sin for eighteen months. It is so much easier today to accept (only) truths, and responses can be superficial. But the old preachers talked of a meeting with God. W. E. Prothero preached in Wales on one big occasion immediately after Lloyd-Jones. His approach was appropriate at that point: 'I am here to tell you that Jesus Christ is in the office now'! He knew it had to be a personal encounter.

d. Concern about apologetics. We spend our time and energy defending propositions and have no time to seek God.

Forgetting God in our zeal for apologetics. The only place for apologetics is a word in our introduction to our message.

e. Preoccupation with the application of the gospel and reacting to the criticism that we lack a social conscience.

But what I found lacking in American 'fundamentalism' was spirituality. Now for a generation talking about application of philosophy, politics and other things. Everybody is now talking about the Christian attitude to things. Some stress that if we want to evangelize the modern man we must familiarize ourselves with the mind of the age.

This has come from the Free University of Amsterdam, that has been a stronghold of Calvinism. The whole emphasis is on what we have to do. Some Seminaries put the whole emphasis on our mastery of contemporary culture. But that is Arminianism!

f. Scholastic theology ... A new deism is with us now. Miracles cannot happen for God does not act like that now. They also reject the possibility of demon possession today and all is explained in terms of psychology. God stopped acting in that way after the time of the apostles and so the devil also gave up!

Christianity then is an acceptance of certain propositions—Deism. They are talking about God yet there is no personal knowledge of the living God. In some centres of Reformed learning there is no place for prayer meetings and they do not believe in revival—See Hodge and Warfield then Kuyper in Holland. An anti-pietistic attitude in Holland.

Acts of God

All this is wrong because it goes against the main message of the Bible. At the centre of the Bible are the wonderful works of God. Right through the Bible—the acts of God. Peter reminded readers of what they knew. God acting in the Garden, the Flood, the Tower of Babel, the call of Abraham, the patriarchs and Jacob at Bethel. Must we go back to Jacob to have personal relation with God. Moses, Joshua and all the prophets. All the time it is God's activity.

In the fullness of time, Jesus Christ. He came as a man. All His emphasis was on the works of God. His praying. He felt more in need of praying than we do! Then the Acts of the Apostles or rather the Book of the Acts of the Living Lord—'the things that Jesus began both to do and teach' (Acts 1:1). He is still acting. What has kept the church alive is God acting in revival. This is His main method down the centuries of building up the church. Revival is nothing but the direct activity of God the Holy Spirit. And as we study the Bible, let us remember that God is still acting which is the message of the Bible itself. If He is not acting then we are helpless and hopeless.

Supreme need

Our supreme need is to realize that God is alive. Robert Bayle at the end of the sixteenth and beginning of the seventeenth centuries established a lectureship to defend the faith. Bishop Butler was involved but Butler is dead and buried. But God acted as in the ministry of George Whitefield. In Malachi, God says to us: 'Prove me now'. I am there!

I have expanded so much energy reasoning the faith, what I am going to do now is not to give God peace until He acts. Nothing will convince people except the phenomenon and manifestation of the activity of God. We must keep this in front of all our preaching. We must concentrate on this for it is the central message of the Bible. Cast yourself utterly on this belief that God will act, He can act and will act in the lives of individuals and churches.

Do we really believe He can still do it? 'Try me', says God, 'Prove me' is his message to us. 'Cast your all upon me'!

APPENDIX 11

Faith healing

Lloyd-Jones's Address—Bala 1971

(Emyr Roberts' notes)

We have to accept the fact that organic diseases are healed sometimes. If it is a functional condition like rheumatism then that is easy to explain. But while we accept the fact of organic diseases sometimes being healed, we need not accept the explanation. In fact, the explanation may have nothing to do with Christianity. Sometimes a cancer condition can be healed.

Many diseases are caused by shock. For example, the commonest cause of gastric ulcers is strain and anxiety. This is true sometimes of cancer ... In our body there is a delicate sensitive nervous mechanism which protects our health. A shock may disturb this mechanism and bring about disease. Likewise, a shock may bring a cure ... What are the things that can bring a cure? Shock, faith, excitement, or it may be suggestive or even evil spirits. The majority of cures relate to functional illnesses.

Dorothy Kearin was in the last stages of spinal T.B. in 1912 when she had a vision. She claims that in this vision an angel spoke to her and informed her she would get up well. That is what she did and she became well. We have to accept the facts. But even organic cases can be cured in the same way. But we should not allow the phenomena to disturb our biblical faith. Kathryn Kuhlman tended to use a psychological approach. We can have temporary healings, but even organic healing— psychological and physical. We look at everything in the light of the Scriptures. We do not re-examine our theology or throw our theology overboard ... Probably the vast majority are functional or temporary improvements.

A man in Westminster had been healed of spinal T. B. by a Christian Scientist.[1] Because of this he could not say anything against Christian Science. Dr Lloyd-Jones (mentioned) a fact about most people who tend to add something to our illness. This was the case of this man—the surgeon had cured the organic condition. The Christian Scientist had cured the residual condition, the psychological additive (?). For two years the man confirmed that after X-ray he had been assured that he had never had spinal T.B.—the whole thing had been functional.

We must not denounce these people in public, but instruct our people in these things.

Test

I believe in the possibility of the Holy Spirit giving healing (like B. B. Warfield), but we must not ascribe healing automatically to the Holy Spirit.

The prayer of faith in James 5 verses 14–15 is itself a gift from God. The apostles never announced they were going to heal; they were given the faith at the time. Andrew Murray took the young man with him, having prayed for his healing and trusting he had been healed (yet) the young man died on the way. This faith is a gift ... There is a certainty in this prayer of faith given by the Spirit at the time.

We are told to test the spirits to prove them. So we can know when the Holy Spirit tells us. We must not quench the Spirit, but we must not believe all spirits. Gift of healing and gift of tongues—no one can say that he can do this at any time ...

APPENDIX 12

Importance of sharing our experiences

Discussion led by Dr Lloyd-Jones—Bala 1973

(Eryl Davies's notes)

Dr Lloyd-Jones chaired this discussion and many of the pastors participated as usual. There was freedom to express their thoughts and experiences as well as their fears concerning initiating an 'experience' meeting in their churches. As was his custom, the chairman interjected often to encourage members to enlarge on their statements or ensure their contributions were relevant. He always provided a masterly summary and concluding challenge at the end of a discussion session.

It is very important for us to share our experiences together.

Why have we dropped this exercise? Should we not restore it in our churches? It once had a prominent part in our churches in Wales two hundred years ago and remained so until the early part of the twentieth century but it degenerated into discussing the sermons of the previous Sunday or giving Bible verses. But the examination of experience was previously considered all-important.

Arthur Pritchard shared how he had started a 'seiat' ('fellowship'/'sharing'/'Society' meeting) after a lapse of twenty years in a small church of only fifty members. In March 1972 he was preaching there on a Sunday afternoon and halfway through his sermon a woman church-elder started weeping and trembling but he thought she was ill. However, he discovered she was under conviction of sin. At the end of the service, she shouted out, 'I am not fit to be a church elder, I am not a Christian if what the preacher says is true'. Over the next four to five weeks the woman changed and experienced grace and salvation.

Only a month or so later her husband and then her married son were also converted as well as another elder's wife. Spontaneously, these individuals expressed a desire to share their experiences and others also wanted to come, with some being under the conviction of sin.

I ask the question: why is there no, or little, sharing in our churches?

I suggest there are many reasons:
1. There is the false idea that a Christian should never be depressed but always joyful and victorious. Many modern

Christian biographies give this false picture of unending victory and blessedness in the Christian life compared with the honesty, sometimes depression, discouragement and sense of sin, of people like Robert Murray McCheyne, Howell Harris and George Whitefield.

2. Sometimes a theological wet blanket (of varying kinds) is thrown on anything which is experiential in Christianity. They are not comfortable with it. This is a most important factor.

3. The experiences of God that Howell Harris had are strange to us today yet normal for Harris. See John 14 and verse 17: 'The Spirit of truth, whom the world cannot receive, because it neither sees Him nor knows Him, but you know Him, for He dwells with you and will be in you'. What then is the relation of these words to the experiences of Howell Harris?

4. Three points can be made in this context about the sharing/fellowship meeting:

   a. There is biblical warrant for this kind of fellowship and sharing together: Malachi 3:16, Colossians 3:16, Ephesians 5:18–19 and Acts 2:42.

   b. A balanced relation must be maintained between sharing/fellowship and the Word and study of the Word. Such fellowship must only be a supplement, in addition, to a Bible study and preaching of the Word. It is not a substitute.

   c. Is there a limit on the numbers involved in an informal

fellowship meeting? The Calvinistic Methodists wisely divided their fellowship groups into small classes or groups.

5. There is a danger of introspection in such sharing meetings so we must shun this.

6. Another fear some have in holding a fellowship meeting is that a leader may feel he is not competent to handle and examine the experiences of others. However, Howell Harris started on this task without any previous experience at all!

7. Or there is a fear of exposing our own hearts or the hearts of others? Christians can be afraid to go beyond the surface of froth and bubble in so-called 'Christian fellowship' and be open and real with one another.

8. Confidence is needed in the individual leading the meeting. The wrong people leading can speak about the wrong things, mislead others and give entirely the wrong impressions to those in the group. Trust is important in anyone leading the fellowship meeting.

9. Do we 'quench the Spirit'? We have our timetables and hate disturbing our programmes and services or disturbing a Christian Union!

APPENDIX 13

Life and teaching

Lloyd-Jones's Closing Address—Bala 1973

Text: 1 Timothy 4 verse 16

(Eryl Davies's Notes)

We need to apply the truths we have heard in this Conference concerning Howell Harris.[1] A study of history should not just be 'objective' and thrilling. It is essential to use it rightly by learning from it. Is that true of us? Do we see ourselves as being the same as those men in the eighteenth century revival in Wales? No, we do not. What is our condition?

It is interesting to reflect on our current spiritual condition but I fear that we are far too much like those Dissenters in Wales before the revival broke out.

What was their condition? This can be described in four ways:

a. They were very able men with considerable knowledge, including theology. But they were very dry and their preaching was doctrinal, not evangelistic. Their sermons were long and full of points.

b. Their church doors were open but they made no attempt to get the people in or reach the people. They had lost every grain of zeal and crusading spirit.

c. Christian doctrine for them degenerated into a scheme of opinions. For them, a knowledge and mental acceptance of the Bible saves. That is Sandemanianism.

d. People in their churches would hear Bible teaching but there was no authority in the preaching. When revival came, the Holy Spirit fell upon preachers. The sermons were biblical and doctrinal but now they were endued with power and authority.

What impression do we give to our people? Are they impressed by our learning and knowledge? Or do we give comfort and grace through the preaching and do so tenderly? Do we think of them in their poor spiritual needs?

I want to consider with you verse 16 in 1 Timothy chapter 4 where Paul wants Timothy to keep a strict eye on himself as well as on his doctrine and teaching. We ourselves often lack balance. When I entered the ministry in 1927 there was a great lack of doctrine but today in our own circles it has gone to the other extreme where doctrine is everything. But it is not Christian experience and godliness as opposed to doctrine. We need both together and in balance

Notice that the apostle Paul places doctrine in verse 16 after taking heed to oneself. We would probably not do that and be suspicious of the order, but not the apostle Paul.

Reasons

Let me suggest some reasons why the apostle does this and does it deliberately under the guidance of the Holy Spirit.

1. The main object of Christian biblical doctrine is to produce this new man in Christ and conform us to Christ's likeness. We are being transformed by means of the truth of God's Word.

2. It is much easier to be vigilant over our doctrine than it is to be vigilant about ourselves and our sanctification. It is more painful to examine oneself and to be real and earnest in seeking Christ likeness.

3. To have the right doctrine but to be careless and unspiritual in one's own life is sheer hypocrisy. The doctrine is not doing us any spiritual good.

4. People judge us and the truth we preach by what we are in our lives and not only by what we say or believe. For example, often our society is outraged when a government minister's private life is corrupt or inconsistent. One's private life is important and we must apply this principle to ourselves as ministers.

5. The supreme end of preaching is the glory of God in bringing people to salvation in Christ.

6. The chief characteristic of a preacher is compassion, not learning, cleverness or eloquence. Compassion was the chief characteristic of our Lord; we must not display even our knowledge of doctrine.

7. There are particular dangers if we put the whole emphasis on doctrine and reverse the order of the text here. For example, there is pride of intellect. 'Knowledge puffs up' writes the apostle Paul, 'but love edifies' (1 Corinthians 8 verse 1). See how some of the Corinthian Christians had a wrong attitude towards knowledge in this first letter. They despised Paul because of his attitude to knowledge as he did not parade his knowledge and boast in it. Paul knew that the kingdom of God was not in word but in power. Without power, we are as useless as our critics.

The sin of Adam and Eve was pride of intellect as they were told by the serpent, 'you will be like God' (Genesis 3 verse 5) in terms of knowledge if they eat the forbidden fruit. Are we free from every display of learning and understanding? We have become drunk on education! The 'new' Evangelicals in America want to be recognized as scholars! But is this not pride?

The disagreement between Howell Harris and Daniel Rowland or between George Whitefield and John Wesley had a doctrinal element, of course, but the real cause was self. If you look at those disagreements, doctrine was not the cause, for after reunion in

Wales the doctrinal element remained and Howell Harris said, 'I was the first man out'.

Now if we do not take heed first to ourselves—and that before the doctrine, as Paul instructs Timothy—then we will experience what the early Dissenters witnessed, namely, God working through others and leaving us to one side so we will criticize what God is doing in and for others.

Questions for self-examination

To aid us in taking heed to ourselves and encourage a balanced self-examination, I recommend to you the twelve questions that Jonathan Edwards used at the end of each day as he examined before God how he had lived. These questions are most helpful.

Did I awake spiritually and with biblical thoughts in my mind?

Have I been nearer to God in times of prayer?

Has my faith been weakened or strengthened today?

Have I walked by faith throughout the day?

Have I preferred other people before myself?

Have I redeemed the time or wasted valuable time?

Have I kept the issues of my heart in the means of grace?

What have I done for the bodies and souls of God's dear people?

Has money been saved by me today for God's work?

Has my tongue been used to speak words of grace and wisdom today?

Have I denied myself?

Do my life and conversation adorn the gospel of Christ?

This is part of what it means to take heed to ourselves. May God give us grace to do this for his own glory.

APPENDIX 14

The place of extraordinary phenomena in Revival

Lloyd-Jones's Address—Bala 1978

(Eryl Davies's Notes)

This is a most important question for us as it concerns the subject of revival. We are reminding ourselves of a forgotten dimension and it is appropriate to do so as this is the centenary of the birth of Evan Roberts.

The churches in Wales today are in a sad condition and without the 1904–05 revival, churches would have been far worse than what they are. The 'spiritually alive' people in churches in Wales when I preached in the country fifty years ago were the revival converts. There is no doubt about that.

Appendix 14: Extraordinary Phenomena in Revival—Bala 1978

I was brought up in a Welsh Presbyterian chapel in Llangeitho—linked historically to Daniel Rowland—where revival was frowned upon. The chief elder and minister had the same attitude towards revival. My father too tended to have this view so I grew up with prejudice and a more intellectual approach to the subject. But in 1913 on reading a small booklet about Howell Harris my outlook towards revival changed. However, I was brought up as a child and early teenager in religion but not Christianity. Later I began to experience something of this realm of the Holy Spirit and in 1927 went into the Christian Ministry at Sandfields, Aberavon and I regularly began to meet in various places more and more of 'the children' of the 1904 revival.

1. Revival itself is a phenomenon. It is something happening that people in the world become aware of whereas we are not aware of regeneration occurring within an individual. I emphasize this fact. Crusades and missions tend to distract people from revival but having heard so much about revival one cannot be satisfied with anything less.

2. Nor is revival the same as renewal in the Charismatic Movement. Renewal is a substitute for revival. Renewal tells us that everyone is baptised at regeneration, therefore people are told that 'all are baptised' and all have great potential within them and only need to surrender. Renewal is what you and I have to do or realize whereas in revival it is something in which we do nothing. The Holy Spirit 'falls' upon us and that is revival. Do not allow anything to stand between us and revival.

Evan Roberts was a phenomenon. He was an ordinary young

man and not unusually gifted either. But he felt a burden and his prayer was 'bend me' and the burden was with him for six months. What happened was the Holy Spirit fell on him and he fell to the ground unconscious in Blaenannerch in Cardiganshire. Some thought he was dead but he soon got up as a new man, claiming he had been baptised in the Holy Spirit.

His teacher was furious because Evan was not studying but the teacher was told: 'be careful, for the Holy Spirit is dealing with this young man!' Then Evan Roberts said he felt commanded by God to go home to the prayer meeting which would be full.

3. For the next ten years and longer, we will have to argue over whether or not God still deals directly and personally with people and gives them messages!

Evan Roberts received messages and it was a phenomenon. One morning when he was staying in his bedroom, a young man called to see him. He had walked sixteen miles from nearby Lampeter and he felt he must see Evan Roberts. He had been privileged to have a great experience of the Lord but his parents had told him to leave their home so he was in great distress. Evan Roberts was informed only of the fact that the young man wanted to see him but he refused to see him because he had been given no liberty by the Holy Spirit. While the young man was desperate Roberts still refused to see him so his aunt pleaded with her nephew to at least give the young man a message. He agreed and without knowing the situation at all, he sent the message: 'When my father and mother forsake me, then the Lord will take care of me' (Psalm 27:10). Those words of Scripture brought great peace and joy to the visitor.

In one meeting in Liverpool, Evan Roberts said publicly there was a man in the congregation trying to mesmerise him. That was true and the man confessed to it publicly.

On another occasion, a revival meeting he was leading was 'dead' with nothing happening. In the pulpit Evan Roberts sat and was in spiritual agony. Eventually he said there was a man resisting the Holy Spirit in the meeting and told him to leave. But no one left. Then Roberts said to one man: 'you are lying—you have not given up smoking, and the pipe and pouch are still in your pocket'! This had an electrifying effect upon the man and the congregation.

I knew a minister in South Wales who was a hopeless preacher and his church was dying. After preaching for the man, I had supper with him and he talked to me about the revival.

He had been a student in Trefecca College (a Presbyterian College near Brecon) when revival broke out. One day a teacher was lecturing on the Atonement at 10.00am and the man remembers him starting the lecture but the next time he remembered was 11.50am when he got up off his knees after being unconscious for that length of time!

The Rev. Dr Conolwyn Pugh was famous in his younger years as a cornet player in Eisteddfodau (local and national Welsh cultural festivals). He was brought up in Porth, Rhondda, and his father was a coal miner. Music was everything to this young man and he was doing well in his music lessons. Then the 1904 revival came. Most evenings he was by himself practising his cornet and only returned home about 10.00pm. But when he returned, the house was in darkness as his family were in the revival meeting and this made him very angry.

One evening he was scheduled to be the chief artist in a music concert in the nearby town of Pontypridd. He was ready for supper but no one was home and in a rage he walked to the church with the motive of making as much damage as possible. But the church was crowded and he managed to get into the backseat on the right hand side. The next thing he remembered was getting up off his knees under the pulpit. Struggling to walk, he walked over people and seats while praying for his father!

Daniel Rowland in the eighteenth century saw one drunken man sobered within a second and saved in a preaching meeting in revival.

The Rev. D. S. Jones, Bridgend, was not an intellectual but he was a godly man. While I was the minister in Sandfields, Aberavon, he came weekly for afternoon tea to our home. Why? Because he was a depressive and discouraged. When he came to us, he talked about revival and that was the cure for him!

He related to me a story about tramps. He had gone home from a revival meeting one evening and was awakened from sleep about 2.00am. He told his wife he was being told to pray by the side of the bed. His wife asked: 'who is telling you to do that?' His answer was immediate: 'God', but his wife thought he was mad and urged him to go back into bed and sleep. He tried but was unable to settle so he eventually got out of bed again. He informed his wife that God wanted him to go to the church at 7-30 that morning where he would find a number of tramps; he was to give them breakfast and speak to them about the gospel.

That is what he did. He found the exact number of tramps waiting for him then, unarranged by anyone, a lady appeared with breakfast for the men! This happened each day.

There was a great sequel to this story. The revival ended in 1906 and D. S. Jones did not know what to do now the revival was finished. He could not really preach and felt it was of the 'flesh' to prepare sermons.

In 1911 he was in a Convention with his brother in London Kingsway and in the afternoon meeting there were several Keswick-type speakers. The meeting was dull and without any spark but suddenly D. S. Jones's brother turned to him and commanded him to go to the front, but he was afraid to make a fool of himself. Eventually he did and stood in the front. At that point, a man in charge of a horse-drawn cab came and greeted him, identifying himself as one of the tramps he had fed and spoken to years earlier! It was this cab-driver, the ex-tramp, who then gave his story to the congregation and the meeting was alive.

People fainted under the ministry of John Wesley but not so much under George Whitefield; they fainted too under the preaching of John Berridge of Everton and folk were carried out unconscious under the heavenly power present in the meeting and these individuals were left on the floor in a barn for two or three hours until they came around!

Jonathan Edwards's wife was also overpowered and rendered unconscious often under the power of the Holy Spirit in revival and overwhelmed by the love of God in Christ. She also levitated on one occasion from one part of a room to another.

Here is supra-normal activity. Some Calvinistic Methodists in the eighteenth century in the Llangeitho area were nicknamed 'Jumpers' because of the ecstasy they experienced under the influence of revival preaching. Daniel Rowland defended this as not being necessarily spurious and felt there should be no interference with the work of the Holy Spirit.

Again, there were reliable reports of 'heavenly singing' in some revivals in Wales as in Beddgelert in North West Wales (1817–1821) when there was remarkable and beautiful singing 'in the air' which often overwhelmed the folk who heard it.

APPENDIX 15

2 Timothy 1:7

Lloyd-Jones's closing message—Bala 1978

(Eryl Davies's Notes)

In 2 Timothy 1, notice especially verse 6 where Paul places a responsibility on the young Timothy 'to stir up the gift of God'. That is something the young pastor is exhorted to do and to be active in. Paul is writing to a discouraged pastor in the New Testament period.

In verse 7 Paul refers to 'a spirit of fear'. This does not refer to a bondage or fear in relation to salvation but a more natural fear. It is a fear of circumstances, conditions and the future. Paul himself was in prison and in ill health as well. Timothy was dependent on this older man and possibly over dependent. There were rumours that Paul was going to be martyred. Then there were rumours and troubles in the churches so Timothy was nervous, apprehensive, tending to despair with a kind of paralysis which fear can produce in us.

Now this is one of our problems today as it is a very difficult time in which to live and preach. There is considerable confusion, criticism, stress, pressure, even ridicule because we are and remain evangelicals. Some people regard us with contempt so we tend to be fearful. Then the future is so uncertain and the fact that revival has not come exposes us to more discouragement. How long will it go on like this?

However, Paul says such an attitude is wrong and a denial of all that we stand for: 'For God has not given us a spirit of fear ...' Timothy has fallen from what he himself knew when in ordination hands were laid on him by presbytery. Now he must stir that gift up which God had given him.

Do we know the Holy Spirit? A man can go into the Christian ministry without knowing the Holy Spirit. This is true of some in Wales, including some who are poet-ministers and heavily involved in Eisteddfodau (Welsh language literary, arts and musical festivals). But do we ourselves know the constraint of the Holy Spirit? Is this true in our preaching? There is a difference between natural oratory and freedom and then being used by the Holy Spirit in preaching.

'Power'

What then has God given to us? He has given us 'power'. In Acts 1 verse 8 the disciples were to wait in Jerusalem until they received power. That is a very surprising statement. They had knowledge and they were witnesses of the Lord's life, teaching, miracles and life-style. The Lord taught them a considerable amount and they witnessed his death and especially his resurrection, then ascension to heaven in triumph. In one sense, they had it all but no, they must stay and they cannot witness until they receive the power of the Holy Spirit.

'Power' is one of the chief characteristics of the apostles' witness and preaching. That is clear in 1 Corinthians 2 verses 4–5 and 1 Thessalonians 1 verse 5. If we are downcast, is it because we are lacking in power? There is a danger of substituting other things for this power. Here are some examples:

a. We may claim that all we need is the Word which is understood as the Reformed faith. That is everything and all we need. Scripture is, of course, sufficient but Scripture alone is inadequate without the working of the Holy Spirit.

b. Others put more emphasis on scholarship and this has been a tendency since the 1870s when learning and degrees have been given considerable prominence over other things. For example, in the 1830s Cardinal Newman saw the Church of England as very mixed. Despite his evangelical conversion in Oxford, he saw that evangelicals were not intellectually respectable and lacked intellectual leaders. He recognised they would have no impact on the University or country so he looked for 'power' which would impact people. Mistakenly, he felt he had found that power in sacerdotalism so the Oxford Movement emerged, influencing the Anglican church profoundly. Newman was seeking power but he found a substitute.

c. Or new and better methods and emphases are sought after, often alongside activities. For example, David Shepherd the South Wales evangelist from Gorseinon started to use a musical instrument like a concertina in evangelistic meetings, but his father who had experienced the 1904 revival was extremely unhappy with this and told his son. The son's reply was very significant: 'yes, but you had the Holy Spirit with you in revival!'

Pentecostals talk more about the Holy Spirit but they are noisy, and often guilty of working up emotions. But someone like Howell Harris in the eighteenth century did not resort to any of these things I have mentioned. All he did was read a book to people in their homes and that was before and after his experience in Llangasty church. However, there was power there. Nothing avails but the power of the Holy Spirit.

'Invigorates'

But what does this power do? The Holy Spirit powerfully invigorates and illumines the mind with regard to the truth of God's Word. But He does more. The Holy Spirit gives 'boldness' and courage as in Acts 4 verses 29–31.

That is a characteristic of believers and preachers in Acts. Howell Harris use to refer to the 'old authority' or power which they knew. Prophecy in 1 Corinthians 14 is preaching the Word but with this authority. When on one occasion George Whitefield was preaching in America, Samuel Davies said of him, 'a poor sermon but there was authority there'. And that is our great need today. Critics and opponents think they can answer and defeat us in argument. But they are no match for the power of the Holy

Spirit! Rather than complain, we must seek a manifestation of this divine power in our lives and preaching.

'Love'

'Love' accompanies, and is a prerequisite of power for it is a loving power which the Holy Spirit manifests, not a carnal, wild and harsh power. There is love permeating this exercise of divine power. In what sense?

To begin with, when the Holy Spirit is working powerfully we know in a more real way God's love to us as in Romans 5:5. This is an antidote to fear which comes upon us and makes us uncertain of God in His dealings with us.

There is also a love for one another. Think of the list which Paul gives in 2 Timothy of people who wronged him. See chapter 1 and verse 15 as well as chapter 4 where he refers to Demas and Alexander in verses 10, 14–15. Then in verse 11 he makes the request: 'get Mark and bring him with you, for he is useful to me for ministry'. Here is an expression of love for Mark in the light of what had happened earlier.

In Acts 15 at the end of the first missionary journey, Paul and Barnabas had a sharp disagreement over whether or not Mark should accompany them on their next missionary trip. Paul refused to accept Mark as a co-worker again because of what Mark had done (Acts 15:36–40). However, Paul now shows love and forgiveness towards Mark and wants his fellowship and assistance in the ministry.

Love the brethren

We must not criticize one another and doubt the brethren. Jealousy and envy are sins. We are to love the brethren as well as our enemies. Being disgruntled and then having a bad, critical attitude will never be covered by orthodoxy! Love the brethren.

Love unbelievers

But this love is also expressed towards unbelieving people. Have we got this love for them? We must not be afraid of the world of people but we are to love them with the love of Christ which the Holy Spirit gives us. Why did the Lord Jesus leave heaven and enter this sinful world of people? The answer is in John chapter 3:16, namely, God's amazing love for sinners.

'a sound mind'

By a 'sound mind', Paul means a disciplined mind in which we exercise self-control of our thoughts and reactions. Is this an anti-climax to what he has already said? No, not at all. Here is application. What he is saying is: 'what you need to do is to pull yourself together; do not give in to your feelings and thoughts of self-pity by feeling sorry for yourself. Discipline yourself. Do not let circumstances overwhelm you!'

This happened in some measure to Moses when he found himself and his people in an impossible situation in front of the Red Sea. There was no way of escape for them as the Egyptian army approached from behind and the mountains on either side then the water ahead. Moses was praying but God told him to get off his knees and strike the water with his rod and see the miracle he would perform.

'Preach to ourselves'

One of our greatest defects is that we do not preach to ourselves as preachers. We must talk to ourselves more! David did that in Psalm 73:15–17. He felt his feet had slipped but he could not give up. Has God called me to moan and complain all the time? No. There is need for us to discipline our thoughts and to think biblically. We have a big gospel, a great God and we are involved in a great work! So here in 2 Timothy 1, Timothy is told to have a 'sound mind' and apply the truth to himself.

When the Calvinistic Methodist preacher, Michael Jones, was due to preach in one Association meeting, the church leaders and a crowded congregation were waiting for the preacher to arrive. Where was he? A young servant girl was sent to see where he was. After she had arrived at the house where he was lodging and approached the door of his room, she returned to report he was talking to someone so did not interrupt him. They sent her back to urge him to come. This time she listened outside his door and heard him say: 'without You, I will not go and preach ...' When she informed the church leaders of these words, they were content. They knew he was in earnest prayer, pleading with the Lord to be with him in power in his preaching for that service.

And that is what happened on this occasion. Do we know anything about this dimension—the presence, power and love of God? Is there authority in our preaching?

Let us resolve to seek him our Living God and his power for ministry.

Bibliography

Andrew Atherstone & David Ceri Jones (eds.), *Engaging with Martyn Lloyd-Jones: The Life and Legacy of "the Doctor"* (Nottingham: IVP, 2011).

W. Ambrose Bebb, *Yr Argyfwng* (Llandybie: Llyfrau'r Dryw, 1956).

John Bencher, *Martyn Lloyd-Jones (1899–1981) And twentieth-Century Evangelicalism* (Carlisle: Paternoster Press, 2002).

Callum G. Brown, *The Death of Christian Britain: Understanding Secularisation* (London: Routledge, 2001).

Roger L. Brown, *Evangelicals in the Church in Wales*, (Welshpool: Tair Eglwys Press, 2007).

Iain D. Campbell & Malcom Maclean (Editors), *The People's Theologian: Writings in Honour of Donald Macleod,* (Fearn: Christian Focus Publications, 2011).

Paul Chambers, Religion, *Secularization and Social Change in Wales: Congregational Studies in a Post-Christian Society* (Cardiff: University of Wales Press, 2005).

Paul E. G. Cook, *Fire from Heaven: Times of Extraordinary Revival* (Darlington: Evangelical Press, 2009).

D. Eryl Davies, *Dr D. Martyn Lloyd-Jones* (Darlington: Evangelical Press, 2011).

D. Eryl Davies, *An Angry God: What the Bible says about Wrath, Final Judgement and Hell* (Bridgend: Evangelical Press of Wales, 1991).

D. Eryl Davies, *The Beddgelert Revival* (Bridgend: Bryntirion Press, 2004).

D. P. Davies, *Against the Tide: Christianity in Wales on the Threshold of a New Millennium* (Gomer Press: Llandysul, 1995).

Dewi Eirug Davies, *Diwinyddiaeth Yng Nghymru 1927–1977* (Gomer Press: Llandysul, 1984).

Gaius Davies, *Genius, Grief and Grace: A Doctor Looks At Suffering and Success* (Fearn: Christian Focus, 2001).

Noel A. Davies, *A History of Ecumenism in Wales: 1956–1990* (Cardiff: University of Wales Press, 2008).

J. Elwyn Davies, *O! Ryfedd Ras* (Pen-y-bont ar Ogwr: Gwasg Bryntirion, 1998).

J. Elwyn Davies, *Striving Together: The Evangelical Movement of Wales—its principles and aims* (Bridgend: Evangelical Press of Wales, 1984).

John Davies, *Hanes Cymru: A History of Wales in Welsh* (London: Penguin Books, 1992).

John Emyr (ed.), *A Father in the Faith: J. Elwyn Davies* (Bridgend: Bryntirion Press, 2012).

John Emyr, (golygydd) *Porth yr Aur: Cofio J.Elwyn Davies* (Pen-y-bont ar Ogwr: Gwasg Bryntirion, 2011)

Joe England, *The Wales TUC 1974–2004: Devolution and Industrial Politics* (Cardiff: University of Wales Press, 2004).

Eifion Evans, *Daniel Rowland and the Great Evangelical Awakening in Wales* (Edinburgh: Banner of Truth Trust: 1985).

Eifion Evans, *When He is Come: The 1858–1860 Revival in Wales* (London/Bridgend: Evangelical Press and the Evangelical Movement of Wales, 1967).

Eifion Evans, *Two Welsh Revivalists: Humphrey Jones, Dafydd Morgan and the 1859 Revival in Wales* (Bridgend: Evangelical Library of Wales, 1985).

Philip H. Eveson (ed.), *When God Came to North Wales* (Weston Rhyn: Quinta Press, 2010).

Geraint D. Fielder, *'Excuse me, Mr Davies—Hallelujah!': Evangelical

Student witness in Wales 1923–1983 (Bridgend: Evangelical Press of Wales/Inter-Varsity Press, 1983).

Timothy George (ed.), *J.I. Packer and the Evangelical Future: The Impact of his Life and Thought* (Grand Rapids: Baker Academic, 2009).

Noel Gibbard, *R.B.Jones: Gospel Ministry in Turbulent Times* (Bridgend: Bryntirion Press, 2009).

Noel Gibbard, *Cofio Hanner Canrif: Hanes Mudiad Efengylaidd Cymru 1948–1998* (Penybont ar Ogwr: Gwasg Bryntirion, 2000)

George Griffiths, *What God Hath Wrought: A Brief Account of the History of the Tro'r Glien Mission Hall, Cwmtwrch* on the Occasion of its Half-Centenary Celebrations, 1962.

Adrian Hastings, *A History of English Christianity: 1920–1985* (London: Collins, 1986).

Doreen Irvine, *Classics from Doreen Irvine* (Eastbourne: Kingsway Publications: Omnibus edition, 2001).

Iwan and Julie Rhys Jones, (eds.) *Diwinydda Ddoe a Heddiw* (Bridgend: WEST/Bryntirion Press, 2012).

D. Martyn Lloyd-Jones: Letters 1919–1981 (Edinburgh: Banner of Truth Trust, 1994).

D. Martyn Lloyd-Jones, *Romans: Exposition of chapters 3:20–4:25:*

Atonement and Justification (London: Banner of Truth Trust, 1970).

D. Martyn Lloyd-Jones, *Preaching and Preachers*, (London: Hodder and Stoughton, 1971).

R. Tudur Jones, *Hanes Annibynwyr Cymru* (Abertawe: Undeb yr Annibynwyr Cymraeg (Union of Welsh Independents), 1966).

J. Douglas MacMillan, *The God of All Grace: J.Douglas MacMillan, Preacher and Teacher* (Fearn: Christian Focus Publications, 1997).

E.L.Mascall, Graham Leonard, Colin Buchanan and James Packer, *Growth into Union* (London: SPCK, 1970).

Michael McMullen, *God's Polished Arrow W.C.Burns: Revival Preacher* (Fearn: Christian Focus Publications, 2000).

D. Densil Morgan, *The Span of the Cross: Christian Religion and Society in Wales 1914–2000* (Cardiff: University of Wales Press, 1999).

D. Densil Morgan, *Barth Reception in Britain* (London: T & T Clark International, 2010).

Iain H. Murray, *David Martyn Lloyd-Jones: The First Forty Years: 1899–1939*: Volume 1 (Edinburgh: Banner of Truth Trust, 1982).

Iain H. Murray, *D Martyn Lloyd-Jones: The Fight of Faith, 1939–1981*: Volume 2 (Edinburgh: Banner of Truth Trust, 1990).

Iain H. Murray, *Diary of Kenneth Macrae edited with additional material* (Edinburgh: Banner of Truth Trust, 1980).

T. A. Noble, *Tyndale House and the First Sixty Years* (Leicester: Inter-Varsity Press, 2006).

James I. Packer, *Fundamentalism and the Word of God* (London: Inter-Varsity Press: 1958).

Colin & Mary Peckham, *Sounds From Heaven: The Revival on the Isle of Lewis, 1949–1952* (Fearn: Christian Focus, 2004).

Robert Pope, *Codi Muriau Dinas Duw: Anghydffurfiaeth ac Anghydffurfwyr Cymru'r Ugeinfed Ganrif* [trans: *Raising the Walls of the City of God: The Nonconformity and Nonconformists of Twentieth Century Wales*]; Bangor Centre for Postgraduate Studies of Religion in Wales, (Cardiff: University of Wales Press, 2005).

D. Ben Rees, *Ymgyrchu Dros Yr Efengyl Ym Môn (1921–1979)* ['Campaigning For The Gospel in Anglesey *1921–1979*'] (Llangoed: Capel Tŷ Rhys, 2010).

Emyr Roberts and Wyn James, *Robert Roberts: Yr Angel o Glynnog* (Bridgend: Evangelical Library of Wales, 1976).

Emyr Roberts and R. Geraint Gruffydd, 'Revival' in *Revival & Its Fruit* (Bridgend: Evangelical Library of Wales, 1981).

Emyr Roberts, *Cyrraedd Trwy'r Glustog* (Denbigh: Gwasg Gee, 1971).

Duncan Tanner, Chris Williams and Deian Hopkin, editors, *The Labour Party in Wales 1900–2000* (Cardiff: University of Wales Press, 2000).

This is That (London: Christian Literature Crusade: 1954).

Arthur Wallis, *In the Day of Thy Power: the Scriptural Principles of Revival* (London: Christian Literature Crusade, 1956).

Gwyn Walters (editors: Eifion Evans and Lynn Quigley), *The Sovereign Spirit: The Doctrine of the Holy Spirit in the Writings of John Calvin,* (Edinburgh: Rutherford House, 2009).

Rob Warner, *Reinventing English Evangelicalism 1966–2001* (Carlisle: Paternoster, 2007).

William Williams, *The Experience Meeting: An Introduction to the Welsh Societies of the Evangelical Awakening,* translated by Mrs Bethan Lloyd-Jones with an Introduction by Dr Martyn Lloyd-Jones (Bridgend: Evangelical Movement of Wales, 1973; New Edition, Vancouver: Regent College Publications, 2003).

Endnotes

Chapter 1

1. The details have been researched since 1995.

2. See the author's popular '*Bite-size*' biography: *Dr D Martyn Lloyd-Jones* (EP Books: Darlington: 2011).

3. For Welsh language readers, see the author's 'Cynhadledd Gweinidogion Efengylaidd Cymru 1955–2008' in *Diwinydda Ddoe a Heddiw,* (Editors Iwan a Julie Rhys Jones; WEST/Bryntirion Press, 2012), 145–185.

4. Some details are recorded by Geraint D. Fielder in *Excuse me, Mr. Davies— Hallelujah!: Evangelical Student Witness in Wales 1923–1983* (Bridgend: Evangelical Press of Wales/Inter-Varsity Press: 1983), 82–85.

5. He was appointed Professor of the Philosophy of Religion in the Presbyterian Church of Wales's United Theological College, Aberystwyth in 1953.

6. *Excuse me, Mr. Davies ...*, 82.

Chapter 2

1. 'I was there! Eluned Thomas and Mari Morgan recall the 1945 Llanelli campaign', *Evangelical Magazine of Wales* (Vol. 37 No.4, August/September, 1998), 7–8.

2. *Y Cylchgrawn* (Vol.1, No. 5, July-August 1949), 46.

3. He died aged 93 in 2013. He also pastored in Caernarfon (1953) and Seion, Llanelli (1958) before moving to pastor churches in California. He was an author, seminary teacher and a BBC Welsh Radio Correspondent.

4. Herbert Evans reporting in the first Welsh language Evangelical Magazine of Wales (*Y Cylchgrawn*). See Vol. 1, No. 1, November-December 1948, 'Yma a Thraw', 39–40.

5. *Cyflwyniad*, page 1.

6. *Y Cylchgrawn Efengylaidd* (Cyfrol 1, Rhif 2, Ionawr-Chwefror 1949), 35–36.

7. Elwyn describes the experience in Welsh in *O! Ryfedd Ras* (Pen-y-bont ar Ogwr: Gwasg Bryntirion, 1998), 18–20.

Chapter 3

1. This began as an independent mission during the 1882 Fair led by Frank and Seth Joshua. The meetings were in the open air, then a tent and a disused Baptist chapel. The mission was so successful that a building was erected in 1884 under the Presbyterian Church of Wales.

2. 'Y Gynhadledd', *Y Cylchgrawn*, Vol. 2, No. 9, 15.

3. 47.

4. *Y Cylchgrawn Efengylaidd* (Vol. 3, No. 2, Autumn 1954), 46.

5. 47.

6. 48.

7. 'Eisteddfod Dolgellau' in *Y Cylchgrawn Efengylaidd* (Vol. 1, No. 6, September-October 1949), 13–15.

8. Iain H. Murray refers to this meeting in *D. Martyn Lloyd-Jones: The Fight of Faith, 1939–1981* Volume 2, (Edinburgh: Banner of Truth, 1990), 210–211.

9. 'Eisteddfod Dolgellau,' 14.

10. A written report to me, 13 March 1996, by Rev. Vernon Salkeld, one of the Cliff College students in this mission and an eye witness. 'Looking back', he added, 'this was a unique and very moving time of blessing and movement of the Holy Spirit'. Mr Salkeld was pastor of Ogmore-by-Sea Evangelical Church in the Vale of Glamorgan.

Chapter 4

1. Inter-Varsity Fellowship (now re-named UCCF, namely, Universities, Colleges Christian Fellowship) is a network of student-led evangelical Christian Unions in UK Universities/Colleges.

2. The Bible Training School which R. B. Jones established in Porth, Rhondda, South Wales, 1919.

3. Reference to the West Wales Conventions and the Keswick-in-Wales Convention in Llandrindod Wells.

4. Rev. 'Nantlais' Williams, Ammanford, 1874–1959, pastored Bethany Welsh Presbyterian Church, Ammanford.

5. *Yr Efengylydd*.

6. Established/supported by men like R. B. Jones, W. S. Jones, W. W. Lewis, O. M. Owen and Keri Evans for the purpose of evangelism. The readers of *Yr Efengylydd* supported this work.

7. Established in 1886 as an evangelistic, interdenominational society. See chapter 6 for links with Duncan Campbell.

8. 1869–1933. Noel Gibbard has written a helpful biography: *R. B. Jones: Gospel Ministry in Turbulent Times* (Bridgend: Bryntirion Press, 2009).

9. An Englishman born in 1873, he pastored churches in Canada, including Jarvis Street Baptist Church, Toronto from 1910 until his death in 1955.

10. '*Observations made by the late Dr Martyn Lloyd-Jones explaining why he kept separate from the pre-war Evangelicals in Wales*'. Undated. There is reference to the 'attached letter' which is missing.

11. W. S. Jones (1860–1933) was a Baptist and ministered in Carmarthen with W. W. Lewis (1856–1938), a Presbyterian and Keri Evans (1860–1941), Congregationalist. All three spoke in the West Wales Conventions.

12. In 1896, the Ministers' and Missionaries' Prayer-Union was formed within the Presbyterian Church of Wales. By 1901, there were 403 members, an

13. Dr Lloyd-Jones observed: 'I felt God's hand was on these young men. I liked their approach ... it was important that it had a Welsh character ... Several of the young men now saw the campaigns and the conference as servants of the church. Under God they were used to produce evangelical ministers and, to a lesser extent, evangelical churches ...'. *Excuse me, Mr. Davies ...*, 158.

14. Andrew Atherstone & David Ceri Jones (Editors), *Engaging with Martyn Lloyd-Jones: The Life and Legacy of 'the Doctor'* (Nottingham: IVP, 2011), 72–75.

15. *Excuse me, Mr. Davies*, 149.

16. *Excuse me, Mr. Davies*, 151.

17. *Engaging with Martyn Lloyd-Jones*, 75.

18. *Excuse me, Mr. Davies ...*, 157–158.

19. *Engaging with Martyn Lloyd-Jones*, 75–76.

20. *Excuse me, Mr. Davies ...*, 158.

21. Other examples will be given in a later chapter.

Chapter 5

1. This term has been qualified in different ways since the 1950s. However,

---

increase of 51 over the previous year. Over the following decade, numbers decreased significantly. Its purpose was to encourage members to pray each Sunday morning for revival and their preaching. By 1901, the Keswick influence on this Prayer-Union was strong.

this is how the term was used at that time. For the Conference, the term continues to retain its original meaning.

2. Minutes of the second meeting of the Evangelical Presbyterian Ministers' Fellowship, January 21, 1955.

3. 2.]

4. The International Missionary Council for Wales was established in 1921 as an interdenominational Christian organisation; to co-ordinate the work of Protestant 'sending societies' and 'field bodies' (overseas). The IMCW, in 1961, was adopted by the World Council of Churches as its Commission on World Mission and Evangelism. The former IMCW was renamed the United Missionary Council for Wales (UMCW). The UMCW Conference declined by the late 1950s.

5. Minutes of the Third Meeting of the Evangelical Presbyterian Ministers' Fellowship, April 22, 1955: 1.

6. Minutes of The Sixth Meeting of the Evangelical Presbyterian Ministers' Fellowship, April 2, 1956.

7. Minutes of the Seventh Meeting of the Evangelical Presbyterian Ministers' Fellowship, October 11, 1956.

8. Minutes of the Joint Meeting of the Evangelical Presbyterian Ministers' Fellowship and the Monmouthshire Ministers' Prayer Group held on January 25, 1957 in Central Hall, Newport.

9. Rev. W. K. Sharman (popularly known as 'Jack') was the minister of Heath Presbyterian Church, Cardiff, 1954–1961. He and his wife were missionaries

in China and married there in 1938. They were among the last missionaries to leave China in 1950. He was ordained into the Presbyterian Church in 1951, assuming pastoral charge of churches in Saltmead and Clive Road, Cardiff, for three years.

10. Minutes of the Meeting of Representatives of the EMW General Committee and the Evangelical Presbyterian Ministers' Fellowship, June 1957.

Chapter 6

1. Adrian Hastings, *A History of English Christianity 1920–1985* (London: Collins, 1986), 290.

2. Callum G. Brown, *The Death of Christian Britain: Understanding Secularisation* (London: Routledge 2001), 214.

3. Noel Gibbard, *Cofio Hanner Canrif: Hanes Mudiad Efengylaidd Cymru 1948–1998*, (Pen-y-bont: Gwasg Bryntirion, 2000), 74–79.

4. Hanner Canrif, 75.

5. This succeeded Urdd y Deyrnas which had functioned effectively at local level in Wales.

6. *A History of Ecumenism in Wales: 1956–1990*, Noel A. Davies (Cardiff: University of Wales Press, 2008).

7. *A History of Ecumenism in Wales*, 199.

8. *D. Martyn Lloyd-Jones: The Fight of Faith*, 431.

9. His research was only published in 2009. See *The Sovereign Spirit: The Doctrine of the Holy Spirit in the Writings of John Calvin*, Gwyn Walters. Editors: Eifion Evans and Lynn Quigley (Edinburgh: Rutherford House, 2009).

Chapter 7

1. June 17–20, 1956.

2. E-mail correspondence 16 August 2013.

3. 'The Revival in the Hebrides', 144–147.

4. *Y Cylchgrawn Efengylaidd* (Vol. 2, No. 6, June-September 1952), 23–28.

5. Colin & Mary Peckham, *Sounds From Heaven: The Revival on the Isle of Lewis, 1949–1952* (Fearn: Christian Focus, 2004), 48.

6. *Sounds From Heaven*, 37.

7. See also *The People's Theologian: Writings in Honour of Donald Macleod*, edited by Iain D. Campbell and Malcom Maclean (Fearn, Christian Focus Publications, 2011), 58–59.

8. *Diary of Kenneth Macrae edited with additional material by Iain Murray* (Edinburgh: Banner of Truth Trust, 1980), 442.

9. Duncan Campbell spent his first five years of ministry in the Faith Mission, an interdenominational evangelistic society established in 1886 and serving throughout the United Kingdom and Ireland with its own Bible College in

Edinburgh. Campbell then served in three pastorates (United Free Church of Scotland), rejoining the Faith Mission in 1949.

10. *Sounds From Heaven,* 137–282.

11. Iain H. Murray claims the charge was justified; see *Diary of Kenneth Macrae,* 444.

12. E-mail correspondence 16 August 2013.

13. The Annual Lecture of the Evangelical Library 1956: *The Faith of the English Reformers: The Foundation of their Doctrine Examined,* Iain H. Murray (London: The Evangelical Library, 1956).

14. *The Faith of the English Reformers,* 5.

15. *The Faith of the English Reformers,* 6–8.

16. *The Faith of the English Reformers,* 9–10.

17. *The Faith of the English Reformers,* 15–16.

18. *The Faith of the English Reformers,* 17.

19. *The Faith of the English Reformers,* 19.

20. Email correspondence 16 August 2013.

21. Email correspondence 19 August 2013.

22. See Appendix One for notes of this address.

23. Notes, Emyr Roberts.

Chapter 8

1. *This is That* (London: Christian Literature Crusade: 1954)

2. Interview on 13 May 1997.

3. An outline of the address is included as Appendix Two.

4. He often used this illustration as in the 1978 Conference.

5. Notes, Emyr Roberts.

6. *D. Martyn Lloyd-Jones: Letters 1919–1981* (Edinburgh: Banner of Truth Trust: 1994), 137.

7. 'Cilgwyn 1958', *Evangelical Magazine of Wales*, Vol.1, No.8, (Aug/Sept.1958), 44.

8. 'Cilgwyn 1958', 46.

9. James I. Packer, *Fundamentalism and the Word of God* (London: Inter-Varsity Press,1958).

10. T. A. Noble, *Tyndale House and the First Sixty Years* (Leicester: Inter-Varsity Press, 2006), 106.

11. Timothy George (ed.), *J. I. Packer and the Evangelical Future: The Impact of his Life and Thought* (Grand Rapids: Baker Academic, 2009), 117.

12. Vol. 1, No. 8, Summer 1958, 10–13.

13. Eifion Evans, *Daniel Rowland and the Great Evangelical Awakening in Wales* (Edinburgh: Banner of Truth Trust, 1985), xi.

14. 'Cilgwyn 1958', 46.

Chapter 9

1. Eifion Evans, *When He is Come: The 1858–1860 Revival in Wales* (London/Bridgend: Evangelical Press and the Evangelical Movement of Wales, 1967), 10.

2. Eifion Evans, *Two Welsh Revivalists: Humphrey Jones, Dafydd Morgan and the 1859 Revival in Wales* (Bridgend: Evangelical Library of Wales, 1985), 52.

3. See Appendix Three.

4. 'Conference at Cilgwyn', *Evangelical Magazine of Wales*, Vol.1. No.10, (Aug.–Sept.1959), 46.

5. E-mail correspondence 16 August 2013.

6. 'Conference at Cilgwyn', 47.

7. Murray, *Lloyd-Jones: The Fight of Faith*, 372.

8. E-mail correspondence 16 August 2013.

9. *What God Hath Wrought: A Brief Account of the History of the Tro'r Glien Mission Hall, Cwmtwrch* on the Occasion of its Half-Centenary Celebrations, George Griffiths, 1962.

10. Converted in middle age, he became an outstanding evangelist in Scotland.

11. E-mail correspondence 16 August 2013.

12. 'Conference at Cilgwyn', *Evangelical Magazine of Wales*, p.48.

13. Interview by author with Gareth Davies, 2 June 1997.

14. Interview by author, 15 May, 1995.

15. Interview by author with Noel Gibbard, 21 May 1997.

16. Personal conversation in the EMW Aberystwyth English Conference August 1984.

17. For Welsh language readers, see *Robert Roberts: Yr Angel o Glynnog*, Emyr Roberts and Wyn James (Bridgend: Evangelical Library of Wales, 1976).

18. Names withheld.

19. 10 June 2013.

20. Prepared by J. Elwyn Davies, EMW General Secretary. Quotations from pages 1–2.

Chapter 10

1. *The Mary Jones Walk* is a walking guide which reconstructs the twenty-eight mile route taken by Mary Jones to Bala from Llanfihangel-y-Penant to buy a Bible. The guide includes a map and illustrations of the route. It is published by the Bible Society in English and Welsh, and is available from

Welsh Tourist Boards or as a download from http://www.biblesociety.org.uk/walkingguide

2. See John Emyr (editor), *A Father in the Faith: J. Elwyn Davies* (Bridgend: Bryntirion Press, 2012) or in Welsh, *Porth yr Aur: Cofio J. Elwyn Davies* (Pen-y-bont ar Ogwr: Gwasg Bryntirion, 2011).

3. Gwilym Humphreys describes the background in 'Eryl Aran' in *The Evangelical Magazine of Wales* (Vol. 1, No. 8, Summer 1958), 19–23. See also the next issue of the Magazine for a follow-on by the 'Editors' with the same title, 'Eryl Aran' (Vol. 1, No. 9, Winter 1958–59), 18–19.

4. A native of Harlech in North West Wales. While training in Bangor for the Baptist ministry, he was converted while walking over the Menai Bridge to Anglesey one Sunday afternoon. From 1953, he pastored two Baptist churches in Bethesda, North Wales, before moving to the Bala area to pastor Baptist churches in Bala and Llanuwchllyn. Gwilym (1924–2010) was a man of prayer.

5. Capel Celyn was a small rural community of seventy people with a school and a chapel located in the eight hundred acre Treweryn Valley, north west of Bala. The village and the entire valley were drowned in 1965 to provide water for Liverpool. In 2005, Liverpool City Council apologised for the 'insensitivity' of its earlier leaders.

6. Joe England, *The Wales TUC 1974–2004: Devolution and Industrial Politics* (Cardiff: University of Wales Press, 2004), 1; John Davies, *Hanes Cymru* (London: Penguin Books, 1992), 574–662.

7. *The Wales TUC 1974–2004*, 1.

8. Callum G. Brown, *The Death of Christian Britain*, 176.

9. Barn 22 (1964), 283 and quoted by Professor D. Densil Morgan in *The Span of the Cross: Christian Religion and Society in Wales 1914–2000* (Cardiff: University of Wales Press, 1999), 228.

10. The nature and influence of 'liberal' theology in churches and colleges can also be seen in Dewi Eirug Davies's Diwinyddiaeth Yng Nghymru 1927–1977 (Llandysul: Gomer Press, 1984).

11. R. Tudur Jones, Hanes Annibynwyr Cymru (Abertawe: Tŷ John Penry, 1966), 320.

12. D. P. Davies, *Against the Tide: Christianity in Wales on the Threshold of a New Millennium* (Llandysul: Gomer Press, 1995), 33.

13. Rob Warner, *Reinventing English Evangelicalism 1966–2001* (Carlisle: Paternoster, 2007), 205.

14. The subject was also handled by Adrian Brake, Mountain Ash, in the 2012 Conference.

Chapter 11

1. J. Elwyn Davies, *Striving Together: The Evangelical Movement of Wales, its principles and aims* (Bridgend: Evangelical Press of Wales, 1984), 5.

2. *Y Cylchgrawn* (Vol. 1, No. 2, January-February 1949), 36.

3. *Y Cylchgrawn Efengylaidd* (Vol. 1, No. 7, November-December 1949), 41–42.

4. Iain Murray explains helpfully the background to Lloyd-Jones's 1966 address, answering many unfair criticisms. See 'Dr Lloyd-Jones: A Review of Criticism,' in *The Banner of Truth* (Issue 518, November 2006), 1–23.

5. A balanced assessment is provided by 'Gildas' in *Y Cylchgrawn Efengylaidd* under 'Codi Cwestiwn' (Vol. IX. No. 3), 84–86.

6. Appendix Four.

7. Notes, Emyr Roberts.

Chapter 12

1. The term describes those who remained in denominational churches but claimed to be baptized with the Spirit. They believed that gifts like speaking in tongues and prophecy are not confined to the apostolic period.

2. The Ministers' Fellowship Sub-Committee Minutes (20 March 1968) confirms completion of the study of this subject when 'final approval for publication' of their document (The Ministry and Life of the New Testament Church') 'was given'. It was published in 1968 by the EMW.

3. Minutes, 1 November, 1965, 7,

4. Michael McMullen has written a popular account of Burns's life with references to his journal, letters and sermons: *God's Polished Arrow W. C. Burns: Revival Preacher* (Fearn: Christian Focus Publications, 2000).

5. Minutes of the Evangelical Ministers' Fellowship Sub-Committee held at Llandrindod Wells, January 14, 1966.

6. *The Span of the Cross*, 248.

7. *Classics from Doreen Irvine* (Eastbourne: Kingsway Publications, Omnibus edition, 2001), 5–8, 126–145.

Chapter 13

1. These were published: *Preaching and Preachers*, D. Martyn Lloyd-Jones (London: Hodder and Stoughton, 1971).

2. He became disenchanted with his Brethren background and denominationalism before entering Restorationism.

3. Arthur Wallis, *In the Day of Thy Power: the Scriptural Principles of Revival* (London: Christian Literature Crusade, 1956). This was re-written radically with a new title: *Rain From Heaven—Revival in Scripture and History* (Bethany Fellowship, 1979).

4. The Ministers' Sub-Committee 'asked the Rev. Elwyn Davies to consult the Rev. Dr D. M. Lloyd-Jones regarding the choice of speaker, and on his recommendation Mr. D. Bentley-Taylor had been invited'. Minutes, September 16, 1968.

5. *Daily Telegraph*, 21 February, 2005.

6. *Evangelicals Now*, April 2005.

7. *The Evangelical Magazine of Wales* (Vol. 8, No. 4, August-September, 1969), 15–16.

8. A personal diary account written and signed by David Bentley-Taylor, 27

June 1969, entitled: *The Evangelical Movement of Wales Ministers' Conference: Bryn-y-groes, Bala, Merionethshire, June 23–25, 1969*. Iain H. Murray was given a copy in 1992 by Bentley-Taylor.

9. Presbyterian Conference members in North and South Wales who seceded in the 1970s, remained in close fellowship for purposes of prayer and mutual support. The five ministers who resigned from the Cheshire, Flint and Denbigh Presbytery between 1971 and 1974 were Glyndwr Jenkins (1971), Gwilym Roberts and Peter Clement (1972), Gilbert Evans and Peter Milsom (1974). They met at intervals to report on their churches, discuss the framing of a Constitution and doctrinal statement, the receiving of members and appointment of elders/deacons, worship, and the sacraments. 'Brief Notes on Meetings of Seceding Pastors, *1981–1985*'. Gwilym Roberts was secretary.

10. 'Cynhadledd y Gweinidogion', 146–147, *Y Cylchgrawn Efengylaidd* (August/ September, 1969).

11. Conference did not propose or establish a new college though members like Graham Harrison, Hywel R. Jones, Philip Eveson and Andrew Davies taught in the London Theological Seminary when established (1977) under the leadership of Lloyd-Jones. Graham Harrison advocated such a college in Conference. However, in 1984 the EMW General Committee, with the Council of South Wales Bible College,Barry, established a new theological college for training pastors and missionaries—the Evangelical Theological College of Wales (which opened in 1985) but renamed recently as the Wales Evangelical School of Theology (WEST). See *Looking Ahead; Trusting God: The substance of an address delivered on 18 May 1996 in Bryntirion to mark the sixtieth anniversary of the founding of the Barry College*, D. Eryl Davies (Bridgend: ETCW, May 1996).

12. An account of this revival is provided by Eifion Evans in *Daniel Rowland and*

the *Great Evangelical Awakening in Wales* (Edinburgh: Banner of Truth Trust, 1985), 309–321.

13. *Daniel Rowland*, 313.

14. *Daniel Rowland*, 320.

Chapter 14

1. Notes, Emyr Roberts.

2. Notes, Eryl Davies.

3. Minutes, 19 September 1972.

4. Notes, Eryl Davies.

5. See Appendix 13.

Chapter 15

1. Minutes of the Ministers' Fellowship Sub-Committee, October 1, 1974.

2. E-mail correspondence 10 July, 2013.

3. *Evangelical Magazine of Wales* (Vol. 13, No. 4, August-September, 1974), 4.

4. Minutes of the Ministers' Fellowship Sub-Committee, 26 September 1973.

5. *Evangelical Magazine* (Vol. 8, No. 4), 4.

6. *D. Martyn Lloyd-Jones: The Fight of Faith,* 700–701.

7. October 1, 1974.

8. *Evangelical Magazine* (Vol. 14, No. 4, August/September 1975), 5.

9. Ministers' Fellowship Sub-Committee Minutes, October 1, 1974.

10. *Evangelical Magazine,* August/September, 1975.

11. *Evangelical Magazine,* (Vol.15. No. 4, August/September 1976), 4.

12. *Evangelical Magazine,* (Vol. 16. No. 4, August/September 1977), 4.

13. Minutes, 28–29 June 1976.

Chapter 16

1. Minutes, 13 October, 1977, Aberystwyth.

2. *Evangelical Magazine* (Vol.17, No. 4, August/September 1978), 4.

3. This was given as the 1904 Revival Memorial Lecture of the Presbyterian Church of Wales, then delivered in English at the Association in the East and in Welsh at the Associations of the South and North during 1978. See 'Revival' in *Revival & Its Fruit,* Emyr Roberts and R. Geraint Gruffydd (Bridgend: Evangelical Library of Wales, 1981), 3–18.

4. For an account of this revival and the one in Bethesda see *When God Came to North Wales,* Philip H. Eveson (ed.), (Weston Rhyn: Quinta Press, 2010).

5. See Appendix Fourteen.

6. Notes, Eryl Davies.

7. *Evangelical Magazine,* (Vol. 17, No.4, August/September 1978), 4.

8. See Appendix Twelve for the message outline.

Chapter 17

1. *Evangelical Magazine* (Vol.20. No.3, August/September 1981), 4.

2. Minutes, 3 November 1980.

3. The full title is: *An Humble Attempt to Promote Explicit Agreement and Visible Union of God's People in Extraordinary Prayer, For the Revival of Religion and the Advancement of Christ's Kingdom on Earth, pursuant to Scripture—Promises and prophecies concerning the Last Time.*

4. Some Baptists in England were encouraged by Edwards's work and prayed from 1784 for revival and global success for the Gospel. They reprinted the *Humble Attempt* in 1789. One fruit of this was the formation of the Baptist Missionary Society and the commissioning of William Carey to India in 1793.

5. E-mail and Questionnaire March 21, 2012.

6. *Evangelical Magazine* (Vol. 19, No. 4, August/September 1980), 4.

7. Published as *The Wrath of God* (Evangelical Press of Wales, Bridgend: 1984),

later expanded as *An Angry God: What the Bible says about Wrath, Final Judgement and Hell* (Bridgend: Evangelical Press of Wales, 1991).

Chapter 18

1. Minutes of the Ministers' Fellowships Sub-Committee, 4 May, 1982.

2. *Evangelical Magazine* (Vol. 21, No. 4, August/September 1982), 4.

3. *Evangelical Magazine* (Vol. 23, No. 4, August/September 1984), 4.

4. *Evangelical Magazine* (Vol. 23, No. 4, August/September 1984), 4.

5. *Evangelical Magazine* (Vol. 31, No. 4, August/September 1992), 6.

6. *Evangelical Magazine* (Vol. 34, No. 4, August/September 1995), 20.

7. *Evangelical Magazine* (Vol. 36, No. 4, August/September 1997), 20.

8. For example, '... pretty well packed to capacity' in 1974 (*Evangelical Magazine*, Vol. 13, No. 4, August/September 1974) 4; in 1975, 'the large number of ministers who were able to attend' (*Evangelical Magazine*, Vol. 14, No. 4, August/September 1975) 5.

9. The substance of the first address was published in *Foundations* (British Evangelical Council [now renamed *Affinity*]; February 1983). See also 'Justification by Faith: What It Means' in *The God of All Grace: J. Douglas MacMillan, Preacher and Teacher* (Fearn: Christian Focus Publications, 1997), 241–254.

10. Minutes, 5 September 1983.

11. *Evangelical Magazine* (Vol. 22, No. 4, August/September 1983), 4.

12. Minutes, 15 June 1983.

13. See chapter twenty seven for more details.

14. Minutes, 10 September 1984.

15. EMW Annual Report, 1984–85.

16. Minutes of Ministers' Fellowships Sub-Committee on 9 September 1985 in reviewing this Conference: 'All the brethren expressed favourable comments and valued the ministry of Rev. V. Higham greatly'.

17. *Evangelical Magazine* (Vol. 25, No. 4, August/September 1986), 4.

18. Minutes, 7 September 1987.

19. *Evangelical Magazine* (Vol. 26, No. 4, August/September 1987), 4.

20. Eryl Davies, *The Beddgelert Revival* (Bridgend: Bryntirion Press, 2004).

21. *Evangelical Magazine* (Vol. 27, No. 4, August/September 1988), 4.

22. His brother, Ivor Davies, gave his experiences of that revival in the 1957 Conference.

23. *Evangelical Magazine* (Vol. 20, No. 4, August/September 1989), 4.

Chapter 19

1. *The Span of the Cross*, 276.

2. The Ministers' Fellowships Sub-Committee, 20 June 1989, felt 'it was time to give attention to an assessment and re-appraisal of the Ministers' Conference ... at the next meeting'. Accordingly, on the 18 September 1989, the Committee discussed *'the future structure of Conference Programme'*. Bala was confirmed as the venue; the first Conference address at 2–00pm after lunch with the final session on Wednesday afternoon.

3. *Evangelical Magazine* (Vol. 29, No. 4, August/September 1990), 4.

4. Ministers' Fellowships Sub-Committee, 8 October 1990.

5. See *Fire from Heaven: Times of Extraordinary Revival* (Darlington: Evangelical Press, 2009).

6. In the 1991 Conference the death of Mrs Lloyd-Jones was noted. She was 'a great encourager, a godly helpmeet to a great man of God ... It seems also as if our link with the "Doctor" has been finally severed. While Mrs Lloyd-Jones lived she was a constant reminder ...' *Evangelical Magazine* (Vol. 30, No. 2, April/May, 1991), 6.

7. Minutes, 9 September 1991.

8. *Evangelical Magazine* (Vol. 30, No. 4, 1991), 4.

9. Ministers' Fellowships Sub-Committee, 7 September 1992.

10. Published by SPCK, London, 1990.

11. Ministers' Fellowships Sub-Committee, 11 October 1993.

12. Ministers' Fellowships Sub-Committee, 10 October 1994.

13. *Evangelical Magazine*, Vol. 33, No. 4, August/September 1994), 20.

14. *Evangelical Magazine* (Vol. 35, No. 4, August/September 1996), 20.

15. *Evangelical Magazine* (Vol. 36, No. 4, August/September 1997), 20.

16. *Evangelical Magazine* (Vol. 20, No. 4, August/September 1989), 4.

17. *Evangelical Magazine* (Vol. 36, No. 4, August/September 1997), 20.

18. The subject of revival is discussed in more detail in chapters 28 and 30.

Chapter 20

1. E-mail response 23 February 2013.

2. *Evangelical Magazine* (Vol. 39, No. 4, August/September 2000), 21.

3. *Evangelical Magazine* (Vol. 40, No. 4, August/September 2001), 25.

4. E-mail response 2012.

5. E-mail response 23 February 2013.

6. *Evangelical Magazine* (Vol. 42, No. 4, August/September 2003), 23.

7. *Evangelical Magazine* (Vol. 43, No. 4, August/September 2004), 22.

8. *Evangelical Magazine* (Vol. 44, No. 4, August/September 2005), 4.

9. *The Banner of Truth Magazine* (Issue 518, November 2006), 1–23.

10. *Evangelical Magazine* (Vol. 46, No. 4, August/September 2007), 8.

11. Notes, Eryl Davies.

Chapter 21

1. Notes, Eryl Davies.

2. *Evangelical Magazine* (Vol. 51, No. 5, September/October 2012), 30.

3. For further information, read a report by a participating pastor, John Orchard: 'Gospel Churches working together', *Evangelical Magazine of Wales* (Vol. 50, No. 5, September/October, 2011), 8–9.

Chapter 22

1. The Conference was held 10–12 June.

2. E-mail 20 June 2013.

Chapter 23

1. *The People's Theologian, Writings in Honour of Donald Macleod*, Iain D. Campbell & Malcom Maclean (eds.) (Fearn: Christian Focus Publications, 2011), 30.

2. *Engaging with Martyn Lloyd-Jones* 10.

3. 'The Lloyd-Jones Legacy', *Monthly Record of the Free Church of Scotland* (October 1983), 207.

4. *Engaging with Martyn Lloyd-Jones*, 77–78.

5. *Engaging with Martyn Lloyd-Jones*, 77.

6. Emyr Roberts, *Cyrraedd Trwy'r Glustog* (Denbigh: Gwasg Gee, 1971), 17.

7. *Cyrraedd Trwy'r Glustog*, 24.

8. Robert Pope, *Codi Muriau Dinas Duw: Anghydffurfiaeth ac Anghydffurfwyr Cymru'r Ugeinfed Ganrif* [*Raising the Walls of the City of God: The Nonconformity and Nonconformists of Twentieth Century Wales*] (Bangor: Centre for Postgraduate Studies of Religion in Wales, University of Wales, Bangor, 2005), 187.

9. Pope, *Codi Muriau Duw*, 45.

10. Densil D. Morgan, *Barth Reception in Britain* (London: T & T Clark International, 2010), 61.

11. Martyn Lloyd-Jones, *Crefydd Heddiw ac Yfory* (Llandybie: Llyfrau'r Dryw, 1947), 11–12.

12. *Barth Reception in Britain*, 245–246.

13. *Barth Reception in Britain*, 197–198.

14. *Yr Argyfwng* (Llandybie: Llyfrau'r Dryw, 1956).

15. 30–32, 51–56.

16. A Welsh Congregational minister, he later lectured in Religious Studies in the University of Glamorgan (University of South Wales).

17. Notes, Emyr Roberts.

18. Questionnaire 23 February 2013.

19. Questionnaire 21 June 2012.

20. E-mail and Questionnaire, 28 January 2012.

21. E-mail and Questionnaire, 21 March 2012.

22. Questionnaire and letter, 26 June 2013.

23. E-mail and Questionnaire, 7 March 2012.

Chapter 24

1. *Religion, Secularization and Social Change in Wales: Congregational Studies in a Post-Christian Society* (Cardiff: University of Wales Press, 2005), 2.

2. 5–6.

3. Duncan Tanner, 'Facing the New Challenge: Labour and Politics, 1970–2000', 264–293, in *The Labour Party in Wales 1900–2000*, eds. Duncan Tanner, Chris Williams and Deian Hopkin (Cardiff: University of Wales Press, 2000).

4. See Chapters 7 and 8 for examples.

5. Completed Questionnaire received 12 June 2013.

6. Completed Questionnaire received 11 June 2013.

7. Letter to author, 7 June 2013.

8. Roger L. Brown, *Evangelicals in the Church in Wales* (Welshpool: Tair Eglwys Press, 2007), 272.

9. Letter dated 1 June 2012; name withheld.

10. He prefers to remain anonymous.

11. Robert Letham, email correspondence 30 August, 2013.

12. Paul E. G. Cook in *Fire from Heaven: Times of Extraordinary Revival* (Darlington: Evangelical Press, 2009), 120–124, provides helpful application in this context.

13. See, for example, chapters eighteen and nineteen.

14. Questionnaire 30 July 2013. He is referring to a Study Conference arranged biennially by Affinity. The addresses are circulated beforehand and presented briefly in Conference with most of the time given to discussion. The comparison is unfair in that Bala is not a Study Conference, but the level of discussion needs attention.

15. See Appendix Twelve.

16. E-mail dated 28 May 2013.

17. Telephone response to Questionnaire, 17 June 2013.

18. E-mail to Steffan Job, 13 June 2013.

19. Questionnaire 11 June 2013.

20. Questionnaire 12 June 2013.

21. Completed Questionnaire, 12 June 2013.

22. Completed Questionnaire, 11 June 2013.

23. E-mail via Steffan Job, 18 June 2013.

24. E-mail 17 May 2013.

25. Questionnaire 16 April 2013.

26. *Evangelical Magazine of Wales,* Vol. 96, No. 4, August/September 1996, 20–21.

Chapter 25

1. See also *Diwinydda Ddoe a Heddiw,* 145–185.

2. Gaius Davies, 'Physician, Preacher and Politician: Dr D. Martyn Lloyd-Jones (1899–1981)' in, *Genius, Grief and Grace: A Doctor Looks At Suffering and Success* (Fearn: Christian Focus, 2001), 372.

3. See John Macleod's reference to his father being 'irritated' over the

'increasing cult of flattery and veneration about the ageing Lloyd-Jones ... it troubled the tough old fellow himself ...' *The People's Theologian, 37.*

4. *Genius, Grief and Grace*, 371.

5. In reviewing the Conference's history in the 1997 Conference, Eryl Davies warned against 'idolising' Lloyd-Jones: *Evangelical Magazine of Wales*, Vol. 36, No. 4, September/October, 1997.

6. Personal reminiscences recorded on tape by Rev. Wynford Davies: 18 May 1997. Andrew Davies's help here is appreciated.

7. John Brencher, *Martyn Lloyd-Jones (1899–1981) and Twentieth-Century Evangelicalism* (Carlisle: Paternoster Press, 2002), 231.

Chapter 26

1. *Cofio Hanner Canrif,* 56.

2. *Engaging with Martyn Lloyd-Jones,* 77.

3. Appendix One.

4. Appendix Two.

5. Appendix Three.

6. See chapter 9.

7. Appendix Four.

8. Appendix Five.

9. Appendix Nine.

10. Appendix Fifteen.

11. Notes, Eryl Davies.

12. Notes, Eryl Davies.

13. See chapter twelve for details.

14. *Engaging with Martyn Lloyd-Jones,* with its eleven authors, is one recent example where much more attention could have been given to the subject.

Chapter 27

1. *Romans: Exposition of chapters 3:20–4:25: Atonement and Justification* (London: Banner of Truth Trust, 1970), xi, 14, 33.

2. See Appendix Two.

3. Appendix One.

4. Iain H. Murray, *David Martyn Lloyd-Jones: The First Forty Years: 1899–1939* Volume 1 (Edinburgh: Banner of Truth Trust, 1982), 180.

5. 'D. Martyn Lloyd-Jones and Post-War Baptist Life', Philip Hill in *The Welsh Journal of Religious History*, Vol. 6 (2011), 96–114.

6. D. Ben Rees, *Ymgyrchu Dros Yr Efengyl Ym Mon* (Campaigning For The Gospel in Anglesey) *1921–1979*, (Llangoed: Capel Tŷ Rhys, 2010), 39.

7. Examples include: John Thomas (Sandfields, 1953), Gwilym Roberts (Peniel, Tredegar, 1955 and again in 1958), Eryl Davies (Ebenezer, Bangor, 1975).

Chapter 28

1. This subject is discussed further in chapter thirty.

2. The author referred to it in reviewing this history in 1997.

3. 'Lloyd-Jones and Revival' in *Engaging with Martyn Lloyd-Jones*, 91.

4. *Genius, Grief and Grace*, 373.

5. See, for example, Appendix Four.

6. *Y Cylchgrawn Efengylaidd*, Cyfrol 19, Rhif 5, Rhifyn Arbennig, 1981, 37. The original interview was in English: 'Twenty-five Years On', *Evangelical Magazine of Wales*, Vol. 14, No. 2, April/May 1975, 8–11.

7. 'Twenty-Five Years On', 8–9, 11, *Evangelical Magazine of Wales*, Vol. 14, No. 2, April/May, 1975.

Chapter 29

1. Further details are given in earlier chapters, especially chapter 24. There will also be further assessment in this chapter and the next one.

2. 'An Historical and Theological Analysis of the Role of the Holy Spirit in

Preaching in English Protestant Writings in Britain 1945–2000'; University of Wales, Lampeter/Wales Evangelical School of Theology, 2003.

3. Written and published originally in French in 1951 and translated into English in AD 2000 by Westminster Publishing House, Seoul. It is a stimulating work.

4. *The Relevance of Preaching*, 232.

5. Published by Epworth Press, London, 1967. The author, Ithel Jones, was Principal of South Wales Baptist College, Cardiff, for a period before returning to pastoral ministry.

6. *The Holy Spirit and Christian Preaching*, 9.

7. *The Holy Spirit and Christian Preaching*, 55.

8. The John Owen Centre, London /Westminster Theological Seminary, Philadelphia, submitted and awarded in 2013.

9. These are: Philip Eveson, 'Moore Theology: A Friendly Critique' (*Foundations*, Autumn 2006). This was also delivered in the Bala Conference 2006; Robert Strivens, 'Preaching—"ex opere operato?"', Westminster Conference, 2007; Stuart Olyott, 'Where Luther Got it Wrong and Why We Need to Know About it,' *Banner of Truth*, 2009:25; Hywel R. Jones, 'Preaching the Word in the Power of the Holy Spirit' (*Foundations* 60, 2011).

10. *The Word and Spirit in Preaching*, 6. Unpublished electronic version supplied by the author.

11. Established in 1856, Moore College in Sydney has been training students

especially for the Anglican but in addition Free Church ministries as well as for mission work. It provides courses too in the United Kingdom and has exercised a growing influence here.

12. *The Word and Spirit in Preaching*, 7–9.

13. Email correspondence 3 April 2014.

14. *The Word and Spirit in Preaching*, 26.

15. *Ordained Servant Online* (Orthodox Presbyterian Church, USA). Robert Letham, 'The Necessity of Preaching in the Modern World,' Part 1, October 2013, accessed 9 October 2013; Part 2, November 2013, accessed 3 November 2013; Part 3, December 2013, accessed 1 December 2013.

16. Chapter II; 3. See also the *Confession of Faith of the Calvinistic Methodists of Wales*, 1823.

17. Ordained Servant Online, December 2013, Part 3, p 2.

18. Stuart Olyott, 'Where Luther Got it Wrong and Why We Need to Know About it', 27; Ralph Cunnington, *The Word and Spirit in Preaching*, 22–25.

19. Ordained Servant Online, October 2013, Part 1, pp. 1–5.

20. Ordained Servant Online, October 2013, Part 1, p. 3.

21. This will be discussed further in the next chapter.

22. Ordained Servant Online, November 2013, Part 2, p. 6.

23. For a more critical analysis see Robert Pope, 'Lloyd-Jones and Fundamentalism' in *Engaging with Martyn Lloyd-Jones*, 197–219. David Ceri-Jones criticises the Evangelical Movement of Wales somewhat superficially, for its 'hostile attitude towards modern biblical criticism'. See David Ceri-Jones's 'Evangelicalism and Fundamentalism in Post-War Wales, 1947–1981' in *Evangelicalism & Fundamentalism in the United Kingdom during the Twentieth Century*, eds. David Bebbington & David Ceri-Jones (Oxford: Oxford University Press, 2013), 292–297. I question several statements made by the author who stretches the terms 'evangelical' and fundamentalist', lacking the balance shown by Robert Pope. The context of statements used by him from the *Evangelical Magazine of Wales* also requires more detailed, careful attention. Again, the 'multiform nature of biblical criticism' with its plurality of methods (A. Thiselton, *Hermeneutics,* Grand Rapids/Cambridge: Eerdmans, 2009, 349) expressing often arrogant and radical presuppositions, leaving little or no place for the supernatural and orthodox doctrines needed to be challenged. Is it not 'the theologian's unique responsibility to ensure that the church's speech and action correspond to the word of God, the norm of Christian faith and practice' (Vanhoozer, *The Drama of Doctrine*, Louisville: Westminster John Knox Press, 2005, 3). Many pastors in Wales also agree with, and testify personally to, Calvin's teaching concerning the 'inward testimony' of the Holy Spirit given to believers concerning the verbal inspiration and authority of Scripture. *Institutes of the Christian Religion,* Bk 1, Ch. VII. 4.

24. Chapter III, Section V, Of God's Eternal Decree.

25. Chapter III, Section VI.

26. Charles Hodge maintains that the means of grace are God-appointed in order to convey grace to people. God works by means—'a continual agency of God in combination with the agency of man, in the development

of the graces of the Spirit, and in attaining eternal life'. Such means 'are absolutely essential' but 'are inefficacious without God's presence ... he gives efficacy to the means of grace ...' *Princeton Sermons* (London: Banner of Truth, 1958), 286–287.

27. Some Reformed theologians exclude prayer in order to safeguard the 'objective channels' of the Word and sacraments which Christ appointed in his church for communicating grace. See L. Berkhof, for example, in his *Systematic Theology* (London: Banner of Truth, 1959), 604.

28. Christian Institutes. IV. XVII.

29. *Westminster Confession of Faith*, Ch. XIV. 1.

30. *The Holy Spirit and Christian Preaching*, 58–65.

31. John Murray, *Collected Writings of John Murray I: The Claims of Truth*, (Edinburgh: Banner of Truth, 1976), v.

32. Pastor of Freeschool Court Evangelical Church, Bridgend, South Wales. He was not present in the Conference during Lloyd-Jones's period but he claims 'his books have had the biggest influence upon me'.

33. Email correspondence 31 July 2013.

34. Collected Writings, Vol. 1, 140–141.

Chapter 30

1. *The Word and Spirit in Preaching*, 6.

2. Ordained Servant Online, December 2013, Part 3, p2.

3. He is a minister of the Orthodox Presbyterian Church (USA) currently teaching systematic and historical theology at Wales Evangelical School of Theology (WEST). He is also Director of Research at WEST and the author of many scholarly books and articles on theology. I am quoting from an adaptation of his lecture on "The Necessity of Preaching in the Modern World" given at the International Conference of Reformed Churches, Cardiff, UK, in August 2013.

4. One example is Carl Trueman in 'J.I.Packer: An English Nonconformist Perspective' in *J.I.Packer and the Evangelical Future: The Impact of His Life and Thought*, ed. Timothy George (Grand Rapids: Baker Academic, 2009), 115–129.

5. It appears as early as 1823 in Hugh Bourne's *History of the Primitive Methodist Church*; see also Iain H. Murray, *Revival and Revivalism: The Making and Marring of American Evangelicalism, 1750–1858* (Edinburgh: Banner of Truth Trust, 1994), 391.

6. James I. Packer, *Collected Shorter Writings of J.I. Packer: Honouring the People of God*, Vol. 4 (Carlisle: Paternoster, 1999), 57.

7. Packer, *Collected Writings*, Vol. 4, 55–58.

8. '... what happens in revivals is not ... something miraculously different from the regular experience of the church. The difference lies in degree, not in kind. In an "outpouring of the Spirit" spiritual influence is more widespread, convictions are deeper, and feeling more intense, but all this is only a heightening of normal Christianity. True revivals are "extraordinary", yet what is experienced at such times is not different in

essence from the spiritual experience that belongs to Christians at other times ...' Murray, *Revival and Revivalism*, 23. See also 'What is Revival?' in *Collected Shorter Writings of J.I. Packer: Serving The People of God* (Carlisle: Paternoster Press, 1998), Volume 2, 57–61.

9. Timothy Keller, *Center Church, Doing Balanced, Gospel-Centered Ministry in Your City* (Grand Rapids: Zondervan, 2012), 60.

10. Keller, *Center Church*, 54.

11. Ordained Servant Online, December 2013, Part 3, p3.

12. Another term which is multi-faceted in its varying references to different geographical groups and emphases within the wider Anabaptist movement from the sixteenth-century Protestant Reformation. Letham does not define the term but refers correctly to the tendency of Anabaptists to exaggerate the distinction between Word and Spirit. In addition, Letham appears uneasy about the methodology of some evangelicals in claiming they approach an 'open Bible' only, without reference to history and tradition. His point merits attention. Interestingly, the title of Douglas F. Kelly's *Systematic Theology* Vol. 1, (Fearn: Christian Focus, 2008) has the following sub-title: *Grounded in Holy Scripture and understood in the light of the Church*. He adds: We 'need the Church in order to see and experience the Word of God in God's own light ...' (from the frontflap cover). The 'open Bible' approach can be viewed simplistically.

13. Ordained Servant Online, December 2013, Part 3, p 5.

14. D. M. Lloyd-Jones, 'What is Preaching?' 258–277 in *Knowing the Times: Addresses delivered on Various Occasions 1942–1977* (Edinburgh: Banner of Truth Trust, 1989). The address was delivered in Westminster Theological

Seminary, Philadelphia two years before his extended lectures there in 1969 which were later published under the title of *Preaching and Preachers* (London: Hodder and Stoughton, 1971).

15. 267.

16. 268–270.

17. 271–272.

18. 273.

19. 275–277.

20. 276.

21. 277.

22. Pierre-Charles Marcel (1910–1992) was a leading French Protestant pastor and theologian who studied under M. Auguste Lecerf (1873–1943), the leading Reformed theologian in France at the time. Marcel also studied under Herman Dooyeweerd in the Netherlands.

23. International Fellowship of Evangelical Students.

24. For example, a long friendship developed from 1942 between the two men and twelve letters written by Lloyd-Jones to Hughes are included in *D. Martyn Lloyd-Jones: Letters 1919–1981* (Edinburgh: Banner of Truth Trust, 1994).

25. Published by James Clarke, London, in 1953 with a new edition in 1982.

26. *The Relevance of Preaching*, 100.

27. Ordained Servant Online, December 2013 Part 3, p. 3.

28. 'Twenty-Five Years On,' 8–11, *Evangelical Magazine of Wales*, Volume 14, Number 2, April/May, 1975.

29. Ian M. Randall, 'Lloyd-Jones and Revival' in *Engaging with Martyn Lloyd-Jones*, 97.

30. Iain H. Murray, *Pentecost—Today? The Biblical Basis for Understanding Revival* (Edinburgh: Banner of Truth Trust, 1998), 18–19.

31. See also George Smeaton, *The Doctrine of the Holy Spirit,* (London: Banner of Truth Trust, 1958), 249–255.

32. Murray, *Pentecost—Today?* 21–25. See also *The Works of John Knox*, vol. I (Edinburgh, 1846), 101.

33. George Whitefield preached in Edinburgh and Glasgow in the summer months of 1741 with significant concern and conversions expressed by some people. By April 1742 in Cambuslang it was estimated that 300 people had been 'awakened' with more to follow.

34. Under the diligent ministry of the Rev. James Robe, his small parish in Kilsyth experienced a powerful revival by May 1742.

35. Murray, *Pentecost—Today?* 23.

36. Murray, *Pentecost—Today?* 24.

37. Hywel R. Jones, 'Preaching the Word in the Power of the Holy Spirit', *Foundations* 60 (2011), 71–90.

38. Ordained Servant Online, December 2013, Part 3, p3.

39. Christopher Catherwood, 'Afterword', in Catherwood (ed.), *Martyn Lloyd-Jones: Chosen by God* (Highland Books, 1986), 275.

40. Ian M. Randall reminds us, however, that he ranked Jonathan Edwards way ahead of all his eighteenth century contemporaries for the reason that he was 'pre-eminently the theologian of revival, the theologian of experience.' See his 'Lloyd-Jones and Revival' in *Engaging with Martyn Lloyd-Jones*, 110.

41. Stuart Olyott, 'Where Luther Got it Wrong and Why We Need to Know About It', *The Banner of Truth* 555 (December 2009).

42. Ordained Servant Online, December 2013, Part 3, 5.

43. Ordained Servant Online, December 2013, Part 3, 7.

44. Ordained Servant Online, October 2013, Part 1, p5; John Calvin, *Institutes of the Christian Religion*, Library of Christian Clasics, trans. Ford Battles, ed. John T. McNeill (Philadelphia: The Westmister Press), 4:12:1.

45. See especially Appendices 4 ('we need prayer but we need something before that. Our first need is to know Him and to know His love …'); 5 ('Acts 6:3-4 are key verses … Prayer is first') and 15.

46. George Smeaton, *The Doctrine of the Holy Spirit* (London: Banner of Truth Trust, 1958), 255.

47. John Calvin, *The Institutes of the Christian Religion*, translated by Henry Beveridge, Book IV. Ch. XX. 146 (London: James Clarke, 1953).

48. *Christian Institutes*, Book IV. Chapter XX. 161.

49. D. M. Lloyd-Jones, Summing Up, *Press Toward the Mark: Puritan Papers 1962* (London: Puritan and Reformed Studies Conference in 1961), 79.

50. *The God of All Grace: J. Douglas MacMillan, Preacher and Teacher* (Fearn: Christian Focus, 1997), 176.

51. For example, Jonathan Edwards, 1703–1758, Charles Hodge, 1797–1878 (America), Philip E. Hughes, South Africa and UK (*Revive us Again*, 1947) and J I. Packer.

52. *The Holy Spirit,* Sinclair Ferguson (Leicester: IVP, 1996), 13.

53. *Collected Shorter Writings of J. I. Packer: Celebrating the Saving Work of God Vol. I* (Carlisle: Paternoster, 1998), 1–7.

54. In John 3, Packer affirms that 'the Trinity is presented in quite a different light—not now as the linchpin of orthodox belief ... but as ... the sinner's way of salvation'.

55. *Preaching and Preachers,* 307. This final chapter entitled 'Demonstration of the Spirit and Power' spans pages 304–325.

56. *Preaching and Preachers*, 308.

57. See also *God The Holy Spirit,* Vol.2, Dr Martyn Lloyd-Jones (London: Hodder & Stoughton, 1997). Chapter 4, for example, considers 'The

Significance of Pentecost' and on page 36 he describes Pentecost as 'The public inauguration of the church as the body of Christ ...' (p.36); 'the great purpose of Pentecost is to give the final proof of the fact that Jesus of Nazareth is the Son of God and the Saviour of the world' (p.40).

58. *1 Corinthians:* Baker Exegetical Commentary on the New Testament, David E. Garland (Grand Rapids: Baker Academic, 2003), 86.

59. Ordained Servant Online, December 2013, Part 3, 4.

60. For example, see Ezekiel 2:2, Micah 3:8 and Hosea 9:7 where the prophet is viewed as 'a man of the Spirit.'

61. A term used by my colleague Tom Holland in conversation with me regarding this theme in Acts.

Appendix 1

1. Professor Nathaniel Micklem (1888–1976), a British theologian who served as Principal of Mansfield College, Oxford. He was also a political activist.

Appendix 2

1. 1766–1838. A popular account of his life with letters and sermon extracts is found in Tim Shenton's *Christmas Evans: The Life and times of the one-eyed preacher of Wales* (Darlington: Evangelical Press), 2001.

2. It assumes that only intellectual agreement with doctrine is required.

3. 1813–1843. He was involved in a major way in the Scottish revivals between 1839 and 1843.

Appendix 5

1. In 1972 they formed the United Reformed Church

2. William Williams, *The Experience Meeting: An Introduction to the Welsh Societies of the Evangelical Awakening,* translated by Mrs Bethan Lloyd-Jones with Introduction by Dr Martyn Lloyd-Jones (Bridgend: Evangelical Movement of Wales, 1973; New Edition, Vancouver: Regent College Publications, 2003).

Appendix 8

1. He is referring to *Growth into Union* (London: SPCK, 1970) co-authored by two Anglo-Catholics (E.L. Mascall and Graham Leonard) and two Evangelical Anglicans (Colin Buchanan and James Packer).

Appendix 9

1. Formally established in 1955.

Appendix 11

1. Founded by Mary Baker-Eddy who reacted against the Calvinism of her parents in America. In 1857 she published her *Science and Health with the Key to the Scriptures*. Suffering and death for her were illusions of the mind. Her teaching is pantheistic. She died in 1913.

Appendix 13

1. Two addresses given by Dr Eifion Evans.

Index

A

Aaron, John 185
Aldis, Arnold 23
Anderson, Andrew 176
Arminianism 37, 38, 69, 200, 324, 340, 354
Armstrong, John 177
Atlee, Clement 57
Azurdia, Art 186, 207

B

Bailey, Jeremy 236
Baker-Eddy, Mary 434
Ball, Andy 200
Barth, Karl 217, 218, 219, 278
Bassett, Paul 159, 160
Baxter, Richard 51
Bayle, Robert 355
Bebb, W. Ambrose 219
Bennett, Dennis 114
Bentley-Taylor, David 122, 123, 124, 125, 126, 127, 128, 129, 130, 131, 406, 407
Berridge, John 375
Bonhoeffer, Dietrich 101, 102
Bradford, John 70
Brainerd, David 135
Brencher, John 243, 244
Brown, James 164
Brunner, Emil 219
Buchanan, Colin 434
Budge, Iorwerth 255
Bultmann, Rudolf 101, 102
Bunyan, John 161, 353
Burns, William Chalmers 116, 117, 120

Butler, Bishop Joseph 355

C

Calver, Clive 103
Calvinism 66, 69, 70, 126, 200, 226, 235, 285, 294, 306, 324, 340, 354, 434
Calvin, John 63, 126, 135, 161, 276, 279, 283, 295, 296, 297, 425
Campbell, Duncan 48, 49, 66, 67, 68, 69, 74, 122, 261, 306, 394, 398, 399
Campbell, Ian 188
Carey-Jones, T. David 166, 175
Carson, Don 198, 201
Carter, Steve 234
Chalmers, Thomas 215
Chambers, Paul 225
Charismatic Movement 166, 168, 324, 371
Charles, Thomas 98, 139, 183, 207
Christian unity 109, 110, 152
Christofides, Andy 187
Churchill, Sir Winston S. 57
Cilgwyn 64, 65, 68, 69, 72, 74, 75, 79, 82, 83, 86, 88, 89, 166, 227, 305, 308, 316
Clark, Stephen 169, 183, 200, 233, 281
Clement, Peter 407
Connolly, Peter 37
Cooke, Gordon 164, 182, 183, 220
Cook, Paul 142, 175
Cotterell, Peter 176
Cotton, Bob 159, 221
Cunnington, Ralph 275, 276, 277, 283

D

Daniel, Graham 149
Daniel, J. E. 218
Davenport, James 346
Davies, Andrew 144, 167, 178, 407, 420
Davies, David 170
Davies, D. Eryl 134, 161, 169, 175, 257, 268, 303, 420, 422
Davies, D.P. 102
Davies, Gaius 240, 241
Davies, Gareth 87, 156, 175, 239
Davies, Glenys 29
Davies, Gwyn 194
Davies, I. B. 24, 29, 41, 49, 51, 52, 62, 63, 73, 77, 227, 268
Davies, Idris 19, 25, 30
Davies, Ivor 75, 76, 261, 262, 412
Davies, J. Elwyn 26, 27, 61, 72, 76, 77, 79, 80, 87, 98, 99, 107, 110, 134, 142, 144, 146, 157, 161, 176, 258, 268, 406

Index

Davies, John M.   139, 207, 222, 223, 257
Davies, Mrs I. B.   47
Davies, Noel   60
Davies, Pennar   174
Davies, Samuel   380
Davies, Wynford   24, 40, 49, 51, 242
Davis, Joe   58
Denning, Malcom   223
DeYoung, Kevin   208
Diana, Princess of Wales   174

E

Ecumenism   59, 61, 103
Eden, Sir Anthony   57
Edwards, Jonathan   135, 139, 158, 159, 166, 281, 285, 293, 324, 347, 368, 376, 410, 431, 432
Elias, Hefin   116, 220
Elias, John   119, 167
Elward, Peter   183, 221
Emyr, John   10
Evangelical Presbyterian Ministers Fellowship   38, 42, 46, 50, 51, 62, 137
Evangelical Presbyterian Ministers' Fellowship   44, 396
Evans, Christmas   311
Evans, Eifion   82, 83, 84, 127, 130, 135, 203, 204

Evans, E. Keri   218
Evans, Gilbert   407
Evans, Herbert   66, 67
Evans, John   98
Evans, Keri   349, 350, 394
Eveson, Philip   10, 170, 178, 184, 185, 221, 275, 407

F

Ferguson, Sinclair   150, 298
Fielder, Geraint   42, 185
Finney, Charles Grandison   285, 346
Frith, John   70

G

Gaitskell, Hugh   57
George, W. M.   23, 24, 41
Gibbard, Noel   87, 104, 127, 143, 170, 238, 246, 271
Gill, Tim   205
Goforth, Jonathan   315, 330
Graham, Billy   61, 314
Griffiths, Ann   98, 144, 248, 254
Griffiths, George   85, 86, 268
Gruffydd, Geraint   129
Gwilliam, John   24

H

Hancock, Thomas 70
Harper, Michael 115
Harris, Howell 97, 135, 136, 266, 294, 341, 362, 363, 364, 367, 368, 371, 380
Harrison, Graham 116, 169, 171, 174, 202, 235, 256, 260, 337, 338, 407
Haykin, Michael 187
Higham, Brian 146
Higham, W. Vernon 49, 51, 52, 117, 168, 177, 412
Hind, Graham 164, 180
Hitler, Adolf 315
Hodge, C. H. 323, 355, 432
Hogg, James 168
Howells, Rees 350
Hughes, A. L. 84, 87, 103
Hughes, Philip Edgcumbe 290, 429, 432
Humphreys, Gwilym 61, 99, 119

J

James, Sir David 109
James, W. R. 49
Jebb, Stanley 117, 256
Jeffrey, Peter 159, 170
Jenkins, Chris 185
Jenkins, Dennis 166
Jenkins, Glyndwr 26, 407
Jenkins, Joseph 347, 348
Jenkins, Omri 62, 64, 87, 143, 238
Joad, C. M. 58
Job, Dafydd 228, 230, 234
Job, Steffan 233
Jones, Bobi 144, 248
Jones, David Ceri 215, 246, 425
Jones, D. S. 374, 375
Jones, Emlyn 41, 49, 50, 88
Jones, Eurfyl 111, 238, 268
Jones, Humphrey 84, 347
Jones, Hywel R. 133, 140, 143, 170, 185, 276, 293, 407
Jones, Ithel 275, 280, 423
Jones, J. D. 48
Jones, John, Talsarn 161, 329
Jones, J. R. 102
Jones, Kim 275
Jones, Leslie 29
Jones, Mary 98, 402
Jones, Michael 383
Jones, R. B. 37, 348, 349, 350, 393, 394
Jones, R. Tudur 101, 174, 217
Jones, S. Malcom 155, 256
Jones, Sulwyn 176, 221, 222, 229
Jones, W. S. 350, 394
Joshua, Frank 392
Joshua, Seth 392

Index

K

Kearin, Dorothy	358
Keller, Tim	285, 286
Kelly, Douglas	176
Kim, Sung Tae	274
Knox, John	293
Kosciecha, Paul	199
Kuhlman, Kathryn	358
Kuyper, Abraham	328, 355

L

Leaves, Mike 234
Leonard, Graham 434
Letham, Robert 276, 277, 283, 284, 286, 287, 288, 291, 292, 294, 295, 298, 299, 428
Lewis, Bernard 183, 194, 205, 228, 229, 235
Lewis, C. S. 58
Lewis, W. W. 348, 349, 350, 394
Lloyd-Jones, Bethan 251, 413
Lloyd-Jones, D. Martyn 9, 10, 12, 15, 17, 18, 31, 32, 34, 35, 36, 37, 38, 39, 40, 41, 42, 46, 47, 49, 52, 61, 62, 63, 65, 66, 68, 69, 72, 73, 77, 78, 79, 83, 84, 85, 86, 87, 89, 90, 91, 94, 95, 100, 102, 103, 105, 106, 110, 111, 112, 115, 117, 118, 121, 122, 123, 124, 132, 135, 136, 137, 138, 139, 140, 141, 144, 146, 148, 149, 150, 151, 155, 156, 165, 171, 186, 211, 212, 214, 215, 218, 219, 226, 227, 229, 230, 236, 238, 239, 240, 241, 242, 243, 244, 245, 246, 248, 249, 250, 252, 253, 254, 255, 256, 257, 258, 259, 260, 261, 262, 263, 264, 266, 267, 268, 270, 277, 281, 284, 285, 286, 287, 288, 289, 290, 291, 292, 294, 295, 296, 297, 298, 299, 301, 303, 305, 308, 316, 318, 321, 322, 323, 326, 332, 337, 339, 341, 345, 352, 353, 357, 358, 360, 364, 370, 377, 406, 407, 426, 429
Lloyd, R. Tudor 250, 256
Luther, Martin 161

M

Macleod, Donald	214
Macleod, John	214
Macmillan, Douglas	165, 223, 297
Macmillan, Harold	101
Macrae, Kenneth	68
Mallard, Paul	200
Mandela, Nelson	173
Marcel, Pierre-Charles	275, 290, 291, 429
Mascall, E.L.	434
Mawdsley, Keith	169
McCheyne, Robert Murray	170, 314

McNeill, John 37
Meeten, Norman 117, 118, 263
Meredith, David 197
Meyer, F. B. 348, 349
Micklem, Nathaniel 305, 433
Milsom, Peter 185, 204, 407
Morgan, Dafydd 84, 156
Morgan, David 147
Morgan, Densil 118, 174, 218
Morgan, G. Campbell 335
Morgan, Geraint 183
Morgan, Hugh D. 23, 88
Morgan, Mari 24
Morris, Dafydd 185
Mullett, Kit 24
Murray, Andrew 359
Murray, Iain H. 9, 61, 66, 69, 70, 71, 72, 84, 85, 86, 117, 140, 141, 155, 186, 262, 281, 292, 293, 362, 399
Murray, John 280

N

Neil, Arthur 119, 263
Nettleton, Asahel 168
Newman, Cardinal 379
Nicholson, W. P. 37
North, Brownlow 86
Noyes, Alfred 58

O

Olyott, Stuart 185, 187, 276, 277, 294, 295
Owen, J. Glyn 18, 20, 21, 23, 30, 40, 42, 66, 68
Owen, O. M. 394
Owen, Richard 66, 147, 156, 159, 162

P

Packer, James I. 24, 60, 63, 80, 81, 88, 214, 262, 285, 298, 341, 432, 434
Palmer, Humphrey 9
Parry, Ian 203, 205, 206, 268
Pastoral Theology 12, 220, 223
Paterson, David 170
Pink, A. W. 219
Plant, Keith 234
Pope, Robert 217, 425
Powell, Bruce 150, 221, 257
Prayer and Preaching 125, 167, 203
Pritchard, Arthur 26, 59, 361
Prothero, W. E. 247, 353
Pugh, Conolwyn 373

R

Randall, Ian M. 262, 291, 431
Rees, Luther 143, 268
Rees, Neville 138, 256, 258, 268

Revival
  Congo   75, 82, 122, 170, 262
  Duncan Campbell 1949–1953
      66–69, 122
  Dundee   117
'Revivalitis'   230
Rhys, Robert   175
Ridley, Nicholas   70
Roberts, Emyr 10, 28, 59, 68, 88, 140, 147, 148, 216, 303
Roberts, Evan   66, 147, 148, 149, 185, 347, 348, 370, 371, 372, 373
Roberts, Gordon   47
Roberts, Gwilym 42, 80, 82, 183, 256, 403, 407, 422
Roberts, Maurice   176
Roberts, Robert, Clynnog   88
Robinson, John A. T., Bishop of Woolwich   101, 102
Rowland, Daniel   81, 82, 88, 129, 135, 146, 161, 175, 266, 294, 311, 329, 367, 371, 374, 376
Russell-Jones, J.   39, 40, 50, 81, 241

S

Salkeld, Vernon   393
Samuel, Leith   23, 29
Sayers, Dorothy   58
'seiat'   97, 111, 361
Sharman, W. K.   51, 396

Shepherd, David   380
Shields, T. T.   37, 343, 350, 351
'society'   97, 98. *See also* 'seiat'
Sookhdeo, Patrick   196
Spurgeon, Charles Haddon   161, 170, 215, 327
Stead, Bill   227, 228
Stewart, Gordon   207
Stone, Tony   117
Stott, John   103
Swann, Derek 42, 63, 81, 116, 133, 139, 158, 166, 168, 183, 268
Swann, Philip   177, 185, 194, 195, 196, 209, 221

T

Taylor, Hudson   117, 324
Taylor, Rowland   70
Taylor, Sherwood   58
Thickens, John   348
Thomas, Geoff   182, 208, 235
Thomas, I.D.E.   26, 39
Thomas, John   41, 42, 51, 52, 66, 88, 422
Thomas, John B.E.   23
Thomas, Meirion   184, 205, 236
Tillich, Paul   101, 102
Tozer, A. W.   206
Troup, Jack   37
Tyndale, William   70

V

Vernon, J. D.   217

W

Walker, Williston   346
Wallis, Arthur   121, 122
Walters, Gwyn   19, 20, 21, 23, 40, 63
Warfield, B. B.   355, 359
Warner, Rob   102, 103
Watson, David C. K.   115
Welch, Roger   207
Wesley, Charles   330
Wesley, John   266, 306, 311, 315, 367, 375
White, Alexander   103
Whitefield, George   135, 161, 215, 266, 285, 324, 356, 362, 367, 375, 380, 430
Williams, Gary   196
Williams, Gwilym O.   174
Williams, Gwynn   177, 194
Williams, H. H.   41
Williams, J. D.   24
Williams, J. O.   31, 32
Williams, John   234
Williams, Nantlais   349, 394
Williams, Rheinallt   19
Williams, William, Pantycelyn   140, 141, 175, 233, 294, 330
Woolwich, Bishop of.
    See Robinson, John A. T., Bishop of Woolwich
Word and Spirit   221, 270–282, 275, 276, 278, 283–302, 286, 287, 288, 298, 299, 428
Wycliffe, John   161